Online Search Services in the Academic Library

Planning, Management, and Operation

Janice F. Sieburth

American Library Association

Chicago and London 1988

Cover and text designed by Gordon Stromberg

Composed by Shepard Poorman in Garamond Book on a DEC VAX-VMS system

Printed on 50-pound Glatfelter, a pH neutral stock, and bound in 10-point Carolina cover stock by BookCrafters

The paper used in this publication meets the minimum requirements of American National Standard for Information Sciences—Permanence of Paper for Printed Library Materials, ANSI Z39.48–1984.
∞

Library of Congress Cataloging-in-Publication Data

Sieburth, Janice F.
   Online search services in the academic library : planning, management, and operation / by Janice F. Sieburth.
      p.   cm.
   Includes index.
   ISBN 0-8389-0490-4
   1. Libraries, University and college—Reference Services—Automation—Management. 2. Reference services (Libraries)—Automation—Management.   3. Bibliographical services —Automation—Management.   4. Information services—Automation—Management. 5. On-line bibliographic searching.   6. Data base searching.   I. Title.
   Z675.U5S54 1988   025.5'2777'0285—dc19   88-888
   ISBN: 0-8389-0490-4   CIP

Dedicated to my parents, Monta and

Emma Boston;

my children, Heather, Scott, Peggy,

Leslie, and Clark;

and especially to my husband, John.

They have provided me with unceasing

inspiration and encouragement.

Contents

Figures *vii*

Preface *ix*

1. Introduction to Academic Online Search Services *2*

2. Planning to Initiate Online Services *24*

3. Setting Up the Search Service *54*

4. Managing the Service *84*

5. Financial Arrangements *116*

6. The Procedure Manual *140*

7. Records, Forms, and Reports *166*

8. The Searcher *194*

9. Online at the Reference Desk *218*

10. Implications for Other Library Operations *238*

11. Microcomputers and Software *248*

12. Online Database Searching by Patrons *272*

13. Diversity, Success, and Change *306*

Index *327*

Figures

1. Sample budget proposal *49*
2. Sample request form *173*
3. Sample request form (cont.) *174*
4. Sample request form for
   undergraduates *176*
5. Sample authorization form *177*
6. Sample search authorization form *177*
7. Sample search appointment calendar *178*
8. Sample billing form *179*
9. Sample search log *181*
10. Sample search log (reference desk) *182*
11. Sample search log (terminal) *182*
12. Sample search plan form *183*
13. Sample search form *184*
14. Sample search evaluation form *185*
15. Sample search evaluation form *186*
16. Sample search evaluation form *187*
17. Sample statistics summary sheet *188*
18. Sample financial summary sheet *189*
19. Sample search summary sheet *190*
20. Sample patron-search costs summary *191*

Preface

Management of online information services denotes planning and control of many different activities: equipment purchase and servicing; online vendor contracts and continuing communication; selecting, training, and coordinating searchers; securing funding and deciding on fees; developing procedures, forms, and records; public relations; making reports; and future development. The online search service is not an isolated unit within the library; it must be integrated into reference activities, absorbed into the budget process, and coordinated with other services and library responsibilities such as collection management. Concurrently, the major focus must be aimed at serving the needs of the academic clientele.

An online database search service may start slowly, with one searcher and a few databases; it will usually expand to include all of the reference librarians, several vendors, and the choice of more than 200 databases. In the intense, rushed work day there may be little time for planning and thinking through the most effective method of organization. Changing search techniques, friendlier systems, greater numbers of larger and more complex databases, choices of software, increased costs of information and decreasing costs of computers—all present great challenges for academic librarians who must be aware of current developments and be able to plan for the future.

This book is primarily intended to assist the manager or coordinator of online search services in the academic library. It covers planning and organization, beginning at the preliminary stage as an online services proposal is prepared, continuing through the establishment of the search service, the expansion of services, to the selection of database systems for patrons to do their own searching. Chapters include the management tasks, the responsibilities of searchers, and the procedure manual that guides the organization and insures consistent patron service. Forms are illustrated to help manage the flow of requests and the collection of data for reports. A chapter on finances deals with the dilemma of finding funds for a potentially expensive service and methods of charging fees. Microcomputers and software are considered in another chapter, and a bibliography of sources is included to encourage keeping up with the information field. The overall approach of this book is intended to be practical and to provide a basis for decision making. Since it is impossible for a printed source to be completely current, principles rather than specific choices have been stressed.

This book was written at the suggestion of Herbert Bloom, senior editor at the American Library Association. He analyzed rough drafts, guided the focus of the book, and advised on content. His interest and encouragement have been instrumental in achieving this final product. Bettina MacAyeal, associate editor, did the final editing, and her comments were very helpful.

My experience as an online searcher began in 1975 at the University of Rhode Island (URI) Library; about the time OCLC was adopted, I began my career as a science reference librarian. Thanks to the Northeast Academic Science Information Center (NASIC), a federally funded project to introduce online searching to academic librarians in New England and adjoining areas, excellent training was available and procedures and forms were developed as needed. Training sessions could last two or three days. A few databases on Dialog or System Development Corporation (SDC) were covered thoroughly, with almost half the time spent on the structure and organization of the equivalent printed index. Management philosophy was discussed, and we followed the established pattern. Even today many of the forms used in Northeast academic libraries are similar, based on the NASIC experience. NASIC staff members even came to the library to help us when we offered demonstrations for faculty in order to answer questions and assist in the uncertain task of connecting up to Dialog.

As the NASIC contract expired, the responsibilities of an expanding online service became greater and I assumed the role of URICA coordinator (URI Computer Access), working with my colleagues to develop schedules, logs, procedures, fees, demonstrations, lectures for classes and better quality services. Most procedures simply evolved, and many ideas for improvements were never implemented because we did not have the time to consider changes. We were indebted to the library's first systems analyst, David Carlson, who installed microcomputers in place of leased terminals, selecting a modem that screened out troublesome line noise. David purchased Pro-Search and encouraged us to automate our collection of search statistics. As other changes were considered, it was not only very difficult to keep up with current online literature, but time consuming and often frustrating to try to find helpful information on a particular search service topic. Therefore, the opportunity to gather together a cohesive manual on search service management was an irresistible challenge.

The material in this book is a combination of personal experience, discussing with other academic librarians similar problems, attending meetings, and reading the literature. I have admired the outstanding and dedicated work being accomplished by academic librarians in research and college libraries across the country and appreciate their contributions to our collective body of knowledge. The selected references listed are those that particularly contribute to the subject matter of each chapter. Examples are primarily from Dialog and Bibliographic Retrieval Services (BRS) because these are the most widely used online vendor systems. I hope that this book will encourage the staff in any academic library without online reference services to establish them, and that it can provide assistance for library administrators and those who manage and/or participate in online search services. Students will find an overview of the complexities of integrating electronic and printed reference sources.

I am indebted to Arthur Young, dean, University of Rhode Island Libraries, who has encouraged the university librarians to meet the challenges of academic status by allowing research time and providing travel funds and support services. He took the time to carefully read and correct this manuscript. Both Dean Young and Mimi Keefe, chair of Public Services, have supplied good examples of the administrative planning that must be accomplished long before implementation of new systems. They have emphasized services for the academic community and their foresight has guided the development of the university library's computer–assisted services.

I am especially appreciative of my intelligent and energetic colleagues in the Reference Department who provide great inspiration as they cope with high pressure schedules, complex questions, and inundations of students, and still manage to make appointments with faculty and graduate students, study search terms and strategy, and perform excellent quality searches.

This book would not have been completed if it had not been for the faithful and very competent assistance of Mary Tate, who worried over spellings, terminology, and deadlines; struggled with her word processing system; and took pride in turning out a high–quality manuscript.

ONLINE SEARCH SERVICES IN THE ACADEMIC LIBRARY

Planning, Management, and Operation

1

DEVELOPMENT OF ONLINE SERVICES 5
GROWTH OF RESOURCES 7
ONLINE INDUSTRY 7
ACADEMIC CLIENTELE 9
EQUIPMENT, STAFF, AND MATERIALS REQUIREMENTS 11
    Searching Equipment 11
    Location Requirements 13
    Staffing the Search Service 14
    Manuals and Support Materials 14
COST FACTORS 15
ORGANIZATION OF SEARCH SERVICES 17
PROBLEMS OF INTEGRATING INFORMATION SERVICES 18
COPING WITH COSTS 19
SEARCHING BY PATRONS 20
THE ACADEMIC LIBRARIAN'S CHALLENGE 21

Introduction to Academic Online Search Services

The computer-assisted retrieval of information from remote databases has generated substantive changes in the information services provided by the academic library. Vast resources are available to the librarian with access to a computer linked to a telephone line and a password that allows communication with another computer's storage of database files, each composed of thousands of records. These files may contain references to articles, books, reports, and other sources of information; numerical data; full texts of articles; or directories of individuals, companies, or associations. The ability to select from these records only the items that contain information relevant to the question being asked provides a powerful tool for assisting individual patrons seeking specific bits of information or comprehensive coverage of everything that can be found on a particular topic.

Access to online resources has developed at a time when individuals in the research community have found it extremely difficult to adequately survey the accumulated literature on a subject and to keep up with the increasing volume of publications that appear every year. Further, most research today is accomplished by individuals or teams working in highly specialized areas, some of which are in rapidly developing fields such as those in medicine, robotics, and biotechnology, where it is essential to keep up with current developments on a worldwide basis. The combination of evolving computer technology, electronic communication systems, and machine-readable databases has resulted in interactive systems that can be searched online and then directed to transmit a selected list of records concerning the most recent advancements in the field of interest.

As more information has accumulated in machine-readable form, these resources have become even more valuable for supporting the needs of scientists and scholars. The resulting online search service has now become an essential component of the information resources of most larger libraries. In order to integrate computer-assisted information retrieval into the public services provided by the academic library, however, there must be a considerable investment in equipment, materials, training of librarians, and continuing funding to pay for the information as it is received. Most databases are supplied by commercial vendors who contract with the producers of indexes and abstracting services to acquire and market their online files. Information can be efficiently extracted, but charges can accumulate rapidly unless effective controls are in place. The problem of costs generated each time a search for information is accomplished has required a different view of paying for online resources from the usual purchase procedures for reference books and materials. Coping with these costs, which can be substantial, has often resulted in charging the patron a fee for the information received, a much discussed and controversial policy.

Online search services utilize a trained librarian, or search specialist, as an intermediary between the patron who needs the information and the databases that store an increasing accumulation of records. The necessity of knowing what online resources are available, the protocols for communicating and interacting online, the content and structure of each database, and the techniques necessary for skilled information retrieval have required librarians to attend workshops, training sessions, and classes to become efficient online searchers. This experience forms the basis for working with faculty and students to execute an online search that satisfies their needs.

Workloads must change to accommodate this time commitment to work on an individual basis with patrons, to develop search expertise (which takes practice), and to make schedules flexible enough to provide a responsive service orientation. These efforts must be supported by public service policies that emphasize effective information services. At the same time, continuing costs must be controlled and monitored to insure that budgetary commitments are not exceeded.

The online search service, first set up to meet the needs of research faculty and graduate programs, is gradually becoming assimilated into everyday reference activities. As database resources have broadened, the clientele has changed from a predominance of those involved in research activities to a wider scope, including teaching faculty in business and humanities and students on all levels seeking literature for class projects, term papers, or other assignments. Librarians have learned to use databases as an extension of the sources utilized at the reference desk—another access tool to augment printed indexes and reference resources.

Online bibliographic searching has been a component of the public services of many academic libraries since the early 1970s. Approached with both enthusiasm and skepticism by public service librarians, the electronic delivery of information has forced a reevaluation of the skills necessary for reference work, made charging for service a legitimate, but still controversial, activity, and has reinforced the librarian's intermediary role in the reference process. This personal involvement with faculty and students in the academic library has enriched the interactive process of reference service, but has also required the individual librarian to learn mechanical skills for working with machines; to acquire more knowledge about terminology, indexing procedures, contents of databases, and abstracting services; and to achieve more depth of subject expertise. Increased job satisfaction among librarians has often been mentioned as a result of these accomplishments, along with a recognition of higher value by patrons and academic colleagues.

DEVELOPMENT OF ONLINE SERVICES

Much of the initial development of online services occurred during the time when academic library budgets were being reduced and any plan to add services, particularly one that was new and incurred costs difficult to determine, required extensive and thoughtful consideration. Some institutions recognized immediately the value of this improved access to information and plunged right into implementing computer-assisted bibliographic retrieval. Others waited for funds, expertise, and assurance that this was a service that could be managed by librarians. Waiting gave the industry time to improve the search procedures, time for the machine-readable databases to become larger and more extensive, time for computers and computer storage to become less costly, and time for librarians to become more accustomed to working with computers and electronic files.

Academic and research libraries often added online databases to their resources as a result of pressure from faculty involved in active research programs. Professors who had worked for government departments where agency databases were being utilized soon asked for the same service in their library. Sometimes a computer search could be ordered by mail or the campus computer center purchased magnetic tapes from the producer of an index and batch searches were performed. Many smaller academic libraries, predominately serving institutions with a more general or applied undergraduate program, may have sent the few patrons needing search services to a neighboring institution. For some librarians serving a medical clientele, online searching began with training at the National Library of Medicine and the use of MEDLARS. Others incorporated ERIC searching into the services of a library serving an active education department.

Sara D. Knapp describes searching at SUNY Albany during the "early days" of the late 1960s before the advent of interactive communication and some of the important changes in technology that have affected the development of an online service. [1] Searching at 120 characters per second on a machine connected directly to a main computer required much patience. Even though there was access to only a few databases and the machine searched one complete strategy at a time without intervention, users were still enthusiastic. It was a totally new concept for most librarians—the service was dependent upon working with a machine and it was very difficult to envision the practical use in the everyday workplace, particularly since each negotiation had a variable charge that could mount up substantially.

By the mid 1970s, computerized searching of bibliographic databases was available in most large libraries. Nevertheless, a survey in 1984 showed that less than half of the academic libraries in the study offered online searching for their patrons. This figure included 83 percent of the universities, 50 percent of the colleges, and 18 percent of the junior colleges. [2] The *Marquis Who's Who Directory of Online Professionals* in 1984 listed 1,929 individuals from academic institutions, 32 percent of the entries. Twenty-six percent spent from one to four hours per month online, while one percent spent more than eighty hours online. [3]

Even among libraries with well-established search services, there is wide variability in the amount of searching being done; the amount of fees, if any; and the location and conduct of the service. Certainly the costs that increase with use, the growing array of resources provided, and the time necessary to work with individual patrons have combined to affect the utilization and implementation of online services. However, as databases have become more diverse and equipment less expensive, even smaller libraries are increasingly accessing online databases for their faculty and students.

Today, patrons are ready to do at least some of their own searching for information. This aspect of online searching, known as end-user searching, presents a challenge for reference librarians to provide an informational retrieval service that combines different approaches and methods. It is exceedingly important that online services be utilized in a manner appropriate to an institution and its clientele, and the organization, utilization, and provision of these online components of an information service must be effective and efficient.

1. Sara D. Knapp, "Online Searching: Past, Present, and Future," *Online Searching Technique and Management*, ed. James J. Maloney (Chicago: American Library Assn., 1983), pp. 3–15.
2. Gayle McKinney and Anne Page Mosby, "Online in Academia: A Survey of Online Searching in U.S. Colleges and Universities," *Online Review* 10:107–124 (1986).
3. Fred Chatterton and Jeff Pemberton, "The Online Professionals—Who Does What. . . . The Marquis/Online, Inc., Project," *Online* 9:15–24 (1985).

GROWTH OF RESOURCES

The development of publicly accessible computerized bibliographic files has been of greatest benefit to those working in the scientific and technical areas. Fast retrieval of up-to-date information on narrow research specialties in actively developing areas of scientific investigation could suddenly be achieved on demand. Databases in aeronautics, chemistry, medicine, and the biological sciences were soon joined by those in education and psychology. This limited number of databases quickly expanded in both quantity and subject areas. The time period of coverage is still variable, but at present may include fifteen or more years. Sources for information on business affairs and management have increased to cover economic data, company information, and a long list of databases on industry, trade, and finance. Databases in the humanities had a slow development, but recently there has been increasing growth in the areas of art, music, and literature. Bibliographic files have been joined by numeric, directory, and full-text databases. Quantity, quality, and complexity have all increased dramatically.

Changes occur so rapidly that it is difficult to maintain an adequate knowledge of the newest databases, the latest improvements in search procedures, and the increasing opportunities for finding information. Two hundred forty-two different databases were used by academic libraries in a survey reported by Martha E. Williams in 1985. However, only seven of them were used 83 percent of the time. [4] While this shows the value of a few basic databases, it also indicates the resource potential that is available as search services expand to meet the needs of a wider group of patrons.

The falling costs of computer technology, the development of telecommunication networks, and the increased sophistication of the database providers have all had a significant role in this development. While most searching is done in the larger research libraries, electronic networks have made abundant resources available to the smallest library, most remote branch library, or outlying campus. Information can be retrieved as needed and documents printed out or ordered online. Many scholars no longer need to travel to larger institutions to have access to worldwide information. Database searching has become indispensable for research in all areas of endeavor.

ONLINE INDUSTRY

The growth of the information industry has been substantial over the past twenty years, and the marketing of databases of bibliographic in-

4. Martha E. Williams, "Usage and Revenue Data for the Online Database Industry," *Online Review* 9:205–210 (1985).

formation has become a big business. The company (vendor) providing the largest number of databases is Dialog Information Services, Inc., with more than 200 files covering subject fields from business and history to chemistry and engineering. Dialog and the System Development Corporation (SDC) established the first markets in the early 1970s and their methods of mounting databases and charging for access to the files have continued to the present time. Fees for use of the early databases were based on connect-time with the company's computer at rates that varied with the individual databases. Additional costs were incurred for printing citations offline, but charging only for use with no minimum fee and no charge for a password insured that even a library with limited use could maintain access.

Bibliographic Retrieval Services, Inc. (BRS) offered the first competition to Dialog and SDC in the mid 1970s by requiring a subscription fee that allowed access to their databases at a standard rate. In order to reduce fees for users, some older files were maintained offline, but searches of these files could be ordered and the results mailed. BRS led the way to increased competition in the online field and additional companies have become database vendors in the 1980s. Most of these, such as Pergamon InfoLine, Wilsonline, and Mead Data Central, offer fewer databases and may specialize in a particular subject area such as law and legal information. Each vendor of databases has its own procedures and protocols for searching and retrieving information from their databases. Charging rates differ and some vendors require subscriptions or charge for passwords. Contracting with one of these vendors allows a library to have access to a range of information resources with one contract, a single billing system, and a uniform search procedure.

The producers of the databases marketed by the online vendors are often publishers of indexes, periodicals, or books for whom the production of the electronic version is a by-product of the publication process. Other producers may only create the online file. Databases are purchased or leased by the vendors and the producers are usually paid royalty fees for the information retrieved from their databases.

Vendors mount these files on their system and arrange and tag the components so that they can be searched using the system's procedures and search language. The charge generated for a database search includes the vendor's connect-time fees, the royalty charges of the producer, communications charges of the networks used to link the library's and the vendor's computers (such as Tymnet or Telenet), and sometimes printing and mailing fees. The search results can be printed in several formats, with the choice of the entire record or selected parts of it; bibliographies can be sorted by title, author, or date; and delivery can be by mail, by immediately printing at the terminal, or by transferring the results to a computer disk. Many vendors have also made it possible to order entire documents through the online system. As vendor's bills are based on use of their databases, the varying needs of a library's patrons make it extremely difficult to judge the budgetary impact. The arrangement is different from buying a book or taking out a subscription, as the charges are not incurred until the database is utilized. The discussion of whether or not to pass on these variable costs to the consumer, or patron, has been heated and continues. Some libraries have absorbed these costs as part of their information retrieval activities, some share the fees with patrons, and others charge users the full cost of a search.

The number of databases available from these vendors continues to grow and there are more choices of systems, each with particular advantages of subject coverage or specific files of interest. Increasingly, vendors are also expanding their markets from institutions to individuals who wish to do their own searching without using the information specialist as an intermediary. A simpler search language, special selections of databases, and different pricing schemes may be utilized in these end user systems.

ACADEMIC CLIENTELE

The type of institution and composition of the academic community will determine the demand for online services. Faculty, graduate and undergraduate students, staff, and administration make up the academic library clientele. Their information needs may be for research, teaching, publications, or decision making. The increasingly computer-literate community will come to expect online information retrieval to be a constituent of the services available to them.

Large research facilities; physical, biological, and medical science faculty; institutes of business and social science; and other programs where knowledge of the latest results of worldwide investigations may be critical, require convenient access to online services. Scientists, engineers, and scholars writing grant proposals, tomorrow's lecture, or a literature review for a new publication will find that an online search will quickly give them a list of pertinent articles, the very latest developments, or confirmation that no one else has reported work on a proposed research topic.

Students in graduate programs writing research papers, theses, and dissertations on very specific subjects usually find that securing information with a computer-assisted search will be quicker and more comprehensive than working with the equivalent printed index. The ability to combine various components of a search topic and to use terminology of the field and names of events or processes for an online search makes it possible to produce results relevant to the student's problem. The graduate student population is an ideal group to benefit from bibliographic searching. Exploring potential research topics, writing reports, publications, theses, and dissertations all may require an exhaustive current literature search. Projects are begun and concluded in relatively short spans of time and the efficiency of an online search can conserve time for essential laboratory work while delivering the most current literature in the specific area of interest.

As databases of information increase in number, size, and scope, the value to the institutional programs will increase and the patron's expectations for responsive services to supply information such as statistics, company financial data, physical properties of chemicals, and the direct results of research in abstracts and full-text articles will multiply. Appropriate sources are available for each academic level. Technical institutes may wish to offer online access to the reports published by engineering societies or to the *Applied Science and Technology Index*. Students in writing programs can utilize databases such as the SOCIAL SCIENCES INDEX or the MAGAZINE INDEX for an online search on a term paper topic. Liberal arts colleges will find increasingly valuable historical and humanities files with information on the arts, music, and literature. Academic librarians will find their own research responsibilities enhanced by their ability to search OCLC by subject, publisher's catalogs such as Wiley, other library serials lists such as the CALIFORNIA UNION LIST OF PERIODICALS, and LIBRARY LITERATURE.

Online bibliographic searching has only just begun to affect services to undergraduate students. Undergraduates do not usually have need for specialized research material, and the strength of online services has been support for research and work in narrow fields of concentration. However, the choice of databases has broadened to provide more general sources, such as magazine and newspaper indexes and the H. W. Wilson indexes, which have long been utilized by college students. Nevertheless, this integration of online resources into general reference use has been held back by concern over costs. Cost has also been a factor when institutions have felt that charges should be passed on to the patron. Where there are fees for service, undergraduate students may find it very difficult to pay. However, absorbing the costs of the searching that might be demanded by these students could make a library-funded service very expensive. Since the printed indexes have served the undergraduate student well, there has not been a great deal of pressure to provide database searching.

Librarians have expressed concern that students who can easily find a few references online will not learn how to use the traditional indexes and abstracts, and will not bother to determine if there are other, more appropriate, resources. Computers, however, attract the attention of students and can be used as a focus for teaching about library research. The procedures for effective database searching such as defining a subject, considering terminology, selecting a best source for searching, deciding on the need for the most recent literature, and judging the quantity of information required are also important principles for searching printed indexes. Computers are increasingly integrated into the academic learning experiences and students as well as faculty will expect them to be part of the process of gaining access to information.

EQUIPMENT, STAFF, AND MATERIALS REQUIREMENTS

Setting up an online search service necessitates an investment of both funding and personnel. Money is needed for equipment, space must be found, manuals and other support materials purchased, and staff time allocated. Planning must include the location of the service within the library organizational structure, procedures for providing searches for patrons, training staff, and managing continuing costs. External variables such as adequate telecommunications in the area, power supply available to the building, and support systems from the campus computer center may influence library decisions.

The equipment used to access the databases must be selected and purchased or leased. The database vendor systems are compatible with most standard terminals or microcomputers, which can be equipped with a modem for connecting with the telephone line. Some knowledge of computers will be necessary to select the most suitable models for the purpose of searching. This process could be hampered by a campus policy that requires all computer purchases to be channeled through a central office to standardize campus equipment; however, the computer center can be a source of valuable advice or could loan a machine on a trial basis. Other needs such as manuals, computer paper, and telephone lines add to the commitment necessary for the library undertaking a search service for the first time. Since academic library budgets are often composed several years ahead, this investment may be difficult to implement from available funds and may require careful planning or an outside source for start-up funding.

Searching Equipment

The first requirement is for a machine that can communicate with a computer. This machine may be a terminal that prints out search statements as they are entered, followed by the return messages from the host computer with the results of the database search. The terminal may already be in use in the library for work with the campus computer, or it may be a machine purchased or leased and dedicated to the search service. Characteristics of the terminal, such as ASCII (American Standard Code for Information Interchange), asynchronous transmission, baud rate (communications speed), printing speed, parity, and duplex, are very important, although most terminals can be adjusted to meet the necessary requirements for communication and interaction. The terminal may be a floor model or it may be more like a portable typewriter, capable of fitting in a carrying case. It may be strictly a printing terminal, or a keyboard may be tied to a visual display unit (VDT) where the search can be monitored on a screen. This type of unit provides better visual observation for the patron and searcher, but to obtain a paper copy, it must be connected to a printer. A printing terminal is the simplest and least expensive machine for a search service, but other applications are limited.

Microcomputers with printers can be utilized as terminals, and their increasing use in many offices and library operations provides a ready source of equipment for online searching. The value of a shared machine, however, may be limited by its availability when the searcher needs it, and this may dictate the need for a dedicated terminal or computer for online searching. A microcomputer can do much more than just communicate with the database: it can be used for storing the search strategy and then sending it quickly to the database computer saving on connect-time charges. The search results may also be stored electronically on a disk (downloaded), which is usually faster than printing out the results. Besides delivery of the information to the patron in either print form or on a disk, the search results can be held on the microcomputer and manipulated by either the librarian or the patron to edit the material and select relevant citations; to eliminate parts of the records that are extraneous, such as locations of authors or coded components; to add notes; and to organize the bibliography in various forms. A microcomputer can also be used for other library applications such as word processing and accounting.

It is next necessary to link the terminal or microcomputer with the telephone line. This step may be accomplished with a modem. One type of modem, the acoustic coupler, is made to accept the handset of the telephone and is either a separate box that plugs into the terminal, or is built into the terminal itself. This type of connection allows the searching terminal to be located anywhere there is a telephone available, from the library office to a laboratory workbench. A modem may also plug directly into the wall telephone jack to make a connection. Newer modems may be programmed to dial telephone numbers and automatically establish the link with the online system.

The speed of message transmission will be determined by the operation speed of the terminal or microcomputer, the modem, and the printer, which must all be coordinated. This speed is expressed as baud rate, where the capability of sending or receiving one character per second is equivalent to 10 baud. Traditionally, interaction has taken place at 30 characters per second (cps) or 300 baud. One hundred twenty cps (1200 baud) is increasingly common and 240 cps (2400 baud) is rapidly becoming available. The local equipment, the distant computer, and the telephone line must all be capable of handling the faster rates. At 1200 baud the rate of interaction is much faster and information is received much more quickly than at 300 baud. Nevertheless, the time to type in a search statement, the pauses generated by the host computer when the system is at peak load, and the hesitations by the searcher when making decisions during an online search will not be changed by the speed of the equipment.

Communications between computer and terminal are determined by sounds that are sent along the telephone line. Any noise or distortion of this sound will interfere with the understanding of the information being sent; the less potential for interruption the better. A telephone handset connection is not as satisfactory as equipment that plugs into the telephone line. The telephone line itself must be good quality and the link with the computer should not go through a switchboard or other intermediary connection. A telephone that is part of a multiphone system that can be interrupted by someone picking up another telephone is to be avoided since this will cause the connection with the host computer to be broken and search results lost.

Location Requirements

Online searching for patrons must be part of the reference services provided by the academic library. Any organizational separation from the location where the patron and librarian interface takes place will interfere with the effectiveness of providing information. Nevertheless, an online search service should have a distinct location where an individual can meet with a librarian, a discussion of the search topic can be carried out, and the search performed. A separate room or enclosure close to the reference desk is ideal. Searching then becomes part of the information services and some separation shows the importance of the patron and librarian interaction. The separateness from the reference desk is especially significant if any fees are charged for a search. It should be clear that free information services are the standard, and that the fee-for-service is an additional option.

The search service may have to be accommodated at a location where terminals or microcomputers have already been placed, or limited to an area where telephone lines and electrical outlets are available. For best results, a quiet area with space for consultation with patrons and enough room for shelving support materials is desirable. If the location is near the reference desk where other information resources are located, the service will be more accessible for the public and more convenient for supporting the information retrieval activities at the reference desk. A location visible to patrons will also help advertise the availability of this information service.

An optimum searching area will have enough room for several terminals or microcomputers, tables and chairs, bookshelves, and a file cabinet. A good environment is a convenient location that is reasonably quiet and where searching will not be interrupted. Any noise generated by a printer and the discussions with patrons should not disturb students using a quiet study area or staff who have other responsibilities. Furniture should include a table and chairs for pre-search preparation, at least enough space and chairs for a small group to observe a search, a bookcase for the manuals and thesauri, and a file cabinet for forms and reports.

Staffing the Search Service

Reference librarians are usually the first choice for staffing a search service, since they already work with patrons seeking information, they are accustomed to interpreting questions, and are familiar with indexes and abstracts. Online searching extends the reference resources they are already using. Subject bibliographers or librarians working with computers can bring other valuable expertise to a search service, but the experience of reference interviews and dealing with patrons is essential for providing effective searches. Workloads of searchers will need to be adjusted to allow the time necessary for training, search preparation and execution, and working with individual patrons. In addition, individuals without any experience with computers may need special encouragement and practice to become comfortable with the mechanics of online searching.

New searchers will need training. One of the best learning experiences is to attend a workshop sponsored by an online database vendor. Frequent introductory sessions are offered in various parts of the country. While these concentrate on the particular system's command language, they also include the basics of developing a search strategy, techniques of manipulating the resulting groups of citations, and methods for producing the results as a printed bibliography. Experienced searchers can provide valuable follow-up support for other members of the staff, and additional training can be obtained from online user groups or graduate schools of library and information science.

Manuals and Support Materials

Manuals to follow the protocols of the database vendors are essential. Usually these include the basic search procedure and directions for combining search terms, sorting results, and printing offline and online. In addition to searching techniques, chapters are devoted to individual databases. Within a database, documents, articles, or directory listings are each represented by a record that may have many components such as author(s), author affiliation, title, source, abstract, date, language, type of publication, descriptors, chemical names, industry codes, numerical data, geographic location, and other pertinent information. Each of these components is a field that can be searched individually. When a word or phrase is sent to the database, the basic subject portions of the record will be scanned for occurrence of the terms unless a specific field is indicated.

The database chapters describe the various fields and provide search examples. Standardized formats for printing the records are also illustrated. Search results can usually be limited to a particular time period, language, or type of publication. It may be necessary to check each database documentation to determine the limits that can be utilized or they may be uniform for all databases in the system. The descriptors that are part of each record are usually indexing terms in the print form of the database. These may be assigned to each reference from a list of words, or thesaurus, that has been specifically composed for the index or database. Descriptors from this controlled vocabulary are then standardized throughout the database, making it very important to consult the thesaurus before going online. Checking each suggested subject term will alert the searcher to different spellings of a word, synonyms, and related words. When discussing the search topic with a patron, the thesaurus listings of broader (more general) or narrower (more specific) terms assist the process of finding the most appropriate terminology for the subject of interest.

The database manuals and the thesaurus for a controlled vocabulary provide essential information for competent searching. Some producers of the more complex databases publish a search manual to guide the formulation of a search statement. There may also be an explanation of procedures for each of the major systems where the database is available. The print index that corresponds to the database can also be used to identify terms and learn about the composition of the records. A dictionary, a general thesaurus for a subject field such as engineering or psychology, a catalog of species names, or a concise encyclopedia can be helpful for spellings, abbreviations, new terms or jargon, or explanations of concepts in a specialized field or area of investigation. Newsletters from vendors and database producers and periodicals that include information on developments in the online field are also needed for an adequately supported online service.

COST FACTORS

Initial costs of equipment and support materials, along with an investment in librarian training have sometimes discouraged smaller libraries from instituting a search service, as the amounts of money needed are easier to absorb in a larger budget. The variable database charges that can quickly add up to a substantial amount for individual searches have helped reinforce the suggestion that information is not free and have made charging for service acceptable, although not universal. Who pays for this individualized service continues to be a debatable topic with legitimate arguments for both patron and service provider. It is only by passing the charges generated by an individual search on to the patron that it has been possible for many institutions to establish an online service. Since the individual search fee is usually based on computer connect time and information received, it has been easy to calculate the cost and link it to the individual who receives the search results. Charging a fee has also allowed many institutions to set up a search service without having to worry about the uncertainties of demand, which could result in very small or very large monthly search costs.

Since a major force for instituting an online search service has been to support funded research on campus, it seemed logical from the beginning to charge back search costs to faculty, who could include these fees in their research expenditures and their grant proposals. Extending this concept to include personal funds has often followed. Various schemes have been devised to adjust charges according to category of patron or different levels of subsidy by the library, with the result that it is difficult to identify a common fee policy among academic libraries. For most situations the initial or capital investment for a search service must be found in the budget or from an outside source to cover the equipment, space, support material, and staff training. Even if an existing microcomputer with a modem can be used, there will still be continuing costs for maintenance, computer paper and ribbons, new manuals, training for more searchers or advanced workshops, and public relations. These expenses are becoming familiar budget items in a library with any amount of automation. Charging back the individual search fees to patrons can cover the additional search expenses and a surcharge or service fee can reduce some of the continuing costs.

If librarians have been doing manual searching of topics for patrons, the time saved and the efficiency of online access will seem cost-saving rather than an additional expense for this individualized service. If funds can be found for totally supporting online database searching, information services can be extended to individuals and their needs far beyond what can be done by the busy reference service, which can only hope to answer specific questions and spend brief periods with individual patrons. A reordering of service priorities will usually be required when budgets must be formulated. Obviously there must be a balance among cost, benefit, and responsibility for providing access to information.

ORGANIZATION OF SEARCH SERVICES

As search services became established, reference librarians or subject specialists who may have first learned to "log on" to OCLC went to training sessions, set up search stations, advertised to the faculty, worked out cost recovery systems, and carted portable terminals around campus. Online searching in most instances became a confirmed part of reference services. In many cases the title "searcher" added one more area of responsibility for the reference librarian to fit into a heavy workload. One librarian may have become a coordinator or manager of the service and learned by trial and error to negotiate with vendors and the library administration, take care of the manual updates, cope with static on the line and equipment failures, set fees, take statistics, and manage other details that have become a part of this fast-changing electronic environment.

David M. Wax, in 1976, wrote a handbook that provided guidelines for introducing and managing an online bibliographic search service. [5] Most of the principles and many of the procedures are still valid. His manual suggested making appointments with patrons; using a variety of forms, examples of which were provided; searching with the patron present; keeping a log of activity; and maintaining flexibility to allow for future developments. This model of a special arrangement for online bibliographic searching has worked well as an adjunct to the provision of other information retrieval services.

The close association with reference services is very important. When reference desks are separated within a large library building or located in branches, it will be necessary to decide whether all searching will be done in a central facility or whether each reference operation will offer their own search service. Consideration must be given to the size of the separate reference service, the level of staffing, the demand for searching, and the funds available for setting up and maintaining each location. However, primary attention must be given to the patron seeking information. If skilled reference assistance is available in a health sciences library or at a humanities reference desk, then online resources must be part of that service. If the departmental or branch library serves primarily as a reading area, then patrons should be referred to a central facility where expert reference assistance, including online searches, can be provided. As online access to information becomes more integrated into the reference function and is in the hands of the patrons themselves, modifications of structure may be

5. David M. Wax, *A Handbook for the Introduction of On-Line Bibliographic Search Services into Academic Libraries* (Washington, D.C.: Assn. of Research Libraries, Office of University Management Studies, 1976).

necessary and even more flexibility of staff and procedures will be needed.

Setting up a search service requires the support of the library administration. Although the goals of a public services unit will not change, nevertheless priorities may have to be adjusted and the characteristics of online searching that make costs unpredictable and controls essential may require a different type of management. There must be a commitment of funds and an awareness of the changing personnel responsibilities that occur. There will also be an impact on other library operations as costs affect the budget, demand for related services and materials increases, and as staff time necessary for training, practicing techniques, and working with patrons becomes substantial.

PROBLEMS OF INTEGRATING INFORMATION SERVICES

Norman D. Stevens suggests that "mental, financial and intellectual barriers will have to be overcome" if an integrated information retrieval system is to be achieved.[6] He points out that reference librarians must learn to automatically include electronic databases among the various sources of information for each question asked. While not always appropriate, it is important that these computer-accessed sources be considered for all information questions and not as just a separate search operation for specific occasions.

Computer-assisted information retrieval is fast, efficient, thorough, and specific to a user's needs. These qualities enhance the traditional reference services in a library; however, other characteristics are different from the resources librarians usually deal with. The information is not there unless it is retrieved by someone who knows the correct procedures. This process can be interfered with if there is a problem with the outside source (vendor), the electrical system, or the telephone. Costs are incurred with each use, and can accumulate rapidly even if no pertinent information is found. Usually only one patron can utilize a machine and a database at a time, and the necessity of charging a fee may limit access to those who can pay for it. In addition, the field of electronic information delivery is changing so rapidly that it is difficult to keep up and to plan for future developments.

Reference librarians must be able to recognize when searching an online database is appropriate. Many information needs are better served by a printed index, reference handbook, or directory. Usually print sources are preferable when the information can be easily located, when the topic is general or the patron uncertain about what he

6. Norman D. Stevens, "Skim Milk Masquerades as Cream: The Myth of Online Data Base Searching," *The Reference Librarian* 5/6:77–81 (1982).

they want, when the subject cannot be defined in words or phrases, when the information is historical or was published in years before database coverage, when there are no databases suitable for the subject, or when browsing will be more productive. Occasionally a patron will have totally unrealistic expectations for an online search. Comparing a database with the corresponding printed index will usually clarify the search process and information retrieved.

Costs for these electronic services arc substantial and yet must be managed so they do not interfere with the delivery of information. The necessity for librarians to accept computers as a tool to be utilized to enhance their skills at the reference desk will take time; however, as librarians realize the value of electronic assistance and as user expectations increase, there is no doubt that an adequate search for information must include all resources available, regardless of the form of storage.

Some of the integration of online databases into the reference process will take place as search procedures become less complex and computers become more helpful. As the number of databases has grown, the amount and scope of information that is available has affected almost every subject interest. The large core scientific databases, available since the early 1970s, correspond to the major general scientific indexes—*Chemical and Biological Abstracts, Index Medicus, Psychological Abstracts* and the three parts of *Science Abstracts*—continue to be basic sources. The multiplication of newer databases are continuing to develop in a number of directions: broader subject coverage in the fields of business, social sciences, humanities, and current affairs; more specialized sources in areas such as advertising, paper chemistry, child abuse, the Middle East, welding, and religion; more data and directory files rather than bibliographic—demographics, properties of materials, the yellow pages, software files, and company annual reports; and increasing sources of full-text databases of encyclopedias, selected periodicals, and news. Managing the integration of these resources into the present-day reference collection will be increasingly important as we proceed into the 1990s.

COPING WITH COSTS

The costs of the electronic delivery of information are considerably more than the charge printed at the end of each database search. Facilities, equipment, supplies, and personnel costs are significant. The uncertainties of individual search costs make expenditures and future allocations difficult to plan. All fiscal and management aspects of an online search service are not new, however. The budgets of academic libraries have already been adjusted to incorporate computer technology, staff patterns have changed to include new computer-related responsibilities, and decisions between printed and other forms of resource materials have been made.

Further adjustments will include lesser costs of computers and related equipment, with more funds needed to keep up with demands and broadening use by individuals and in more locations. Changing vendor fee schedules are difficult to predict, but will probably be increasingly based on information received. Continuing education for librarians will be another cost factor as different skills are needed, new technologies develop, and vendor services change.

It appears doubtful that most academic library budgets will expand significantly and, therefore, there will have to be some difficult decisions made regarding the priorities for services that can be offered. Decisions about fees-for-services will not become any easier, but the incorporation of online searching as a regularly budgeted item will establish this aspect of information retrieval as a necessary option for providing adequate reference services.

SEARCHING BY PATRONS

By the mid 1980s, a trend evolved that will move direct control of online bibliographic retrieval back to the user. Continued development of database systems has utilized the interactive capability of the computer to help a searcher make decisions and to guide the search process. An individual who has never searched before can respond to questions about a subject that will help choose a database, assist in the selection of search terms, and follow through on searching and retrieving relevant records. Whether these systems are controlled by the online database vendor such as BRS After Dark or Knowledge Index (Dialog), provided by software such as *Pro-Search*, or by a link with an intermediary computer system (EasyNet), is not as important as the fact that the patron or untrained librarian can perform satisfactory searches on simple topics, can retrieve some information on most subjects, and can often find all the necessary information without additional assistance. Although there is considerable doubt that this will replace the librarian as intermediary, it makes sense that some individuals will wish to search indexes with the computer just as they have always searched paper indexes.

As online searching becomes more integrated with the reference process, giving the patron the choice of searching an index with the printed copy or a computer terminal will seem logical. Patrons will need guidance and training, but they will already be comfortable with computers, so instruction on the use of terms, constructing a search strategy, and finding sources online will be just as important as it is in bibliographic instruction today for printed materials. The broad perspective of bibliographic search services divided among subscriptions to paper indexes, computer searching with the librarian as intermediary, and end-user searching for the individual will provide options for the most appropriate response to the information needs of the patron. The choice of search method can be guided by the skilled and experienced librarian for the most productive results. Patron satisfaction will depend on the speedy delivery of correct information. While cost will often be an element, the results are the critical factor.

THE ACADEMIC LIBRARIAN'S CHALLENGE

Online access to remote sources of information has opened new vistas to librarians who provide reference services for their patrons. Not only have computers improved access to materials held in the library, but they can assist in the identification of unique sources from all over the world that are held in many other locations. Scholars at all levels—researchers, teachers, and students—will benefit from the vast scope of resources available at their campus library. The transformation of information delivery can be observed by the rapid growth in the number of available databases (over 200 from Dialog alone), the new types of databases (directory and full-text) that are becoming more numerous, the increased sophistication of computer-literate patrons, easier to use computer systems, and the increasingly varied content of databases that can supplement resources in almost every subject area.

The academic librarian's greatest challenge is to keep up with this changing panorama of technology, resources, and information needs. Identifying what information is needed by patrons is a first step; finding the best source and method of access is next; and efficient delivery to the patron is the final critical element. Computers have not changed the mission of the reference librarian, but have opened up new possibilities for success. The librarian is at the focal point of information retrieval with a responsibility to know the best method of finding needed data. This status will continue to challenge the intellect of librarians, the methods of bibliographic instruction, and the relationships with patrons.

In the complex field of information delivery, there will be new demands on traditional resources and new skills needed for librarians. It will undoubtedly mean more training, more experience, and more continuing education. Support for the professional information provider has come from vendors, colleagues, professional associations, and online user groups formed in local, state, and regional locations. MARS, organized in 1976 as the Machine-Assisted Reference Section of the Reference and Adult Services Division of the American Library Association, has been an outstanding source of conference programs while working to provide information on library use of online services and to establish standards in the field.

Academic librarians have set many examples of excellence, innovation, and resourcefulness as the online information field has expanded. The challenges of managing the developments in technology and the marketplace will continue as academic librarians strive to provide effective information services in a world where information is an increasingly valuable commodity.

Bibliography

Cogswell, James A. "On-Line Search Services: Implications for Libraries and Library Users." *College and Research Libraries* 39: 275–280 (1978).

Doll, Russell. "Information Technology and Its Socioeconomic and Academic Impact." *Online Review* 5:37–46 (1981).

Lee, Joann H. "The Academic Library." In *Online Searching: The Basics, Setting and Management*, pp. 114–127. Edited by Joann H. Lee. Littleton, Colo.: Libraries Unlimited, 1984.

Mosby, Anne Page, and Gayle McKinney. "Status and Future Directions of Online Search Services in Georgia Academic Libraries." ERIC Document ED245709, 37 pp. (1983).

Neufeld, M. Lynne, and Martha Cornog. "Database History: From Dinosaurs to Compact Discs." *Journal of the American Society for Information Science* 37(4):183–190 (1986).

Root, Christine, and Maryruth Glogowski. "Online Searching in SUNY Libraries." ERIC Document ED242323, 35 pp. (1983).

Sandy, John. "On-Line Databases Vital for Scientific Research." *Science* 216:1367 (1982).

Williams, Martha E. "Data Bases—A History of Developments and Trends from 1966 through 1975." *Journal of the American Society for Information Science* 28:71–78 (1977).

2

ESTABLISHING GOALS AND OBJECTIVES *26*
  Establishing a Computer-assisted Search Service *27*
  Contributing to Campus Research Projects *28*
  Integrating Online Searching into the Library Reference
    Services *29*
  Acquainting Students with Electronic Services *31*
  Enhancing the Capabilities and Efficiency of the
    Librarians *31*
  Serving Additional Groups or Individuals *32*
DEFINING THE CLIENTELE *33*
DETERMINING LOCATION *35*
  Physical Environment *36*
  Administrative Placement *37*
STAFFING THE SEARCH SERVICE *39*
ESTIMATING COSTS *40*
  Initial Investment *40*
  Variable Search Costs *43*
  Continuing Costs *45*
DECIDING ON A FEE POLICY *46*
BUDGET PROPOSAL *48*
PROJECTING THE IMPACT ON LIBRARY OPERATIONS *48*
PRESENTATION OF THE PROPOSAL *50*
  Library Administrative Support *51*
  Academic Administrative Support *51*
  External Funding *52*
SETTING A TIMETABLE *53*

Planning to Initiate Online Services

An academic library may be considering the addition of computer-assisted bibliographic searching to the services it offers because of the need for better and more efficient information retrieval for faculty and students doing research, the desire to offer more personalized information services, the additional resources available online, or the wish to keep up with current technologies. The first step in implementing such a recommendation is to formulate a proposal that will recognize the objectives, costs, impact on other library services, and the decisions that must be made. The proposal may contain a review of the literature to demonstrate the current status of the online searching field or a survey of online services in several libraries of similar size. The steps required for the establishment of a search service should be included in the proposal and decision points with choices appropriate to the institution should be emphasized.

An online services proposal includes the following elements:

Goals and objectives of the search service to place it in the context of the type and size of institution, the services already provided, and the information needs of the community.

The clientele the library serves—faculty, research staff, graduate students, and undergraduates.

The physical location(s) and placement in the library's organization.

Estimated cost for equipment, manuals and supplies, training of searchers, and the obligation for continuing expenses.

The projected impact on library operations already in place, including budgets, workloads, and services.

The institutional or library support expected. Proposed financing of the service may include securing a grant to cover start-up costs and charging fees for service.

A timetable for accomplishing the planning, the purchase of equipment, training of searchers, and phasing in the search service.

ESTABLISHING GOALS AND OBJECTIVES

Long-term goals for the inclusion of online searching among other services provided by the academic library are not any different from those already in place for meeting the information needs of the academic community. Online searching enhances and improves these efforts. More specifically, the goals may include:

Establishing an online search service to improve the quality of research on campus.

Providing expanded and personalized information services for faculty and students.

Broadening the scope of library resources.

Integrating online services into the information retrieval provided by reference services.

Increasing the effectiveness and efficiency of the information retrieval process.

Acquainting students with electronic services to enhance lifelong information gathering skills.

These goals should be kept in mind as more immediate objectives are established.

Objectives are specific proposals that can be examined or measured to determine if they have been achieved. They should result in attainment of the goals and will be influenced by the nature of the library and its environment. Library characteristics affecting the objectives include the type and size of the academic institution and its programs; the amount of faculty research; the makeup of the student body and number of graduate programs; specialized institutes or laboratories on campus; the size of the library; the number of staff; and the desire or necessity to provide services to individuals, businesses, and other groups from outside the campus community.

Objectives to help accomplish the goals of supporting research and improving information services include:

Sponsoring an open house to introduce the new service.

Online demonstrations in departments and/or colleges.

Production of a brochure.

Personal contacts of research faculty by searchers.

Collecting statistics on the patrons using the service to determine where more publicity and education are needed.

Collecting statistics on the interlibrary loan requests generated by searches to document the impact of the new service.

Collecting statistics on the databases used to observe the areas for more support material and advanced searcher training.

Determining the costs of individual searches, the average charge for a search, and observing the costs relative to the information delivered.

Evaluating patron satisfaction after six months.

Surveying searchers' opinions on procedures, equipment, results obtained, and amount of training received.

Having a plan with a time schedule and a number of objectives to be accomplished will benefit the library beyond reaching the stated goals. The library staff will recognize that there has been careful planning to establish this service, and that efforts are being made to improve information delivery. The library's image in the campus community is enhanced as new technologies keep up with developments in other fields, and as closer relationships are developed between librarians and patrons participating in this personalized service. A discussion of goals follows.

Establishing a Computer-assisted Search Service

A search service is an organizational unit that provides individual consultation and information retrieval. Although it is primarily aimed at research faculty and graduate students, any member of the academic community is able to consult with an information specialist (or reference librarian) to obtain a bibliography or specific information. Fast, thorough, up-to-date online information retrieval can determine work already accomplished on a topic of investigation, provide background for a research proposal, or establish methods or data needed to solve a research problem. Appointments are usually scheduled to allow the patron and searcher the opportunity to discuss the search problem undisturbed. By working together, a list of appropriate terms can be assembled and a strategy developed so that a database search will result in the information needed.

Besides its value to research programs, the availability of online searching will enable faculty to have personal assistance for the preparation of a bibliography for a class lecture, a list of recent articles for writing a review article, or the retrieval of data for presentations. Librarians can assist graduate students by using an online search to identify other work that may have been done on a proposed thesis topic or to complete a comprehensive review for dissertation research. Even the student who does not know where to begin on a term paper can choose to have an online search performed to produce a few references, while simultaneously receiving special guidance regarding sources and locations of material.

A search service is organized to provide personal attention for patrons with skilled assistance and searches on demand or on an appointment basis. Search results are available immediately or within two to five days. The online databases accessed by the service greatly expand the reference resources available in the library and usually contain information more up-to-date than a printed equivalent.

Contributing to Campus Research Projects

Faculty members writing grant proposals can usually improve their submissions by including a computer search on the topic to show that the same work has not been done previously, or to show a background of established documentation for their proposed outline of work. Access to an online database such as CRIS which lists research programs funded by the Department of Agriculture can be a requirement of a grant proposal for that agency. With emphasis in many disciplines on funded faculty research, the ability to quickly produce a bibliography or information on very specific subjects can save time for the individual researcher not only in the grant proposal stage, but also in the development and execution of the research project. In addition, an online search can provide a survey of similar work in the field and help assess the impact of the planned study.

Academic institutions with a substantial research component may have faculty working on the basic sciences from gene splicing to atomic particles, staff developing new techniques for studying viruses and diseases, and graduate students carrying out engineering studies on the seabed storage of nuclear waste. The very large databases in chemistry, physics, biology, engineering, and medicine can provide a massive amount of information on most subjects in the basic scientific fields and the ability to retrieve current and retrospective citations.

Librarians can work closely with research faculty providing up-to-date comprehensive literature appropriate for their areas of interest. Researchers may want a broad search, viewing everything related to their subject. They often find that the information in the abstracts is sufficient to tell them who is working in their field and the major results being achieved. Others want to have their own terms searched and are certain that there are no other words that could be used. A few references on their topic may be sufficient to give them an indication of current research.

Scientists often depend on their colleagues, their knowledge of other current work relating to their research, and their own subscriptions to relevant journals to keep up with the literature. It is often when they are exploring a new area of research, trying a new technique, or when they need assurance that they possess all the current literature for a paper that they will ask for a literature search to be run. Graduate students, on the other hand, frequently work on topics that concentrate on one aspect of their adviser's major interest or a related area new to the investigation. They need some background on the basic literature that they often find by starting with a recent publication and securing the articles cited.

Librarians can produce substantial printouts that have great relevance to a research topic, and some scientists will be very anxious to read the results. Others may find that all the articles are printed in a foreign language or published in obscure journals difficult to obtain. A search resulting in a few items of interest may reflect the lack of published work in the field or may be due to the patron's lack of understanding of the search process, the searcher's inability to understand the topic, poor technique, or use of an inappropriate database. These disappointments may result in a researcher avoiding further bibliographic research, deciding that calling a friend for a reference to a recent article is a better and more productive process. Researchers may also be very impatient if they have to wait to borrow a book or find an article. In order to cope with these different attitudes toward the literature, it is essential that searchers give priority to and provide a responsive service. Care must be taken to understand the attitudes of patrons in order to decide when a comprehensive and careful search is needed or when a quick scan of the literature is the best response. The ability to order documents online also provides assured support for the researcher requiring critical information quickly and cost-effectively.

Patrons who need to keep up with the latest developments may be interested in arranging for an SDI (Selective Dissemination of Information) service. Their search strategy can be stored and run automatically by the vendor against each database update, or performed at intervals in the library to supply new literature citations on a regular basis. Online services encourage the close collaboration of researcher and librarian. To be of greatest value to these patrons, a search service must be conveniently located, searchers must be well trained and able to discuss terminology and research topics, and the search service must be one component of the overall information retrieval provided.

Integrating Online Searching into the Library Reference Services

A search service must be closely linked to reference services for maximum effectiveness; electronic databases then become one element in the search for information. Used to complement and enhance printed indexes, databases can be searched quickly; they cover a span of years; and the computer provides a means of easily finding specific information. Several databases can be searched in succession for broad coverage of the literature. Indexes that are heavily used in the printed form are strengthened by the additional access points available online, such as searching by colloquial or scientific terms; specific names of tests, methods, or phenomena; classification codes for industry, general subject or geographic area, author affiliation, journal name, and type of document. Several of these components can be combined in one search statement to find information on subjects difficult or impossible to secure from a printed index.

Databases may also represent collections of indexes such as CAB ABSTRACTS which includes all the abstracts published by the Commonwealth Agricultural Bureaux, or INSPEC which combines *Physics Abstracts, Electrical and Electronics Abstracts* and *Computer and Control Abstracts* in one database. Other databases contain information not available in a printed form such as industry standards, business and financial information, and files that have been assembled by a company or professional society to meet their own needs (STANDARDS AND SPECIFICATIONS, FINANCIAL INDUSTRY INFORMATION SERVICE, or FAMILY RESOURCES). Particular programs on campus may depend on the library to supply specific information easily found in online databases, such as the latest government regulations on the development of drugs, lists of specific types of companies for surveys, or literature on the newest applications of robotics in other countries.

When equipment was very expensive and databases were limited to scientific topics and when librarians had little experience with computers, it made more sense to consider a centralized search unit where a few full-time searchers could take advantage of the equipment and benefit from repeated searches. Now that microcomputers can be found in most offices and laboratories, and librarians have experience with computer-assisted operations from word processing to catalog databases, and now that the scope of resources available from databases reaches into every subject area, it is vital that the computer-assisted search process be a strong component, not just an optional resource adjacent to reference services.

Integrating online sources into the information retrieval process may cause a change in the composition of the reference collection. An online source may replace a printed index that is either too expensive or of such limited interest that it is not possible for the library to justify the cost of a subscription. The library may also choose to forego a costly cumulative index for an important abstract (such as *Physics Abstracts*) when the yearly printed indexes are available and the equivalent database can be searched online to cover a number of years. Few academic librarians have been able to provide bibliographies on specific topics for faculty or students when the only procedure available was to search printed indexes. By utilizing the computer, librarians can speed up the search process and provide patrons with the answers to their questions, rather than just point to sources. The overall goal must be integration, where the choice of a printed source, a quick online search, or a more lengthy interview with the patron and expertly executed online search of the literature is determined by the patron's information needs.

When online database searching is new to the institution, however, there is an advantage in centralizing the service and concentrating on particular subject areas until more experience is gained. As more librarians are trained, procedures established, and confidence developed, having a terminal or computer for providing search services near each information desk will be the logical and required arrangement.

Acquainting Students with Electronic Services

Whether students are being taught library research in groups in the classroom or on an individual basis near the reference desk of the library, access to both printed and online information sources offers maximum learning potential. Utilizing both a printed index and its online version in a discussion of bibliographic research with a class will reinforce the use of subject terms, the need for a clearly defined problem, and the steps for formulating a search strategy that can be useful for either the printed or online source. There are advantages for each approach to information retrieval, and this contrast is significant for the student's future academic work.

Teaching about database resources at a department faculty meeting or in the class or seminar room can easily include an online demonstration on a portable terminal. A demonstration of a database search is also an enticement for encouraging a faculty member to bring a class to the library. Graduate seminars, advanced classes requiring literature reviews, and undergraduate courses where students are responsible for research papers are all groups of the academic population that will benefit from the exposure to resources available online and the value of the computer in retrieving information.

Enhancing the Capabilities and Efficiency of the Librarians

Librarians answering questions at the reference desk will have additional resources to consult when online systems are available. Time consuming efforts to complete or correct an article citation can be replaced by a quick database search. Articles on topics too new to be found in printed indexes are easily secured online. Librarians can provide information services for individuals and work with them to produce a review of the literature on a research topic or the background for a thesis proposal. Several databases can be searched in sequence, a number of years covered, and an extensive bibliography printed out immediately. Online practice and experience are necessary for optimum efficiency and the confidence to select the best method for securing information.

Reference librarians who become familiar with electronic databases will find that they learn a great deal about the equivalent indexes. Practice with thesauri, examining abstracts, comparing indexes and databases for subject content, and the need for careful consideration of terminology are all experiences that increase knowledge of both printed and electronic sources. For an online search, the patron's description of a subject must be converted into specific search terms that precisely define the topic. These terms must conform to the vocabulary of the selected database. The search is then carried out in logical steps that group synonyms and search concepts and then combine them to effect retrieval of a number of records. The searcher as well as the patron quickly observes the results of the search strategy and is able to determine whether the information retrieved is appropriate.

Since the process is dependent on precision of terms and understanding of their application, searchers will be much more successful when working with researchers if they have background and experience in the subject area. A librarian with an undergraduate degree in history will have difficulty finding chemical names or using zoological classifications. A science reference librarian may have problems trying to do an adequate search of the humanities literature. While the fields can be learned, there is an obvious advantage to building on a subject specialization when working in research areas. In addition, since most online searching requires the searcher and the patron to work together to find information on a subject, the librarian has an opportunity to increase communication between the library and departments. More knowledge about faculty interests and activities will assist in planning library services. If searchers are also involved in collection development, the more personal interaction with faculty and students over search topics will help increase awareness of changing subject interests and the development of new programs and projects on campus.

Advanced training of librarians in search techniques, content, and organization of databases will add to their expertise as information specialists at the reference desk. The availability of a search service to take fullest advantage of the training and experience of the librarians cannot help but enhance the library's reputation as a service-oriented, effective, information-retrieval facility.

Serving Additional Groups or Individuals

When the online search service has become established and experience has been gained, some academic libraries may wish to extend this service to the community outside the campus. Some institutions, particularly those that receive public support, may be expected to provide information services for local businesses and industry. Governmental units, community hospitals, small neighboring colleges, local inventors, writers, and small independent research units are other potential patrons. It will be a logical extension of online searching services to reach this group. The characteristics that make online information retrieval of great value to the research community will also provide effective support for scholars and industry.

The goals and objectives to be achieved by acquiring access to online databases define services that should be reviewed regularly, and resources that can be expanded as experience is gained. While online searching requires librarians to achieve more expertise, more training, and more computer skills, they must still continue their responsibilities at the reference desk, answering telephone questions and assisting patrons. A proposal to add an additional service must include a careful review of priorities so that a search service does not overburden individual librarians to the detriment of their job performance. In addition, as the service grows, there must be flexibility of workloads and, when necessary, more public services personnel. The goals and objectives when planning a search service must aim toward enhancement of the overall reference and information services, first for the campus community and then for additional groups.

DEFINING THE CLIENTELE

Research faculty are likely to be the first patrons to ask about an online search service. Their interest may be sparked by the frustration of trying to find needed information in a printed index, or the necessity of keeping up with the most recent advances in their field. The intensive competition for grant or contract funding, the accumulation of scientific work as publications proliferate, and the impact of high technology on research methods require access to the resources available through remote databases. It is not only easy to justify establishing an online search service for these research-oriented patrons, but funded research can, in turn, support database searching when projects include an allotment for literature searching or overhead money can be tapped for library support.

Research in the social sciences and business fields is assisted by database files of statistics, directories, and bibliographic citations. Faculty working in these subject areas may wish to find examples of new social programs, tests for reading levels, articles on potential corporate mergers, or a mailing list for a survey of business establishments. Literary themes or styles, art criticism, music methodology, and teaching experiments can now be explored in the humanities literature as art, music, and historical databases are increasing in number.

Graduate students may utilize a literature search service even more than faculty. Guided by their faculty advisors and often funded by research money, they may be working on particular aspects of larger projects and their time for library research is limited. A literature search will show their thesis or dissertation committee that they have thoroughly investigated previous work in the field. A follow-up search when they are ready to finish or publish the results of their research saves both time and effort. Professors will often send their new graduate students to the library for an online search to learn the procedure and so that they can take advantage of a quicker start on their literature review. Graduate students may also be responsible for much of the searching needed by their professors, who are too busy to come to the library. The graduate programs on campus, the levels—masters or doctorates—and the numbers of these students will help determine the demands on the library search service.

Teaching faculty will utilize a search service to update lectures, find case studies, or print bibliographies for their students. Student class projects and papers with research components can also be assisted with an online literature search. Faculty may wish to have a demonstration of an online search included in a bibliographic instruction session to acquaint students with library resources and the various means of access. Publication requirements of faculty members, whether writing a textbook or researching a review article, seeking grant sources or finding a few figures for next week's speech, will all add to the potential use of online searching.

Most academic libraries serve broad subject interests; however, branch libraries and particular programs in an institution—a medically oriented service for the elderly, a curriculum development center, or a cellular biology research unit—are subject area concentrations that should be considered when determining the potential for online services. It is possible to focus on serving these special units or areas of study, service, or research to provide an initial impetus that can then be expanded to include a wider segment of the academic community.

Service to undergraduates may be a special concern for the smaller college; however, undergraduates from all academic institutions now face a stronger emphasis on writing and academic excellence. The librarians' support of better scholarship may include an online search for students developing a class presentation, researching a lab report, or writing a term paper. So many students have had experience with computers that they will be increasingly enthusiastic about online-assisted information retrieval and, in fact, may find outlining a search topic for the computer a logical and interesting approach to library research. Other students will be eager to learn the techniques so they can apply them to searching with their own microcomputers at home.

Administrative staff, development officers, and other management officials of an academic institution will find literature searches valuable for preparing information used to develop new projects on campus, finding grant sources, investigating possible candidates for honorary degrees, surveying policies on other campuses, or determining the patent potential of a particular research project. Producing a quick bibliography on these topics will impress personnel who often do not think of asking the library for assistance.

Identifying potential individual users of online searching can begin by observing those asking questions at the reference desk, patrons using the indexes, and faculty and students frequenting the journal stacks. These regular patrons will be particularly interested in and appreciative of the capabilities of a search service. An academic institution with a population of foreign students will often find this group eager to utilize the results of an online search. With the assistance of a librarian to prepare the search terminology, and to help select the best sources for the information needed, many of the problems associated with English-language indexes can be overcome. The search not only puts students in direct contact with a librarian, but helps them formulate a search strategy and provides those with language difficulties a start toward finding the information they need.

The clientele for a search service may also include those faculty and students, both graduate and undergraduate, who are anxious to do online searching themselves. Whether or not they have their own microcomputer, they can quickly learn a system with simple searching protocols. This group may well include individuals not interested in the appointment, preparation, and procedure necessary to search a topic with the librarian as intermediary. They may not need a great deal on a subject, just ten references for a term paper or the most recent work done in the field. Others may be long-time library users who understand their subject and the appropriate indexes from extensive use and who are very capable of extending their own bibliographic research techniques to this electronic approach.

The clientele, then, includes the broad range of library patrons from the academic community seeking information. While originally geared to research needs, the increased range of subjects covered by online databases provides information on many levels.

DETERMINING LOCATION

The location of a search service within the administrative structure of a library and its physical location, which may be centralized in the building or library system or dispersed to separate subject areas or branches, requires careful consideration. The most important factors in the placement of the service are the resulting quality of service for the library clientele and the efficiency of the information retrieval process. Since online searching is part of the reference services the library provides, it should be closely linked both administratively and physically.

Physical Environment

The characteristics and ambience of a search service location will influence the response of patrons and the morale of the searching staff. Enough space and furniture, convenience, and adequate planning for the future are important aspects. Particular considerations include:

Building Location · An active searching program will benefit from being near reference material and the reference desk. This placement allows convenient access to online resources for answering reference questions, and facilitates the utilization of other sources to supplement the search results. If the search service is within sight of the reference desk and in a public area, the physical location can be used to help identify the service and make it easier to alert potential patrons to its availability. On the other hand, if the location is too open, without any barriers to protect the desk, terminal, and telephone, it will be more difficult to safeguard the equipment, and it may put stress on librarians when they are doing a search in full public view. A hidden or out-of-the-way location may be so inconvenient as to be a deterrent for responsive and convenient service. To be most effective, however, there should be a defined space for the search service, one used only for this purpose.

Noise is another important factor to consider when evaluating potential locations. Although care should be taken to purchase a quiet printer, discussions about search topics and the activity associated with the search process may be annoying to those working at a reference desk or trying to study in the vicinity. In addition, concentration is needed when developing a search strategy with a patron and any interruption at the terminal will increase costs—a particularly important consideration if the patron is being charged for the connect time. Therefore, there needs to be some separation from, as well as convenient access to, reference activities.

Space Requirements · A separate room or area with partial or transparent walls will provide an environment suitable for the search negotiation and execution, as well as security for equipment. Space is necessary for a table and chairs, bookshelves, and files. The search area should also be large enough to handle small group demonstrations and, if the space is to be shared with other operations, arrangements must be flexible and allow priority for the search service. A contained, exclusive area may also be important if some potential users need to have privacy or confidentiality when discussing their research topic. Alternatives to a separate room should be considered carefully. Searching at a librarian's desk, in an alcove, at or behind the reference desk may be necessary choices, but the disadvantages of possible interruptions, the need for nearby manuals and resource material, and the intrusion of this activity on others should be appraised.

Planning for space needs should include consideration of future expansion. Additional searching terminals and room for adding equipment at a later date for patrons to do their own searching may be important for the library and its clientele. Terminals for this purpose might appropriately be located either within the room set aside for searching, or plans may be made for an adjacent area.

Utility, Equipment, and Furniture Needs · A high-quality telephone line and adequate electrical connections for the equipment are primary essentials. Terminals or microcomputers may already be available but may need a modem for connection to the telephone line. If possible, a terminal should be purchased and dedicated to the service. If a microcomputer must be shared, there should be an understanding that database searching must have priority. Convenient storage space for manuals and other materials, along with furniture for consulting with patrons and for their observation of the search process, are important. These elements are needed, therefore, for the initial phase of operation:

> two or three telephones or jacks
> adequate electrical outlets
> one or two terminals or microcomputers
> acoustic coupler(s) or modem(s)
> table for consultations
> three or four chairs for the searcher and patrons
> shelving for manuals, thesauri, and other materials
> file cabinets for forms and records

Additional electrical outlets and telephone jacks for adding more machines in the future may be economical to include in the beginning stages. Extra chairs will be useful for group demonstrations. Another terminal for the reference desk or a portable machine to use in different locations may be an additional priority for flexibility in serving patrons.

Administrative Placement

The organizational placement of a search service is usually either integration into the reference department with reference librarians searching as part of their provision of information services, or separation as a special unit responsible to the head of the library or the head of public services. Integration is the most logical choice for providing effective information services and for utilizing the experience and expertise of the reference librarians, although there may be some instances when a separate unit providing search services would be advisable. These would usually be related to staffing—primarily workload—and the willingness of reference librarians to learn online searching. Some institutions may choose to hire a part- or full-time person who has the expertise and can concentrate on search services.

Integration · Integrating the search service with reference activities adds the computer to other tools used by reference librarians for information retrieval. Online sources add great depth to the reference collection and the convenient access makes more efficient use of the librarian's time. By having an active role in the search service, these librarians are aware of the potential of computer-assisted searching in the information retrieval process, and this knowledge can be communicated to patrons whenever appropriate. In addition, reference librarians who become searchers increase their expertise in subject specialties, gain additional skills with computers that can be incorporated into other tasks such as word processing, increase their knowledge of printed indexes, and have an opportunity to work more closely with individual patrons.

Online searching can be integrated into branch libraries when full reference service is provided there. These associated units can now offer their clientele broader resources and personalized service at the touch of the keyboard. The smaller college library may have only one or two reference librarians responsible for answering a broad range of questions. Online databases will add to their information tools, and patrons can be offered online search services as extensive as those of any larger institution.

A potential disadvantage of integrating online searching into reference activities is that one more time-consuming activity is added to an already very busy operation. There may be inequality of responsibilities as some subject specialists do more searching and others may not get enough practice. It may also be difficult to provide searches as quickly as requested when they must be fitted into reference desk schedules and other activities. These problems can be lessened by adding staff to the reference unit as online searches increase. Supplementing the search service with facilities for patrons to do their own searching is a possibility for providing this service and reducing the workload and time demands on reference personnel.

Separation · An organizational pattern that concentrates online searching in a separate unit detached from other information services could put emphasis on responsiveness, searches on demand, by appointment, or during specified hours. Personnel for this unit could include new staff members with online searching experience, subject bibliographers or other librarians, both from within and outside of the reference department. If the number of searchers is kept to a minimum, they receive the maximum amount of practice, have job descriptions with searching as a major emphasis, and are able to give priority to this responsibility. Staff could be selected for their capabilities as searchers and to take advantage of subject specialties. The location of a separate unit would not have to be near the reference desk and could be in a centralized location to serve a multiple branch library system. With less distractions, expertise could be developed, searches could receive high priority, and emphasis could be placed on developing a specialized clientele or attracting a new user group.

The primary and most serious disadvantage of this organization is its separation from the reference operation. A patron has two places to go for information and, unless procedures are very clear, this may be confusing. It is usually up to the librarian to decide if a subject is suitable for an online search, and sometimes this cannot be determined without experience with both printed and online resources. Searchers not part of the regular reference staff will not be as familiar with the resources of the reference collection and may not be accustomed to working with faculty and students. Separating the online search service from reference desk activities requires an emphasis on good communication to avoid duplication of effort and to provide the best service for patrons. This can be a viable short-term arrangement, but should be considered the first step toward full integration.

STAFFING THE SEARCH SERVICE

Searching responsibilities may be part- or full-time. Searchers are usually reference librarians, but could be subject bibliographers, staff interested in working with computers, or individuals hired especially for this purpose. Skills associated with good searchers are the same qualities usually identified with good reference librarians—a facility for working with the public, subject expertise, experience with the reference interview, and logical and deductive thinking. Searchers should be accustomed to using indexes and thesauri, familiar with student and faculty interests, and comfortable using computers.

The staffing decision may be influenced by the number of professionals in the library, the workloads already in place, the necessity to adjust service or staffing priorities, funds available for hiring searchers, and interest and training of existing personnel. Since the primary demand for searching will be from patrons involved in research, reference librarians already working with these individuals will be the first choice to become searchers. Training two searchers at first allows them to work together to learn and improve search techniques and to develop procedures best suited for the library. With two trained individuals available, the patron's search is more likely to be scheduled at a convenient time. If the staff is limited, one person may be assigned the task of doing all the searches, or an experienced searcher may be hired to initiate the service before reference librarians receive training.

The personnel decision may be affected by the funding available for beginning the service. If a grant or specially allocated funds have been secured, the budget may include an amount for all the reference librarians to be trained or for a temporary position that can be filled by an experienced searcher. If funds are limited to the current library budget, it may be necessary to train one searcher at a time. Regardless of the personnel selected, it is vital that the reference staff work closely with the searcher(s) so that procedures assist the integration of database searching into the information retrieval process.

ESTIMATING COSTS

Equipment, space needs, support materials, search fees, public relations, and staff training are cost elements for setting up a search service. These costs can be divided into three segments: those involved with the initial investment, primarily the equipment, space, manuals, and initial training to set up the service; variable costs related to use, including the telecommunications, online, and printing charges for individual searches, which can fluctuate widely; and continuing costs, including regular training for keeping up search skills, manual updates, support materials, public relations, and in-house use of online databases for practice time, demonstrations, and search problems.

Initial Investment

Setting up a search service will require funds for site preparation, equipment, introductory training, and materials. Total investments can vary widely and depend on the building facilities available, the choice of equipment, the number of searchers receiving training, and the amount of support material needed. Costs can be modest or substantial and will not be affected as much by the size of the library as by the need for building improvements and the choice of equipment.

Costs can inflate rapidly if a microcomputer is used with all the potential software options, if a more elaborate office is desired, or if extensive building renovation, electrical rewiring, and telephone service are required. Since this capital investment will also be approximately the same for each location established as a search center, these costs may influence the number of locations set up at the initiation of search services.

Site Preparation · There will be minimum costs to prepare an online search service location if some rearrangement in the building will provide satisfactory space. A desk or table with two chairs in a corner, out of the traffic area, where discussion and printing noises will not disturb anyone would be a minimum requirement. An unused office near the reference area would be much better. Convenient access to the reference desk and the reference collection is important. There must be a telephone with an outside line that is not part of a switchboard operation and that cannot be interrupted by someone else. Electrical outlets for a terminal and any extra lighting should be available. The usual ambience of light, heat, or cooling should be observed.

However, if possible, a more permanent and more expansive facility is desirable and some building accommodation may be necessary. A room with partial walls or some glass panels may be built into an open area near the reference desk, or some bookshelving may be moved to make space that can be enclosed. The room should be large enough for several tables, chairs, bookcases, and files or even larger to accommodate a small class of twelve to fifteen students and six to eight microcomputers. Furnishings may be regular tables and chairs or computer work stations; ergonomic chairs may be used. Telephone lines and electric wiring must be adequate and the facility should be planned so that security is provided for the equipment.

Equipment · Terminals and computers are becoming less costly as they are becoming faster, with more data storage capacity. A microcomputer with software to assist the search process, a portable terminal for demonstrations or for use at the reference desk, and a spare terminal to use in case any machine problems develop during a search would provide the equipment for almost any situation. However, all this equipment is not necessary to begin the operation of a search service.

A printing terminal with an acoustic coupler or modem to connect to the telephone line is the simplest form of equipment. The slowest terminals are available with a communication speed of 300 baud (thirty characters per second) and are adequate for the initial operation of a search service. As the searchers become more skilled and the number of requests for searches increases, the use of faster equipment will be desired, so if possible a 1200 baud machine should be acquired at the beginning.

A microcomputer is an even better investment. It permits the maximum flexibility for searching with software programs that can increase the efficiency of the search process, take care of accounting, and provide the results on a disk or in printed form. It can also be used for other purposes in the library. A printer is an essential part of this arrangement. The campus computer center can provide advice on the purchase of equipment and can often obtain terminals and microcomputers for reduced prices.

Support Materials · System manuals are a necessary purchase for each vendor utilized. The basic manual provides the system commands and guidelines for developing searching techniques. Separate chapters devoted to each database are part of the system manual and can usually be purchased separately. The basic manual and chapters for those databases that are expected to be used the most are a minimum purchase. Brief descriptions of other databases in the system that do not seem appropriate to the library's needs may be sufficient for occasional searches. Database outlines such as Dialog's Bluesheets or BRS's Aid Pages include the components of the records in the database and the various access points. These can assist searching, but do not replace database chapters for search guidance.

Additional support material will depend on those databases anticipating the greatest use. A thesaurus of terms such as *MESH* or the *ERIC Thesaurus*, used in the construction of the equivalent printed index, will be necessary for adequate searching of the databases. A small collection of dictionaries and both general and specific thesauri to cover several fields can be useful. Many databases have search manuals published by their producers. Some, such as Predicasts *PTS Users Manual*, are important to have when numerical codes have been used to supplement the search terms, when searches in this field are expected to be complex or comprehensive, or when the subject matter is particularly difficult or specific.

Supplies such as paper and ribbons for the printer, record books, and paper for preparing forms and reports are needed. Printing a brochure describing the search service is a good method of introducing it to the academic community. Extra diskettes for a microcomputer and subscriptions to online journals to keep up with developments in the field are helpful additions to resources for online searching.

Initial Training for Searchers · Basic training on system language and search techniques will be necessary for new searchers. Vendors of databases provide workshops on the use of their systems and this training, combined with study of the manuals and online practice, will be sufficient to begin the new library service. If possible, two librarians should receive training so that the hours of availability for searches is as extensive as possible, vacation time can be covered, and so they can share problems and questions while working together to improve their searching techniques.

Variable Search Costs

Each search performed for a patron will generate different costs dependent on a number of factors. Charges for individual searches are unpredictable and fluctuations in the demand for searching make planning and budgeting very complicated. For this reason and also because of the potential for incurring very high costs, many libraries have chosen to pass this charge on to the patron receiving the information.

Many factors can influence this charge per search, including: the search topic and its complexity; the databases accessed; the amount of information needed by the patron; the skill of the searcher; and the type of equipment used. Even the time of day will make a difference, as the response time from the vendor during the search can be slower during peak use periods. These human and machine influences on an individual search affect the charge from the vendor. The charge, usually printed at the end of the search, is composed of a number of variable components, including: the cost of the communications network per hour of use; the connect-hour rates for each database accessed; and the per-record charge for the information received. Characteristics of these cost components encompass:

Communication Charges · The location of the nearest connection with a vendor or a communication network such as Telenet, Tymnet, or Dialnet may depend on the part of the country and the distance to a major city. Vendors can be called directly if they are close enough, but most institutions will use one of the networks that offer a cost-effective link with the host computer. There is some difference in the hourly rate of these companies (in the range of eight to fourteen dollars) and their charge is usually added directly to the vendor's bills. The library's telephone charge to reach this connection is an additional cost that may be absorbed as part of the overall library operations.

Vendor Connect-time Fees · Database charges are primarily based on connect-time with the database vendor's computer. The rate will vary depending on the database being accessed. Many vendor connect-hour fees are a combination of the vendor's charge and royalty fees of the database producer, although some price lists will separate these figures. The hourly charges can range from $25 to $300 per hour. Various contract arrangements with the vendor will affect the charging rates with the highest cost (described on the basis of cost per hour) for a contract with no subscription or initial contract fees. Rates are usually reduced as volume of use increases and if subscriptions are prepaid.

Subscriptions are usually based on a minimum number of hours of connect-time with the vendor's computer. It is necessary for an online service to be in operation for a while in order to estimate a reasonably accurate amount of time that will be used per month or per year. While most vendors have several different arrangements available for their customers, a few may require a subscription, an initial contract fee, or an annual payment and, due to the wide variations, it is important to check thoroughly the entire range of fees from each source considered. The availability of a local network or group of libraries that can take advantage of lower rates by subscribing as a unit should be investigated. This will not only allow access to the lowest level of costs, but may also reduce the amount of negotiation necessary with the individual vendors.

The simplified versions of Dialog and BRS, the Knowledge Index and BRS After Dark, are examples of database access at a much lower rate than the largest volume discount for the major online service. Designed for home computer use, they are an economical source of online information for libraries wishing to provide facilities for patrons to do their own searching, or finding it practical to use these less expensive systems for training searchers. The hours of availability and the number of databases may be limited. However, searching procedures are simplified and these systems can be a cost-effective method for novice searchers to begin on their own and to have some online practice.

Type/Display/Print Charges · The information received by the online searcher in the form of a bibliographic citation, abstract, or other record content, is another component of the vendor search charge. This cost is not affected by the type of contract with the vendor. The charge for the record obtained will be dependent on the database used and may vary with the portion of the record printed. For other databases there will be a standard fee any time the source of the citations is included. Depending on the database, the charge may differ for offline printouts or printing online. The online print charge will be the same for displaying on a screen, printing, or transferring the records to a disk.

The Dialog citation charges vary widely, ranging from no charge to forty-five cents per citation, to twenty dollars for an annual report, or fifty dollars for a complete patent. For some searches these display and print fees quickly become more significant than the connect-time charge.

Personnel · The time librarians spend on each search must be included as a changeable cost component that will largely depend on the experience of the searcher and the complexity of the search. While the time online may be brief, the time spent preparing the search terms and discussing and composing the search strategy before going online may be substantial. Usually personnel time is absorbed by the library, but can be separated out as a direct and variable search cost.

Other Variable Factors · Some database charges are reduced for subscribers of the equivalent printed index. Added costs may include those for mailing offline prints, printing on gummed labels, or other specialized output such as tables of data or specialized reports. Special services such as SDI, automatically mailing the results of running a stored search on the newest update to selected files, have additional charges.

Continuing Costs

After the search service is operating, the library budget will need to cover continuing outlays for equipment maintenance, utilities, personnel time, training, support material, and in-house use of database searching. These continuing costs can be predicted from the level of service offered. There are two categories: expenditures specifically related to the search service and those that affect items already in the library's operating budget.

Search Service Recurring Costs • These expenses primarily relate to the use of machines, supplies, continuing education of searchers, and public relations. Terminals, computers, and printers will need maintenance or service contracts. New equipment must be purchased. Computers will require additional diskettes and different software packages may be utilized. Additional manuals and database guides with updates will be necessary as new databases become available, changes are made in the vendor's system, and as the library's service expands into new subject areas. Supplies include computer paper, ribbons, and other office materials. Advanced and review training for searchers must be a continuing commitment, and this should be supported by providing online time for practice. Training will also be necessary for new searchers as they are added to the searching staff.

Some money should be included in the continuing funding to handle problems associated with searches for patrons; online time for reference questions and in-house searching for demonstrations, library research, and bibliographic instruction; and printing for brochures, forms, and public relations material and advertising. There may be costs associated with membership in local or regional networks or online user groups, and allocations will be needed for conference attendance and subscriptions to online journals and newsletters.

Related Library Operating Costs • Staff, utilities, space, and telephone charges for the search service affect the library's operating budget. Personnel costs are probably the largest element in this category. The time needed by search personnel will increase as the service grows. Salaries for the searchers and support staff can be substantial. Usually these expenses are difficult to separate from the overall budget and are commonly absorbed by the library. In most situations, new staff is not added, the service is added to other responsibilities of the reference staff, or there is a reallocation of duties in other positions.

DECIDING ON A FEE POLICY

Before a budget can be put together in an online services proposal, there must be a decision about whether or not there will be some cost recovery expected from patrons. The ethics of charging fees for service has been thoroughly discussed with opposing viewpoints unresolved. The practical aspects of implementing a service may depend on recovering enough funds to keep the operation from overly affecting the library budget. The ability to charge patrons for specific information retrieved for them, the fact that these costs can be charged to research funding or department educational funds, and the cost-effectiveness of this form of information retrieval make the fee system acceptable in most cases. Some disadvantages, however, include poor public relations, the new responsibility for librarians to handle cash and make financial arrangements, the difficulty for some patrons to pay, and the precedence of charging for services.

The impact on the library budget is most difficult to predict for the variable cost of the individual search. If the vendor's charge for each search is passed along to the patron, the library budget will only need to include a minor amount of these unpredictable costs for housekeeping functions such as practice time for the searchers, adjusting fees when there are problems, and in-house searching. Some libraries may feel the need to recover more than this portion of the total costs, while others may wish to subsidize the patron's fee. Some cost recovery formulas based on the vendor's charges for individual searches include:

partially subsidizing the patron charge for the individual search
charging patrons the vendor's search fee
charging the patron the search costs plus a surcharge.

While the most common arrangement is the second option, charging the vendor's fee for each search, decisive factors in making the decision may be the commitment of the library administration to establish this information retrieval service and the limits of available funding. It is probable that in the research environment of a university or large college library the major users, the research faculty and staff, will have funds that can be used for online database searching. These moneys are then a small portion of the research funding used for literature to support additional grant seeking, for determining previous work on similar projects, and for background information on the subject to support publication of the results. Patrons from the research community may require complex searches and extensive printouts that can be costly and can easily reach $60 to $100 or more each. In a small college library, where the principal patrons are teaching faculty and undergraduates, brief searches on less costly databases may average less than $20. The many variable factors, however, make generalization difficult.

Although charging off a little less, a little more, or the exact amount of the direct search costs is a convenient arrangement, there are many other fee structures designed to cover at least portions of the search costs. Different categories of patrons (faculty, students, off-campus users) may be charged various rates; there can be a standard fee based on an "average" search; or only a portion of the search cost, such as type or print fees, can be charged. The most effective method of calculating a search fee is to base it on the vendor's charge so that the method of charging can remain the same despite changing database and vendor fees. In addition, when the cost is printed at the end of each database search, patrons will observe that the charge is specifically for their search and is based on the characteristics of their topic and the information received. If these variable search costs are recovered, the budgetary impact of large fluctuations in monthly totals and an expanding amount of searching will be minimized.

If the library proposal is to cover all the costs, there must be an estimate of the amount of searching that will be done and an approximate amount each search will cost. This may be very difficult to determine when the search service has had no previous experience to base the proposal on. If the estimate is 500 searches for the first year at $10 each, then $5000 must be included in the budget proposal. A start-up grant may include this category of funds with plans to institute some cost recovery when the money has been expended. This arrangement will give the searchers practice and experience before they have to charge individuals, and is an effective method of introducing an online search service. It is important, however, to inform patrons during the free period that charges will be instituted in the future. Once a search service is established and becomes a viable part of the information retrieval process, usage will gradually increase even without extensive advertising. The maximum number of searches performed will likely be determined by the amount of time the searchers have for appointments or the availability of the terminal or microcomputer.

The rate of growth, however, is influenced by many factors. One of the most important is the amount of necessary cost recovery and the ultimate charge to the patron. Advertising, enthusiasm of librarians, and the commitment of the searchers to offer a responsive and efficient service will also affect the rate at which the amount of searching increases. Scientific research and contract funds on campus, the activity of those seeking grants, the size of graduate programs, the time of the semester, and term paper pressure are all outside influences that ultimately have a great effect on the amount of online searching activity.

BUDGET PROPOSAL

The budget portion of an online services proposal includes many variable factors; however, some general estimates can be made on both a modest and a more elaborate scale, taking into account different sizes of institutions and clientele, various vendors, and alternative arrangements for search fees. It could be assumed that one library could add some furniture to an area that would be satisfactory for the search service, purchase a printing terminal and modem, buy a minimum number of manuals and search aids, train two librarians, contract with Wilsonline, and offer free searching. In contrast, another situation could include some building renovation, purchasing a microcomputer with printer and software, obtaining extensive manuals and search aids, training two searchers, contracting with Dialog and charging fees to recover the search costs. Even within these two schemes, there are many choices that can be made.

A sample budget proposal composed for a two-year plan is shown in figure 1. The range of estimated costs illustrates many of the factors that must be determined as a search service is organized.

PROJECTING THE IMPACT ON LIBRARY OPERATIONS

Adding online searching to the services already provided by a library will have an impact in many areas of a library's organization. The positive effects include greater patron satisfaction, expanded resources, faster and more efficient literature retrieval, increased skills of the librarians, an enhanced image in the academic community, and a positive effect on the morale of the reference staff as they are able to offer improved information services and to work more directly with patrons to assist in the research process.

It is possible, however, for this service to also have a negative impact on the rest of the staff if it is not introduced in a manner that helps these librarians understand just what an online search service is, what it produces for the patron, and how it extends the information resources of the library. Searchers can help solve this problem by giving demonstrations for the rest of the staff and discussing the types of searches being done. Staff in a library where terminals or computers are used for cataloging new acquisitions, where there is an online circulation system, and where microcomputers are being used in the accounting and administrative offices will not need as much introduction to the mechanics of online searching as those where the departmental operations have not acquired computer support.

The workload of reference librarians can be altered substantially when searching becomes part of their responsibilities. Time must be allotted to work on an individual basis with patrons and these sessions must be given priority at times when immediate results are needed. If appointments are made, they must be scheduled along with reference desk time, and other duties must be fitted in as time permits. Calculating charges and collecting money are usually new procedures. Everyone at the reference desk must be able to explain the value of a search, what databases are available, and potential charges. Whether all the reference librarians or just a few of them are searchers, the time consumed will certainly impact on the workload of everyone in the department. If searching is to be done by a separate unit, the effects on

Online Services Budget Proposal

First year:	Estimated Range of Costs	
Site preparation, furniture, telephone	$ 300	$ 2,500
Equipment:		
terminal or microcomputer	500	3,000
Modem	100	1,000
Printer	500	1,000
Software	—	300
System manuals, search-aids, supplies	200	600
Basic training for two searchers plus travel	200	350
Online time for practice, search backup	100	400
Search costs, fee charged	—	—
Search costs, free searches	1,000	10,000
(Number searches × cost per search)		
Public relations	50	500
Second year:		
Equipment service contract	0	500
Advanced training, two searchers	0	350
Online time for practice, search backup	100	400
Search costs, fee charged	—	—
Search costs, free searches	1,000	15,000
(Number searches × cost per search)		
Public relations	100	500
Library operations: Utilities, telephone fees,		
Building space, Personnel	Absorbed by Library	

Figure 1. Sample budget proposal

personnel may come in other areas. This changing workload will encourage the examination of priorities by the reference staff and a regular review of the information services being provided so that new methods and new sources can be absorbed and used effectively.

When the library decides to make terminals or microcomputers available to the patrons who wish to do their own searching, this step should not adversely influence the search service being provided for research faculty and students. On the other hand, end-user searching will complement and broaden search services and will ease the impact on the reference librarian/searcher for the simpler and more routine searches. It will also mean that there will be more and different questions for the reference desk about computers, software, search procedures, and strategy.

Online searching is one more service to increase the visibility of the library in the academic community and may bring additional people to use the facilities. The bibliographies generated can increase use of journals and other portions of the library collections. The immediate effect of increasing the number of interlibrary loans has been widely recognized and can be expected as bibliographic printouts bring up a broad range of information sources. Requests for new journal subscriptions will include those on online searching itself as searchers feel the necessity to keep up with the developments in the field. There could be a substantial impact on budget allocations if much of the cost of this service is absorbed. Even if the direct charges are passed along to the patron, the amounts needed for terminal(s), telephones, training, and support materials will compete for available funds. Increased services for patrons and greater efficiency and productivity of staff must be balanced against the other demands on the library budget.

PRESENTATION OF THE PROPOSAL

Approval of the proposal for an online search service must be secured from the library administration and a plan devised for the best method of funding the initial implementation. Library budgets are often completed years ahead of time and so any immediate adjustments to include additional expenses may be difficult. Various alternatives must be considered to secure these funds, which could cover up to two years of operation. Requests to an outside granting source, a campus incentive fund, support from departments, reallocation from the library budget, and patron fees could all contribute to the plan. After the approach is decided upon, a presentation made to the president, academic vice-president, the provost, or other administrator can emphasize the increased information services for the campus community and the valuable applications for many academic and research units.

Library Administrative Support

The library administration must participate in the policy decisions necessary for the successful implementation of a search service and review the procedural and budgetary aspects. The change in job responsibilities for some of the librarians, the handling of money for service, the additional equipment and space requirements, and the necessity for continuing costs will require many adjustments in workloads and budget. To build support for the necessary changes, both the internal and external constituents of the library must be educated to understand the potential for increasing services for the patron and using new methods to provide these services as efficiently as possible.

The library administration must make the decision about the amount of cost recovery necessary from patrons. This decision should be made at a preliminary stage to allow for sufficient planning if patron fees are to be implemented. The direct online costs are the most flexible and unpredictable part of the online search budget. A few commands and many dollars are added to a search cost. An error by the librarian, a misunderstanding with the patron, or an extensive in-house search may add multiple amounts to the vendor's bill. It will take serious consideration to determine the costs the library can support and whether or not the patron should be expected to contribute. Even if the library chooses to provide free searches, it is usually necessary to have some restrictions in place in order to control costs. These may be as simple as allowing the reference librarian to judge if a topic is suitable for a search or as complex as limiting each search by time online and the number of references received. The potential for uncontrolled and rapidly inflating costs requires that there be some generally understood controls or restrictions.

Enthusiasm by the library administration for this service and its information retrieval capabilities will greatly assist the implementation and resulting adjustment in library operations. The library staff will be responsible for passing this enthusiasm along to patrons who can benefit from an online search.

Academic Administrative Support

A search service may be implemented by the library without seeking approval of higher authority in the institution. This is particularly true if no additional funding is sought or the implementation is part of an overall plan to use computer systems throughout the various units of library operations. If, however, additional funding is being asked for, or online searching is used as an example of the improved services the library is providing for faculty and students, a formal presentation is desirable.

If the decision has been made to charge patrons for searches, the fee proposal, along with some examples of costs, should be part of the presentation. The precedent has already been set on most campuses where computing costs and other support services such as photography or drafting are charged to research grants or departments. Departments where online services will be particularly valuable for faculty and graduate programs can be utilized as a support group for the library proposal to offer this service. A portable terminal used for a demonstration of a search on a topic of interest to the administration, such as the establishment of an endowed chair or the work of other institutions to increase writing skills of students, will make an impressive introduction.

External Funding

A request for funds to establish a search service may be submitted to a granting source, the campus research office, friends of the library, an alumni group, or an administrative educational fund. There will be a difference in approach between a local or campus source and an outside foundation or funding agency. The campus development or research grant offices can advise on procedures and potential grantors. It is often necessary to demonstrate an impact on a broader community, innovative methods or procedures, or a model for other institutions in order to receive funds from a broad-based source. Making online searching part of the implementation of new technologies such as an online catalog or CD-ROM (Compact Disk—Read Only Memory), applying searching to a specific area of popular interest such as improving undergraduate education, or introducing online services for a broad segment of the community may be recommended. Applying for money from a campus source allows a different approach—usually more focused—to show applications for the academic community, such as support for researchers in a fast-moving field like biotechnology or assistance to graduate students.

A letter of inquiry to a funding agency will confirm a potential source of funds. This would be followed by the proposal, which should indicate definite objectives, adjustments in the current library environment, logical procedures, and evaluation after a year of service. Contributions from the library should be emphasized and may include personnel costs, equipment already owned, furniture, and purchase of support material.

The addition of a new information retrieval service will enhance the image of the library and emphasize its progressive role in the campus community. If a grant can be found to provide the initial costs and a trial period, the library administration will be better able to judge the continuing costs and will have more information for considering the budgetary impact.

SETTING A TIMETABLE

After approval of the proposal by the library and academic administrations, implementation should be planned in a logical sequence. Funding and budgeting are a critical first step. When this is accomplished, the equipment must be ordered, the site for the service prepared, telephone and electric lines installed, and furniture acquired. If six months are allotted for this to be accomplished, another three months (or some of the installation time) should be planned for securing vendor contracts and training staff. A month or more of a trial operation with introductory searches at a special rate will give the new searchers some practice and advertise the service. A program of evaluation to insure efficient procedures as the service becomes established and to allow feedback from patrons will help set a pattern for enhanced service to the community.

Bibliography

Freides, Thelma. "Current Trends in Academic Libraries." *Library Trends* 31:457–74 (1983).

Grimes, Nancy E. "Costs, Budgets, and Financial Management." In *Online Searching Technique and Management*, pp. 123–34. Edited by James J. Maloney. Chicago: American Library Assn., 1983.

Martin, Jean K. "Preparation of Proposals for Online Bibliographic Services in Academic, Government, and Industrial Libraries." *Science and Technology Libraries* 1:7–15 (1980).

Saffady, William. "Availability and Cost of Online Search Services." *Library Technology Reports* 21:1–111 (1985).

3

SELECTING THE DATABASE VENDOR(S) *55*
    Online Vendor Characteristics *56*
    Database Resources *57*
    Search Costs *61*
    Vendor Contracts *62*
    Other Comparisons *63*
CHOOSING THE EQUIPMENT *67*
    Terminal or Microcomputer *68*
    Modem or Acoustic Coupler *69*
    Printers *70*
SELECTING THE SEARCHERS *70*
TRAINING SEARCHERS *72*
ORGANIZING SEARCH RESPONSIBILITIES *75*
SEARCH PROCEDURES *76*
    Scheduling Searches *76*
    Preparing for Searching *77*
    Delivering the Results *78*
    Forms and Record Keeping *79*
DEVELOPING QUALITY SEARCHING *79*
    Support Materials *79*
    In-house Support *80*
PUBLIC RELATIONS *80*
    Informing the Staff *81*
    Informing the Campus Community *81*

Setting Up the Search Service

Once the decision has been made to initiate a search service, the next steps in setting up the operation include choosing the vendor(s), selecting equipment, appointing the searchers and training them, purchasing manuals and support material, planning the introduction of the service to the academic community, and informing the library staff. The location of the search service should have been determined during the proposal process. A corner near the reference desk, an office behind the reference collection, or a newly enclosed room next to the index area will be prepared and furniture secured. Lighting, electrical outlets, and telephone lines must be checked for adequacy. After selecting a single vendor, modest equipment, and two searchers, the service can be introduced and expanded as procedures are developed, experience gained, and demand increases.

SELECTING THE DATABASE VENDOR(S)

Thousands of databases are available to a searcher who makes arrangements for passwords. Each of these databases may have a different method of searching and use different terminology for commands. Most libraries elect to contract with a commercial online vendor who has mounted a group of databases on one computer system to provide access with a single password and a standard system language. The largest commercial vendors are Dialog Information Services and BRS. Other vendors may offer a group of databases with a particular subject emphasis or may be publishers of indexes, such as the H. W. Wilson Company, who market their own files produced along with such print indexes as *Readers' Guide* or *Library Literature*. Some databases are available from several of the vendors; access to others is limited to a single source. The same database may be organized differently by each vendor, and the charges for accessing it will usually vary according to the vendor's policies. New material is added to the files regularly and this may take place daily, weekly, monthly, or annually. Update frequency will differ among vendors but will depend to a great extent on the publication schedule of the corresponding index or edition of a directory. Normally the update is available online before the printed copy is received in the library.

The vendor acquires the database from the producer and makes the necessary adjustments so it conforms to the organization of the online system. The components of the records in the database such as title, language, descriptors, or source are tagged for identification and retrieval. The vendor's procedures to log on to the system, to log off, to change from one file to another, to search for articles on a subject, or to type out results are very specific and the searcher must know the correct process or have a manual to follow. Some system languages may be easier to learn than others and each offers some advantages for searching and manipulating the results. Searchers may prefer one system over the others, and it can be very confusing to search several systems in sequence and difficult to maintain search skills in multiple vendor languages.

Database vendors may offer other services that are valuable to an academic library. For example, their system may include access to an electronic mail network; documents may be ordered online; instruction workshops and update sessions may be offered; and there may be extensive hours of availability. Although searchers can dial directly to the vendor's host computer, most libraries will use a communications network such as Telenet or Tymnet. These networks are accessible with a local phone call and link the searcher's telephone with the vendor at a low hourly rate. Some of these lines may be limited to certain transmission speeds.

The online search service should start with a single vendor that offers databases most closely matching the interests of the academic community. Searchers will be able to gain experience with the system, develop procedures for scheduling and executing online searches, and become better acquainted with the clientele. From this foundation other vendors and databases can be evaluated and added as patron interest is determined and additional resources are needed.

Online Vendor Characteristics

Resources:

number of databases
subject areas of concentration
unique files
database types such as directory, numerical, full-text
materials covered—newspapers, magazines, software.

Costs:

contract options
minimum use or sign-on fees
individual database charges
reduction of fees for increased usage
extra mailing, print, or management fees.

Features:

complexity of search language
structure of files—back files, segmentation
variable print formats for database records
comprehensive manuals, updated regularly.

Reliability:

response time
amount of system failure or unavailability.

Services:

extensive hours of operation
service desk for immediate assistance
SDI (Selective Dissemination of Information)
document ordering
mailing labels
newsletter
user feedback.

Training:

introductory
specialized
advanced
practice files.

While all of these factors are important, the subject areas and types of databases supplied by the vendor are a primary consideration. Reliability of the system must be maintained at a quality level. Costs will probably vary more by the type of contract than by a difference between vendor systems.

Database Resources

The character of the institution and the needs of the library's clientele should be major considerations when reviewing the databases and services available from the various vendors. Subject interests of researchers and teaching faculty, emphasis of graduate programs, and classroom assignments for undergraduates may dictate the databases needed. Resources that supplement the library's holdings may also be very important. Database access can take the place of expensive subscriptions to printed indexes or may provide support for a few faculty who have specific interests that can be met by the occasional use of an online database. Databases can also supplement library holdings by providing additional access points for extensive journal collections and heavily used printed indexes.

Database Information · Libraries are usually interested first in obtaining access to bibliographic databases. Most of these are by-products of index production; the usual result of a search of a database is a bibliography. The information included for each bibliographic reference is a database record. The record will usually include the same components found in the equivalent index: author, title, source of publication, date, and abstract. Other information from the index that is also often included in the online record: the first author's location, type of publication, language, indexing terms, major descriptors, and identifiers. Occasionally, the abstracts of the printed form may not be available, and additional information may be added to a record such as the numerical codes that indicate subject classification, an industry grouping, names of organisms, or specific chemicals. Two or more printed indexes may be combined into one file (ERIC includes both *Resources in Education* and *Current Index to Journals in Education* and CAB ABSTRACTS contains records of twenty-six abstract journals from the Commonwealth Agricultural Bureaux). Individual records are numbered by the vendor, and the reference numbers used in the printed index may also be included.

The number of records in a database file varies from a few thousand to several million. Large databases such as AGRICOLA (*Bibliography of Agriculture*), INSPEC (*Physics Abstracts, Electrical and Electronics Abstracts*, and *Computers and Control Abstracts*) and MEDLINE (*Index Medicus*) now cover more than fifteen years of publications. As they increase in size, databases have often been divided into segments, usually by time period, by the online vendors. For instance, CA SEARCH (*Chemical Abstracts*) on Dialog is in six files: 1967–71, 1972–76, 1977–79, 1980–81, 1982–86 and 1987-present. Until recently, it was necessary to search these files separately to cover the entire time period and the more than 6,500,000 records. Advancements in computer storage technology have now made it possible for many of these large files to be searched as a single unit.

Some files are being expanded backward in time; GEOREF is a significant example of a database that now covers the geological literature from 1785 to the present. The time span of other files varies and some contain just the newest information in the field. PRE-PSYCH and PRE-MED are databases that are updated weekly and retain only three months of citations before they are transferred to the PSYCINFO (*Psychological Abstracts*) and MEDLINE databases, respectively.

Databases, like their printed counterparts, contain references to various types of material; some, such as Wilsonline's SOCIAL SCIENCES IN-DEX, provide citations limited to articles in periodicals, while others such as INSPEC include conference proceedings, government publications, patents and books. Articles in newspapers may be identified and retrieved using other databases such as the NATIONAL NEWSPAPER INDEX. Although a searcher can choose to print out the list of records in various sequences (e.g., alphabetically by title, author, or journal name; by report number; or in order by a numerical field), search results are usually listed in reverse chronological order. The advantage of this procedure is that the patron can choose to read the first ten or twenty records, which will be the most recent material.

Nonbibliographic databases are additional online resources. These include directories such as the FOUNDATION DIRECTORY, BUSINESS SOFTWARE DATABASE, and SCHOOL PRACTICES INFORMATION FILE and some statistics and data files such as Predicast's TIME SERIES or FORECASTS for economic information, CENDATA for census figures, the MERCK INDEX for data on chemicals and drugs or the ELECTRONIC MATERIALS INFORMATION SYSTEM for properties of materials used in microelectronics. Increasing numbers of full-text databases are becoming available such as the COMMERCE BUSINESS DAILY, IRS TAXINFO, the HARVARD BUSINESS REVIEW and articles in chemistry journals from the American Chemical Society. Full-text databases usually allow searching of all the significant words in the publication(s) and the capability of printing out an entire page, a paragraph, or tables of data. Full text encyclopedias and handbooks make the entire content of reference books searchable and available for instant retrieval.

Not all databases have printed equivalents. They may have originated as a company or government agency file, such as the PHYSICIAN DATA QUERY DIRECTORY for 10,000 physicians and organizations devoted to the care of cancer patients, TRADEMARKSCAN for active trademarks, or CHILD ABUSE AND NEGLECT from the National Center. These databases may be either bibliographic or directory files. Vendors have their own databases, such as the CHRONOLOG NEWSLETTER or DIALOG PUBLICATIONS from Dialog, or FILE from BRS which includes descriptive material about the BRS databases to assist in determining subject emphasis, types of publications included, and current costs.

Subjects covered by databases were originally concentrated in the sciences. Medicine, engineering, and the physical, biological, and social sciences have a relatively long history of database access. Business, finance, and company information has become extensive. Humanities databases are now available in the arts, music, and literature. News, law, patents, and biography are additional subject areas representing the very broad coverage of database resources.

Database Availability · If broad subject coverage of databases is important for the library, a first choice among the available vendors will be Dialog. This largest online database company offers access to more than 200 different databases. Dialog has strong holdings in science and technology, business information, social sciences, humanities, political science, and library-related databases. Relatively new files, such as SOVIET SCIENCE AND TECHNOLOGY, BIOBUSINESS, HEILBRON, MAGILL'S SURVEY OF CINEMA, EVERYMAN'S ENCYCLOPAEDIA and PETERSON'S COLLEGE DATABASE, and further expansion into business information sources show continued development of subject areas and diversity of types of databases by this vendor.

BRS is a strong second choice with more than ninety databases. An increasing number of files covers medicine, business and finance, education, social sciences, and humanities. Their exclusive files include ARTS AND HUMANITIES SEARCH, OCLC EASI REFERENCE, ACS JOURNALS ONLINE, CATALYST RESOURCES FOR WOMEN, ROBOTICS INFORMATION DATABASE, and RESOURCES IN VOCATIONAL EDUCATION. The availability of a single file, such as the subject access to OCLC, may be a compelling reason for a library to choose BRS to begin their online service.

The Pergamon Orbit InfoLine system is the result of the recent combination of the ORBIT (SDC) and Pergamon InfoLine search services. The combined databases emphasize strengths in the technical and business fields. ORBIT databases on patents, Pacific islands, automotive and petroleum engineering, accounting, and labor complement those on InfoLine, which include British companies and trademarks, chemical engineering, and a number of specific industry files.

Other general database vendors from Canada and Europe offer still more depth in scientific research areas, international affairs, and other scholarly resources. Some of these major companies are: BLAISE-LINE (British Library), CAN/OLE (National Research Council of Canada), DATA-STAR (Swiss/English), ESA-IRS (European Space Agency), QL Systems (Nova Scotia), QUESTEL (France), and STN (service centers: Fachinformationszentrum, Germany; Chemical Abstracts Service, USA; and Japan Association for International Chemical Information, Japan). Usually accessible through Telenet or Tymnet, marketing in the United States for these vendors has increased considerably during the past few years, and they will undoubtedly maintain a presence in the marketplace. Their specialties must be examined in relation to the needs of the academic institution.

Besides these major search services, each of which offers a selection of databases on a host of subjects, there are many smaller producers who have chosen to market their own products or to maintain a particular subject concentration or a certain type of resources. One of the more recent entries into the field is the H. W. Wilson Company with WILSONLINE, the online source for their various indexes such as *Readers' Guide to Periodical Literature, General Science Index, So-*

cial Sciences Index, *Humanities Index,* and *Business Periodicals Index*. These databases are especially significant for providing increased access to library resources for undergraduate students. Since the printed Wilson indexes are used extensively for term paper research and other curriculum projects, the online versions will complement this usage and may be the first choice of the smaller college.

Other database vendors with specialized resources include Dow Jones for business information, VU-TEXT for newspapers, NewsNet for newsletters, Mead Data Central and West for legal research, Chemical Abstracts Service for *Chemical Abstracts*, NASA and NLM for government-sponsored databases, and many other business, legal, and public interest online search services. Most of these are geared to a particular clientele and should usually be considered supplemental to a general database vendor. CAS-ONLINE, for instance, may be very important for a chemistry library serving chemists who need access to the special features of this database for searching chemical structures and for those abstracts not included in the *Chemical Abstracts* files mounted on other database vendors.

Selecting a vendor with a variety of databases of interest to the library's patrons and then adding specialized vendors chosen for their specific databases or type of material available online is a realistic strategy to take advantage of the variety of resources available.

Search Costs

After examining the subject areas and selection of databases offered by the online database vendors, cost will most likely be the next consideration. Comparisons are usually based on the hourly connect charge of individual databases. Vendor catalogs generally list the maximum price of a database, which can be reduced by various contract plans.

There are many contract options available. The large database vendors, Dialog and SDC, have always offered a plan of access with charges based on computer connect-time at rates that vary with the database. There have not been any start-up or subscription fees. When BRS entered the marketplace, they required a subscription based on the estimated number of hours of expected use. In return, the customer had access to their databases at a much reduced rate. At the present time, most database vendors offer a choice of contracts that include all these options. In general, the simplest and most convenient plan is paying monthly only for the amount of database use. This plan, without any commitment of money or guaranteed amount of searching, is the most costly. The charges may be reduced when the user pays ahead, subscribes to a specific amount of online time, or when a large volume of searching is done.

Vendor Contracts

Usage Based Contract · Monthly payments with no subscription or minimum amount of searching required are billed at the maximum cost per connect hour. This no-commitment contract may include a one-time fee for a password or a small annual service fee. Although more expensive, this arrangement is a good option for trying out a system or making it available when limited use is expected.

Committed Amount of Connect Time · This contract has a monthly or annual minimum amount of connect hours that are expected to be used. There is no prepayment, but the minimum must be paid whether used or not. This contract is a cost-saving option if the volume of use matches the minimum time arrangement. As larger amounts of usage are promised, there are further reductions in database rates. Dialog, for example, requires a minimum of $5,000 annually in connect time for this contract, with better rates at higher levels. This option is an especially good plan for high volume users, or for library networks.

Prepaid Subscription Plans · Contracts paid in advance offer the best discounts. Arrangements are often available for various subscription amounts with the more money paid, the lower the database fees. For instance, for BRS a $35 hourly database rate can be reduced to $20 per hour with a subscription of $2,400 for 120 connect hours. The lowest subscription fee is $750 for 25 hours at a database charge of $30 per hour. These plans are suitable for the institution that decides to budget a prescribed amount at the beginning of the year and has enough experience to judge the level of searching that can be expected. Good planning is needed as unused time is lost and additional searching over the contracted amount may be charged at the highest rates.
    A first year contract for an academic library wishing to phase in a search service could be at the highest rate paid as the system is used. If there is considerable use expected, the lowest subscription rate could be secured until data is gathered about the amount of searching being done and a projection can be made for the next year. Another option is joining a network or group of libraries that can secure lower fees for the individual participants based on high volume use by the group.

Database Charges · Besides examining contract options, the connect-time charge for specific databases can be compared among vendors. Several databases that are expected to be used most frequently the first year can be selected and the costs from different sources determined. Database fees include the vendor's connect-time charge, the communication network cost, and royalty fees of the database producers. These rates vary widely and are frequently changed. The royalty fees are based both on connect-time and citations retrieved. Charges for typing, displaying, and printing citations have become a significant expense particularly in the sciences and business, reflecting the trend toward paying for information received rather than for the time spent online. With the utilization of microcomputers and software to aid in search preparation, in speeding the delivery of the results, and for later manipulation, the online connect charge is reduced and the total cost is often more dependent on the amount of information retrieved.

William Saffady has produced an extensive comparison of the charges of the various vendors, which shows that while BRS has the lowest average online rates, there were no significant differences among four of the major search services. [1] Additional vendor fees may include those for mailing printouts, SDI, or for specialized services such as printing mailing labels or tables of data. Costs may be reduced for some databases such as SCISEARCH or SOCIAL SCISEARCH when the library subscribes to the corresponding index.

The simplified systems, such as Dialog's Knowledge Index or BRS After Dark have significantly lower connect-time charges for their databases. This lower cost must be weighed against the slower guided command language, less convenient hours, and restrictions of flexibility of search procedures and choice of files. However, these systems may be a viable choice for libraries that want to offer online searching for patrons to do themselves.

Other Comparisons

When examining the features of various online database vendors, the following list identifies characteristics that have importance for online searchers:

Search Language and Displays · The search commands should be easy to learn and remember. This process will be facilitated if natural language is used, rather than a code that must be memorized. The availability of an online thesaurus will be valuable for some databases, and online help information will assist inexperienced searchers or those unable to keep their search skills up-to-date. Flexibility of search and sort procedures and diversity of print formats are desirable. It should be possible to select and print out any portion of the individual database record. Line numbers used for manipulating the sets of records should be clearly printed or displayed, and the list of executed com-

---

1. William Saffady, "Availability and Cost of Online Search Services. Part 2. Cost of Online Searching," *Library Technology Reports*, 21:37–111 (1985).

mands should be easily recalled at any time during a search. System messages, when errors occur, should be easily understood.

Specific features such as prefix and suffix truncation, the ability to search for an indefinite or specified number of additional letters added to the beginning or the ending of the word-stem, will be valuable for some types of searches. The capability of searching for phrases or the sequence of words either next to each other, in a certain order, or within specified parts of the record is an important feature, as well as being able to easily restrict search results to certain years or a sequence of document numbers. The procedure for limiting records to English language or to a particular date should be the same for all databases so the procedure is easy to remember. Any limits to the number of records that can be retrieved in one statement, or to the number of statements utilized in one search, should be noted. Most systems have a large data storage capability, so that restrictions to the amount of information retrieval is no longer a concern, but these can be important elements in a complex and lengthy search.

The ability to scan several databases or groups of databases with one query to help determine the most appropriate choice for a particular topic can be an effective search procedure when the subject is cross-disciplinary and there are many database choices. Storage of all or parts of the search strategy for recall to use in a second or third database should be a simple procedure. It should also be possible to store the search terms both temporarily and for indefinite periods of time. The system search language should be simple, logical, consistent, and flexible. Changes in procedures or commands that improve the search system are regular occurrences when a company is taking advantage of new technology and improved equipment. The database vendor must communicate these changes clearly and quickly to users and provide timely supplements to manuals.

Database Files · All files should be available for online access. Since backfiles on some systems may be only searched offline, the interactive capability is lost and a different procedure must be followed for searching these databases. The time span of bibliographic files should be as extensive as possible and the segmentation into parts by time period or other categories should be noted. The ability to search only the current portion of the database may be an advantage if the subject dictates that up-to-date information is the primary concern of most patrons. If comprehensive coverage is more valuable, the capability of covering the entire file in one search is desirable. Updates to the files must be regular and timely. The latest update to a database can be compared to the receipt date of the corresponding issue of the index to help judge availability of new information.

Different types of databases on a system will provide a wider scope of resources for library use. Directory files may be especially important if the reference collection is limited. Full-text files will be valuable for patrons both for the ability to print out specific paragraphs or tables of data and for sources the library may not hold. The nonbibliographic files can be an important source of data for some research areas. Other databases may be particularly suited for assisting library operations. The activity of the vendor in acquiring new databases, updating files, and improving customer services in a planned and organized manner is a sign of continuing vitality and increasing usefulness.

Each record in the system should have consistent labels for fields and specific formats for displaying the records; these should include the same components in each database. Similar components and structure of databases across the system—such as listing authors' names in the same format—are very important when several databases are searched in sequence.

Manuals · Clearly written, up-to-date manuals are indispensable. A systems manual should be free of jargon and easy to follow in a step-by-step procedure. The format and printing style of the manual and a good index are important so that if a problem arises, the correct portion of the manual can be quickly found. Updates to the manual should be supplied as soon as any changes are made in the system, and they should be easily incorporated. A brief chart of the essential search commands, kept next to the terminal, is very helpful.

Separate database manuals or chapters should describe the contents of each file in detail, how it compares to the corresponding printed form, the relationship to other databases, the major subjects of the material, and the types of documents included. Any unique characteristics of the database structure or its contents should be stressed. Suggestions for use of particular features, techniques for effective searching, and sample searches that give examples of topics particularly suited to the database are especially helpful. This support can assist the novice searcher or illustrate the procedures for patrons. Summary sheets, preferably one page, highlighting the database features should be available for quick review and consultation.

Reliability · Minimum downtime and consistent speed of response time are critical for providing dependable service. Experienced searchers may be the best source for this information, since it is the person sitting at the terminal or computer who must deal with the problem of delayed response or the loss of a partially completed search. The search vendor must have enough computer storage capacity and enough access routes via various telecommunications networks so that there are no delays at peak time of use in either logging on to the system or in response time. The system expansion capabilities must be such that as the user group expands there will not be overload problems.

Services · A toll-free service desk telephone number, staffed by experienced personnel for up to twelve hours a day, is an important feature of a vendor's service. The answering staff should be able to advise on technique and be knowledgeable about all of the databases and procedures.

The search service itself should be available for searching for lengthy hours. Dialog has recently announced that it is operational for twenty-four hours on Monday through Thursday. While most libraries will not need this capability, nevertheless, evening and weekend hours of operation may be important for some situations.

Vendors should be prompt in communicating with users about system problems and changes in databases or procedures. This can be accomplished online as part of the log-on communications or with an optional news message. A regular newsletter sent to each password is important to report manual changes, suggest searching techniques, and provide other system news. There should also be a feedback procedure for system users to communicate their suggestions and problems. BRS has a user advisory board and committees that consult with the company on new developments and consider suggestions and requests.

The availability of SDI (Selective Dissemination of Information) from as many databases as appropriate to supply regular updates for patrons may be a popular service for library clientele. This current awareness service should be easy to set up and adjust, and the system should automatically send a search of the most recent file update to the patron. Document ordering online can be useful, although the costs from various suppliers should be compared. The procedures need to be simple, the service speedy, and the charges clearly defined. There should be appropriate sources of documents for each database. Specialized reports or print capabilities in tabular or other organized formats from business files using market or demographic information and other statistical data may be of interest. Output from a directory database may be printed on mailing labels and special reports may be available when searching numeric databases.

Training Provided · Vendor-sponsored training is significant for the library introducing a new search service or adding a new vendor to a service already established. It is important that training sessions be available at convenient locations in various parts of the country and at regular intervals. There should be a selection of workshops offering various levels of instruction with opportunities for improving skills, developing specialties, and reviewing new improvements to the search system.

Introductory sessions may be one or two days and often can be followed up by specialized workshops on particular databases or database groupings by subject. These sessions are especially helpful when they include free search time at the training location or at the individual's home terminal. Costs of introductory training may range from $60 to $125 for a full-day session and be around $55 for a half day on advanced techniques.

Training files can be very useful for new searchers who are developing search techniques and need extra practice time. When available, they are usually offered at low rates. Files such as Dialog's ONTAP, available at $15 an hour, can be used for in-house instruction or for searchers who need to try out a new file, keep up their skills, or experiment with a search strategy. ORBIT offers a self-instruction workbook package and online time to use with it for $125. Video cassettes and other training aids may be available.

In evaluating the various features of the database systems, it may be difficult to judge some of the differences in language and technique without considerable experience. Specific features will be more valuable in some situations than others or simply more convenient. For instance, the logging on process, the clarity of error messages, the selection of proximity operators (which denote the position of one word in relation to another), the ease of saving a search and recalling it, the ability to disconnect from a system and then reconnect without losing a search underway, the consistency of author listings, and even the format of the individual citation will be different. Only by using several systems and comparing them can the advantages be determined.

There will also be different results when searching the same database mounted on different vendor systems. The time period covered may not be the same, the updates may come at different times, and the searchable fields for each reference may differ and may contain variable amounts of information. The search systems can all be learned rather easily and all have many variations and some unique features. Consultation with the literature or an experienced searcher will help assess the more practical advantages or disadvantages. It is first necessary to decide on the databases and services that are important for the institution and then determine which online vendor can supply them.

CHOOSING THE EQUIPMENT

The equipment needed for establishing a search service includes a terminal or microcomputer that will produce a printed output, and a modem for connecting to the telephone line. Some considerations for selecting this equipment, which may be borrowed, rented, leased, purchased, or already owned by the library, are:

Terminal or Microcomputer:

standardized, compatible with online vendor systems
printing capability, may have video display unit
convenient keyboard
speed of interaction
floor, table, or portable model
availability of software.

Modem:

attached or separate unit
communication speed
additional capabilities.

Printers:

part of terminal or separate unit
printing speed
availability of supplies
quiet operation
printing quality.

General Features:

reliability
servicing available.

Terminal or Microcomputer

A printing terminal dedicated to the search service may be the simplest and the least expensive machine to use. A copy of the search is produced as the search takes place and the speed of transmission of signals may be determined by the model, or there may be keys for selecting a choice of interactive speeds such as 30 or 120 characters per second. The video terminal is usually faster, but a separate printer will be needed to produce a permanent record of the online search. A comfortable keyboard with easily identified control keys can be chosen in a portable, table, or floor model. "Smart" terminals have some microcomputer capabilities built in which will provide extra features such as automatic telephone dialing. Terminals, however, are increasingly being replaced by microcomputers for searching, since costs have fallen dramatically, new machines are more powerful, more software has become available, and microcomputers are used for many other purposes such as word processing, record keeping, and management tasks. Most modern machines are built to meet current standards and considerations such as as ASCII coding, parity, and full duplex mode. If there is a question, compatibility can be checked with an online vendor. Reliability is extremely important and performance reviews of terminals and microcomputers and the experiences of regular searchers should be utilized. Academic computer centers or online user groups can supply additional advice.

A microcomputer with appropriate software provides options such as sending a multistep search strategy in one action (uploading), an interface to simplify the search language (for inexperienced searchers or end-users), transferring the results of a search to a disk (downloading), and providing automatic record keeping.

A quiet terminal or printer should be a priority since it will usually be located in or near a public service area. If searching is to be done in different locations and only one machine is used, a portable terminal is an obvious choice. This small-size machine can also be kept at the reference desk and locked in a drawer if security is a problem. A video display terminal (VDT) or computer monitor provides better visibility for observers, is especially useful for demonstrations, for scanning items retrieved, and for use with some of the software to work out search strategy ahead of time. It should be noted that databases with fees for typing records usually charge the same rate for displaying the records, which can be lost if not stored or printed out.

Modem or Acoustic Coupler

In order to connect the searching equipment to a distant computer, a modem is needed to translate signals from the terminal into electronic messages transmitted over telephone lines. One type of modem is the acoustic coupler that will accept a telephone handset to link the machine to the telephone line. This device may be built into a portable terminal that can then be hooked up to a telephone at any location. The acoustic coupler is mostly used at slower speeds (30 cps) and is more susceptible to line noise than a modem that plugs directly into the telephone line and is activated by pushing a button on the terminal. The modem may be an internal part of a microcomputer or may be an external box with wires running to the computer or terminal, the electrical plug, and the telephone line. An external modem may require a serial interface card inside the microcomputer. The modem must be compatible with the terminal and both must operate at the same speed of data transmission. Some modems can be programmed to automatically dial the telephone numbers when going online.

Communication rate is a consideration when selecting a modem and other equipment. Thirty or 120 characters per second (300 or 1200 baud) are the most common. Faster rates are developing, with 2400 baud presently available. At higher baud rates line noise causes more interference even though a modem is less susceptible to this problem than an acoustic coupler. The faster transmission rate does not affect the connect-time used for typing in a search request or the pause that may occur at peak times when the vendor's computer system is especially busy. However, the receipt and printing of information occurs at the much faster pace.

Telephone lines must be high quality to reduce static that will garble messages. If line noise is a problem, a modem should be capable of filtering out the extraneous sounds. Direct outside lines are essential. They should not be extensions or tied to a switchboard, as interruptions can break the connection to the database. If the faster speeds are desired, the availability of convenient communication network nodes for these rates should be investigated. Although the lines are constantly being expanded, those capable of transmitting at speeds higher than 1200 baud may be limited.

Printers

A print product is a requirement for an online search service in order to provide the patron with a copy of the search results. This can be achieved by using a printing terminal for searching or by attaching a separate printer to a microcomputer or video terminal. The printing speed must be compatible with the transmission speed of the terminal, print quality should be as legible and as neat as possible, and quiet operation is important. Simplicity and reliability are especially critical when the printer is to be used by several searchers. Ribbons should be easily replaced and the paper must feed through dependably, as a paper jam can result in lost search results.

Equipment can be rented, leased, or purchased; renting or leasing is a good option if a trial period is desired. It may also be possible to borrow a terminal from the campus computer center or to purchase one through their facilities at a reduced cost. Servicing the machine(s) is always a consideration along with the cost and availability of paper and ribbons. It may be tempting to utilize a machine that is already in the library; however, this arrangement can only be satisfactory if other uses are minimal, if it has an acoustic coupler or a modem, and if it is kept in a convenient location. Availability is a key issue here since any difficulties or delays in securing a machine work against the goal of providing rapid access to information. It is especially important to look at the overall features of the searching equipment and to favor machines that utilize standard operating systems so that assistance and advice can be easily obtained. Machines should be easy to learn, have good manuals, and have simple, straightforward procedures for adding paper, putting in new ribbons, or getting help from the manufacturer.

SELECTING THE SEARCHERS

The individual characteristics of good searchers usually match those of proficient reference librarians. The experiences of working with patrons, interpreting requests for information, teaching bibliographic instruction classes, and helping researchers or students use indexes—all help prepare a librarian for the analysis of a search topic, composing a search strategy, and explaining the procedures and results to patrons. Personal qualities important for searchers include:

good communication skills
ability to think logically and analytically
ability to organize options and make decisions quickly
interest in working directly with patrons
expertise and background in a subject area
enthusiasm about working with computers.

Individuals with a facility for analyzing problems should find the organization of keywords for a computer-assisted literature search a challenging exercise. Complex search topics require considerable skill in the selection of appropriate terms; in developing a flexible, effective strategy; and in being able to make quick decisions online. These capabilities are important for individuals who must provide efficient searching of specialized subjects with reliable results.

Experience and enthusiasm about working with computers are definite advantages. While it is not necessary to know how a computer works or to be able to program, it is important to feel comfortable at the keyboard so that more concentration can be applied to the search itself, rather than the mechanics. Librarians with subject backgrounds, experience in doing research, or an interest in computers may supply special expertise to online searching. If they are recent library school graduates they may have already had good training.

There is a substantial advantage if the searcher has worked with enough faculty and students doing research to understand their literature needs. Sometimes a few of the most up-to-date articles will provide all the information required or give sufficient access to older publications. Another problem may require comprehensive retrieval of information on the topic. In still other cases, the retrieval of no literature on the subject indicates that the thesis problem is going to contribute to an untested area of research and the student is happy with the results, even if the searcher is a bit uneasy at finding no citations and may wonder if the strategy should have been revised. Often a patron knows what information she or he needs, but does not know how to translate the problem into search terms. It is important for a searcher to be able to work with researchers and scholars and, utilizing experience at the reference desk, to help determine the subject matter and then probe further about the topic to be sure the search terms are organized to secure pertinent information for the patron.

Coping with patrons, who may be critically watching a search, takes experience and confidence, particularly when the patron is paying for citations that give them no new information or do not seem relevant to their problem. The patron may have insisted on a particular approach or there may have been inadequate selection of search terms, errors in search strategy, or the choice of an inappropriate database. These factors can result in poor public relations and will be discouraging for the searcher. For these reasons, searchers need institutional support of time and online practice to gain experience. They should be encouraged to participate in advanced and specialized workshops to learn the newest search techniques, to try out new databases, and to keep up with developments in the online field.

The number of trained searchers needed for adequate service may be difficult to determine. Since it is important to keep up searching skills and to get enough practice, it is probably best to phase in the number of searchers, adding new individuals as needed. A minimum of two searchers will provide sufficient hours of availability and cover vacation times, allow consultation with each other for problems and techniques, and enough searching to develop expertise. As the volume of requests increases, additional searchers can be secured. It is important that their library responsibilities allow them to give priority to this patron-oriented service.

The first choice of individuals for training as searchers will be the present reference staff, who have worked with faculty and students, have used indexes and reference materials, and who have a familiarity with the type of questions asked. Usually these librarians are eager to add to their reference skills and to broaden the resources available to them. It is possible that in some cases, when the workloads of the reference librarians are particularly demanding, a searcher could be borrowed from a nearby institution or an experienced part-time librarian could be hired to initiate the service and to develop the operating procedures. This individual could work with the reference staff to help integrate the online search service into the reference activities as other priorities are adjusted. A temporary position used in this manner presents an opportunity to try out a search service without upsetting established routines.

TRAINING SEARCHERS

For staff with no experience in computerized bibliographic searching, a good introduction is to receive training by the vendor chosen for the search service. Learning to be a searcher is not difficult if the individual has used computers previously and is accustomed to looking for information in printed sources. It is very important, however, for searchers to have a thorough basis of search techniques including selecting search terms, utilizing Boolean logic and manipulating results, understanding the content and structure of files, printing procedures, and enough practice to be able to think and respond quickly while online.

Skill in typing or previous use of a computer for word processing is easily transferred to online searching. The return, break, delete, and other keys usually have the same function regardless of the application. A paper jam in the printer or changing a ribbon will require patience and a willingness to learn about the mechanics of the machine. Assisting patrons with printed indexes is good practice for searching the online version, as both are based on terminology. It is usually more critical in the online search to use specific terms and synonyms, different spellings, and sometimes acronyms or abbreviations. This dependence on words requires some understanding of the terminology of the subject area or knowledge of appropriate sources to consult. An experienced searcher knows how to read an abstract of a relevant article to select important concepts, how to find additional search terms in an online record, and what other resources can be utilized for an intelligent discussion of the problem.

Familiarity with the printed index, which corresponds to the database to be searched online, is also helpful for understanding the structure of the record in the database. Records are composed of segments such as accession number, author, title, source, year, abstract, descriptors, etc., and may include industry codes, geographic locations, or chemical identification numbers. It is very important to know the particular record components for the database being used to insure precision and accuracy in searching. The content of these records is determined by the publisher or producer of the index and database. The structure of the database and the methods of accessing different parts of the records are decided by the database vendor, who arranges the record contents, codes the components for retrieval by the system commands, and may divide the database into two or more sections if it is a very large file. Searchers need to know which databases include an online dictionary of subject terms and how to use it effectively. Instruction in online searching should include sufficient emphasis and discussion of the content of the database records and the way the database is organized.

The mechanics of searching primarily involve organizing the terms into concepts of the problem and using Boolean operators, "or," "and," and "not," to arrive at the desired list of citations on the subject. This process requires some understanding of the way the computer searches for terms, and knowledge of the various options available to the searcher for entering terms (truncation, word relationships, searching only portions of the record such as descriptors), the means of limiting the results (time period or language), and the different possibilities for printing out the final bibliography. These basic procedures should be learned at a training session that presents the search process in a manner that is logical, concentrates on the important commands, and allows the searcher to start with the basics and to follow up with advanced technique as experience is gained.

A number of options for beginning instruction in online searching are:

vendor-sponsored introductory sessions
workshops by online users groups or other organizations
library school courses
in-house learning with experienced searcher
self-instruction with manuals, workbooks.

Training by the online vendor has many advantages for the beginning online search service. The workshop concentrates on the system that will be used; classes are offered at frequent intervals and at various locations; and an excellent introduction to search techniques, significant features of the system, and the characteristics of some of the individual databases are included. Extra practice time is usually part of the session or may be allocated for later use. If a large number of staff are to be trained, arrangements can be made for representatives to come to the institution. This option can be rather costly if the number of searchers is small; however, several libraries could cooperate on a training session at a central location. This concentrated course on one vendor's system should be viewed as a good method of learning a single system, but not necessarily providing a balanced view of the online field or covering a wide choice of databases.

Vendor's advanced workshops often concentrate on subjects such as company information or science and technology; specialized techniques such as searching for cited references; or the different approaches needed for full-text or numeric databases. These sessions are very useful to broaden searching experience, to improve search skills, to keep up-to-date on new procedures, and to learn additional strategies for information retrieval.

Library school courses usually include a broad view of the online searching field and provide comparisons of the various vendor systems available for libraries. A course is much more lengthy than the other training options, but allows time to practice with guidance and to discuss different methods of approaching search topics. There is undoubtedly more theory on information science, building databases, indexing fundamentals, and the related topics that form the background on which online searching is based. This academic approach is particularly valuable as a means of providing a basic understanding of the field and the forces that are constantly changing it. The location of a library school may present a problem for conveniently taking a course and the time requirement and scheduling by semester may be difficult to coordinate with a work schedule.

For more personalized training geared to the searcher's needs, it is possible to provide in-house instruction if there is an experienced searcher available. Training can be done in groups or on an individual basis. The instructor must have enough background and experience to present the fundamentals of searching procedure and the use of appropriate databases, as well as good communication skills. It takes time to prepare material and work with new searchers. Self-instruction manuals and workbooks can be utilized, along with vendor practice files. In-house training is probably the least costly and the most convenient, although the scope of the training may be limited. Care must be taken that the instructor is a good teacher and that enough time is devoted to basic skills and online practice. Regardless of the method of instruction, a trained, experienced searcher available for consultation, answering questions, and helping solve problems, is a valuable asset in establishing a competent search service.

To help searchers gain confidence, they should be able to begin working with patrons in an atmosphere that makes the cost of a search a less important factor than the quality of the results. This can be accomplished by having a period of free searches before fees are instituted or by providing institutional support to pay for errors and problems and to subsidize inefficient searches.

ORGANIZING SEARCH RESPONSIBILITIES

The many available databases provide bewildering choices for beginning searchers. Not only are there many databases to choose from in most subject areas, but different types of databases require different procedures and vocabularies. Despite this complexity, the same basic technique is used for searching all databases within a vendor's system and the searcher can be a generalist, providing literature retrieval on any subject where an appropriate database can be found. This is certainly satisfactory for brief searches, for finding information on term paper projects, for subject areas where the terminology is clear and reasonably free of jargon, or searches for the individual who just wants a sampling of the recent literature.

However, to provide expert service for scientists and scholars, searchers must be able to provide authoritative and accurate assistance. Since research topics usually involve specific terminology and precise areas of investigation, the searcher will benefit from an understanding of the field of study whether in the sciences, business, or humanities. It is important for the searcher to participate actively in the discussion of search terms, suggesting appropriate database(s) and organizing the search procedure to insure the retrieval of relevant literature. It is valuable for the searcher to have a subject or database responsibility in order to develop expertise and experience in a specific area. Specialized assignments can be distributed according to the librarians' current responsibilities. Reference subject specialties, collection development areas, or departmental interests can be followed in assigning search subjects. Even when the library staff is small and the searchers must cover all areas of interest, it is often advisable for one to become the specialist in business, chemistry, or other fields where either the terminology (chemistry), the complexity of the databases (MEDLINE), or the number of choices of databases (business) require extra training and study.

Instead of a subject division, responsibilities can be divided on the basis of database concentration. Several of the major sources, selected according to the probable interests of patrons, will answer most of the demand as the service is becoming established. When the individual searcher concentrates on thoroughly learning a few basic databases, this experience can be applied to searching the more specialized files that are infrequently used. These major databases can be selected by considering the primary clientele and their needs. After the introductory system training and some experience, an advanced session on the major database(s) or subject area can strengthen searching expertise. Where there are a number of searchers serving a clientele with broad interests, specializing in a few databases instead of a subject area may be an appropriate method of organization.

SEARCH PROCEDURES

Initiation of the search service can begin when the equipment is in place, the beginning searchers trained, and a preliminary outline of searching procedures ready. Procedures that should be formulated include:

scheduling searches
search preparation
search execution and delivery
forms and records.

The developing service philosophy should be reinforced by procedures that encourage promptness in scheduling searches, include the possibility of searches on demand, clearly establish any limitations on the types of searches or clientele, and emphasize placement of online databases among the other information sources of the library. The searchers must be clear about the priority they should give to searches, the amount of time they can take for preparation, the amount of record keeping and, when necessary, the procedure for payment by patrons for the service.

Scheduling Searches

The patron should be present while the search is being performed. This is sometimes difficult or uncomfortable for new searchers until they have developed confidence, but the interactive process is enhanced and the search results are more likely to be relevant to the patron's need if they have participated in the entire development and execution of the search. The potential for educating the patron about the search process, use of terms, and even library resources is increased. Personal contacts for librarians on campus and a better understanding of research investigations can also result and can play a role in making the librarians more aware of the information needs of the campus community. A chart for appointments near the terminal provides a method for the searcher and the patron to secure enough undisturbed time to carry out the search.

While there is a better opportunity for patron satisfaction when the individual is present to clarify and articulate the search topic, there is also the expectation that individual searchers will develop technical expertise and subject knowledge so they can be an active participant in the intellectual portion of the search development. As in other reference work, librarians' knowledge of sources (databases) and their analytical skills, combined with the patron's familiarity of the subject area, can produce the best results. Usually about an hour must be set aside for a search with a patron in addition to any preliminary preparation time. This time may be reduced as searchers receive more practice and patrons have a better idea of the search process.

In some circumstances, searches may be more cost-effective and more efficient if they are batched and accomplished at a convenient time without having the patron present. Critical to this procedure is the ability to satisfy the information needs of patrons. This arrangement may be appropriate when searches are done consistently within a limited subject scope, when patrons can describe exactly what they need, and when the searcher is using a familiar database or databases. The convenience of the patrons, their use of the information, and the complexity of the searches can all influence the scheduling of searches.

Some faculty members may send students to the library to do a search for them. The faculty member is busy or may think that it is good experience for the student. While this can provide adequate results, more often there is uncertainty about the information needed. Having the student consult with the faculty member after a preliminary search with a sample printout may be necessary to be sure the subject has been correctly defined. Encouraging the faculty member to come with the student for discussion of the topic is a better procedure.

Preparing for Searching

Learning online techniques and preparing strategies for search topics will require more of an individual's time than may be expected when the search service is first established. Both searchers and patrons must learn to deal with problems differently and to give careful consideration to key words and search parameters. Limiting the service to a few databases at first until the searchers have some experience may help build confidence and expertise. Nevertheless, adequate preparation for each search is essential.

Inexperienced searchers can request an outline of the search topic from the patron ahead of time with any qualifications of time period, language, and amount of information needed. With this in hand, terms can be checked in dictionaries and thesauri, the indexing of the topic can be examined in a printed index or abstract, and a preliminary search strategy developed. By working with an appropriate database manual, a step-by-step procedure can be written out to include logging on, search steps with qualifiers and limits, and the format for typing or printing the results. After reviewing this with the patron and discussing alternative strategies, the number of decisions that must be made while online can be reduced and, if necessary, various options can be ready. If the search topic is not well-defined or the concepts are complicated, the searcher can try the strategy in one of the online practice files.

If the patron is not present during the search, it is even more important to understand the information needed and to clarify the subject during a presearch interview. If this part of the procedure is not done by searchers, they should be familiar enough with the selection of databases, development of search strategy, and the choices for delivery of results to be able to ask the correct questions and to record the essential details. For this procedure it is important to have a detailed form to fill in for the needed information. (See chapter 7, figures 2 and 3.)

Delivering the Results

The search planning stage should include decisions about the resulting bibliography or information retrieved. The patron may wish to view titles of some of the items before printing the citations. Are only English-language documents needed? Should the abstracts be printed? Are only the most current references needed? The citation and descriptors may give enough information about the content of an article for the patron's usage. An abstract may save time and in some cases provide enough details so that there is no need to obtain the entire document. If a comprehensive search is desired, the search strategy may be saved and rerun against another file.

The resulting bibliography can be typed, printed offline, or downloaded onto a disk, depending on the preference of the patron. Alternatives may be limited by communications speed of the equipment, length of printout, and availability of software for downloading. Storing the search strategy for later updates and ordering documents online may also be appropriate.

Forms and Record Keeping

Procedures in place at the beginning of the search service for recording the activity of online use, financial arrangements, and comments of patrons will help with evaluation, planning for further development, and justifying costs to the administration. A simple log for recording each search and some of the details will provide a basis for determining the amount of information useful to the institution. A form for the patron to fill out about the search topic will help define the problem and the amount of information needed. A billing form may be needed if a fee is charged. (Examples of forms can be found in chapter 7.)

Preliminary evaluation of both procedures and expertise of searchers can be based on the number of searches accomplished; the numbers of faculty, staff, graduate students, and undergraduates who have used the service; the departments they represent; the databases used and the costs of individual searches; and comments noted by the searchers after each search session regarding any difficulties. Problems can include telephone line noise; difficulty in reaching a communications network; slow response by the vendor; or malfunction of the equipment. The search may have had unsatisfactory results when nothing relevant was found and the patron was sure there should be information on the subject, when the wrong database was used, or when the topic was more appropriate for a printed index. Patron satisfaction can be determined by a brief survey asking for comments on the value of the search results and eliciting suggestions for better service. A more extensive survey sheet can be distributed at the conclusion of each search, or sent out to patrons at the end of a trial period. Review of these evaluations will provide information for improving the operation of the search service as well as for planning future expansion.

DEVELOPING QUALITY SEARCHING

After the searchers have received their initial training, it is important that they have the necessary support on the job to develop their searching skills. Good quality, reliable equipment; manuals and search guides to consult; enough time and funding for online practice; and the encouragement of colleagues who can share searches and consult on problems are all vital for developing a quality search service.

Support Materials

Vendor manuals are essential to have next to the searching terminal. Good quality manuals are easy to understand, include examples of searches, and clearly identify the options and access points with illustrations at each step. A complete set of database manuals may not be needed when subject interests of the clientele served are limited. A basic search manual of the system procedures and chapters for the appropriate databases may be sufficient. Usually a single-page summary of the contents and structure of other databases will provide enough documentation for occasional searches. There should be a mechanism for searchers to request the purchase of other reference materials such as thesauri or specific database manuals as they are needed.

In-house Support

Planning for an online search service should include support for the searcher to assist in developing technical skills, to encourage effective interaction with patrons, and to produce high quality search results. Regular in-house discussions about the search interview, determining appropriate topics for searches, reviewing search techniques, and examining search strategies will reinforce training sessions and help resolve problems. A discussion of previous patron searches will provide practical applications relevant to the institution's clientele. Pairing beginners with experienced searchers will help them learn procedures and how to interact with patrons. A skilled searcher can be available for consultation on complex searches or when unexpected results are obtained. Working with patrons is an additional learning experience as topics are discussed, search strategy developed, and the results reviewed together to determine if the desired information has been obtained. Practical search techniques are quickly developed.

Regular evaluation is important, and review of log records and patron surveys can contribute to this process. Enough funding should be provided for the service so searchers can not only practice, but can rerun searches, try different approaches, and test out different databases. Searchers must have enough time in their daily schedules to prepare and review searches, and to read manuals, vendor newsletters, and relevant literature. Newsletters and online journals are needed to keep up with the changing online field and to provide information on new databases and search practices. The library should also support the attendance of at least some searchers at conferences and workshops. These experiences can be shared so the newest equipment, databases, and innovations can be discussed.

PUBLIC RELATIONS

Public relations starts with the enthusiasm of the library staff and extends to the campus community—administrators, faculty, staff, and students. Formal efforts can be minimal, allowing the service to develop slowly, or extensive advertising may be used to encourage more searching by the academic community. The library may be anxious to publicize the new computerized information service or limits on staff time and experienced searchers may require a slower introduction.

Informing the Staff

Every staff member who deals with the public should know when a search is useful and something about the diversity of databases that are available. He or she should also be able to tell patrons how they can arrange to have a search performed, what preparation is needed, an approximate amount of the time it will take, how soon it can be scheduled, and whether or not there is a fee. All staff members should understand the necessity for giving priority for searches and how this may affect other responsibilities of the searchers.

Librarians, whether searchers or not, can promote the information services of the library by mentioning the availability of online searching when they are working on campus committees, discussing collection development with faculty, or assisting researchers and students. In order to promote the service they must understand what information is available online and how it is used by the academic community. Scheduling a brief search for each staff member is one method of developing awareness and at the same time impressing them with the amount of readily available information. A few recent papers on the treatment of diabetes, references to articles in magazines on physical fitness, some studies on online catalogs, and a list of microcomputer software reviews, all quickly retrieved online, will do more than any general descriptions or brochures.

An open meeting or lunch-time seminar can also be used to familiarize the staff with the new service and its potential. An in-house library newsletter can report on recent activity and give some examples of topics on which searches have been performed. Library staff members will provide some of the best advertising as they answer questions and mention the service to patrons.

Informing the Campus Community

All publicity can be delayed until the search service has become established; then a carefully planned public relations campaign can help phase in the search activities so that demand does not exceed capabilities. A selected target clientele, such as a single college or department, can help focus the publicity on a few databases that will provide a good sampling of online resources and examples of search results. A department offering a graduate program can be contacted to interest them in sponsoring an online literature search for each student's thesis or dissertation. Research faculty will usually have students working on various aspects of their projects and online searching will contribute to both the student's literature review and the research effort. By selecting a specific department or research program for introducing online searching, the searchers can experiment with various public relations approaches before publicizing the service on a broader scale. Personal contacts with regular library patrons will also provide an opportunity to demonstrate the value of an online search. These patrons will especially appreciate the efficiency and the additional access points for an index that they use a great deal, or the availability of a database that represents a new source of literature.

A notice to the faculty suggesting that they bring a few search terms to the library for a scheduled demonstration can generate considerable interest. One searcher can provide a brief search while another is describing the procedure and answering questions. If a portable terminal is available, the demonstration can be done at a faculty meeting or during a departmental seminar. Using a search topic suggested by one of the participants will make the presentation as relevant as possible.

It is important that the delivery of results meets patron expectations right from the beginning. Too much publicity at first may result in an overload of requests that cannot be speedily accomplished, and the reputation of the service could be jeopardized. A modest public relations effort and the placement of the search service in a public area where it will be noticed by patrons coming to the reference desk should help interest to increase gradually and enable the reference or public services departments to adjust work schedules when needed.

Once the searchers have gained confidence, a greater impact on the campus community can be made if a period of free searches can be offered. A month, six months, or a year without fees will bring in a wide variety of patrons and give the librarians practice without the anxiety of charging patrons while learning to use the system. This is an excellent way for searchers to become adept and comfortable, since a wide variety of patrons and subjects will provide a sufficient volume of searching for practicing skills. Some limits may need to be placed on the amount of searching done for each individual patron. This can be as simple as five to ten minutes online and ten to twenty-five references, or left to the discretion of the searcher. Free searches can be done for a selected group such as those writing Ph.D. dissertations, masters candidates, or seniors working on research projects. If a patron fee is to be instituted, there should be a prominent notice of the temporary status of the cost-free service.

Other methods of reaching potential patrons can include bibliographic instruction for advanced classes; students can be given a copy of a sample search and the lecture on sources of information can include a comparison of the printed and online versions of an index. Librarians at the reference desk can also be encouraged to suggest an online search to patrons with appropriate questions. The best publicity will be gained from satisfied patrons.

Publicity may not be necessary for a reference unit that has a good interaction with their patrons in the research community. As online searching becomes a more integral part of the reference services, its use to extend the library resources and to increase the access points of heavily used indexes will be logical and productive. On the other hand, if a fee is charged, patrons may need some convincing that it will, indeed, be worth the cost to do an online search.

A brochure or other printed material can be prepared and distributed at the reference desk, mailed to faculty, sent to individuals, or placed in various locations. At the introductory stage this material should first identify the service with a name or library logo, explain clearly what the results of an online search are, and the value to the patron. There should be information about the procedure to obtain a search and a statement about cost. Posters and fliers can be utilized and an effort should be made to integrate information on the search service into all the library promotional material.

Phasing in the publicity and encouraging the gradual increase in use of the search service will allow the searchers to gain the experience they need to produce quality searches. There will be a solid basis for the continued expansion of the service and the development of a reputation for valuable assistance for the academic community.

Bibliography

Cooper, Douglas W. "Computer Literature Searching: Start-Up and the First Year in a Small Liberal Arts College." *Reference Librarian* 5/6: 129–38 (1982).

"International Comparative Price Guide to Databases Online." *Online Review*. February and August issues.

Lee, Joann H., and Arthur H. Miller. "Introducing Online Data Base Searching in the Small Academic Library: A Model for Service without Charge to Undergraduates." *Journal of Academic Librarianship* 7:14–22 (1981).

Pensyl, Mary E., and Susan E. Woodford. "Planning and Implementation Guidelines for an Academic Online Service: The M.I.T. Experience." *Science and Technology Libraries* 1:17–45 (1980).

Saffady, William. "Availability and Cost of Online Search Services." *Library Technology Reports* 21:1–111 (1985).

4

COORDINATOR/MANAGER *86*
FACILITIES MANAGEMENT *87*
 Environment *87*
 Vendor Contracts and Communication *88*
 Equipment and Supplies *89*
 Security and Controls *90*
 Keeping Records, Writing Reports *92*
MANAGING SEARCHERS *93*
 Selecting and Scheduling Searchers *93*
 Distributing Search Topics *95*
 Scheduling Searches *98*
FISCAL MANAGEMENT *100*
 Budgets *101*
 Monitoring Costs *101*
MANAGING FOR QUALITY SERVICES *103*
 Efficiency of Procedures *103*
 Improving Searcher Expertise *105*
 Patron Access and Information *106*
 Advisory Committee *108*
 Evaluation *108*
 Keeping Up-to-date *111*
MANAGING PUBLIC RELATIONS *112*
MANAGING DEVELOPMENT *114*

Managing the Service

Decisions have been made, space and equipment provided, contracts signed, and the initial operation of the service begun. It is time to put someone in charge, to develop firm policies, establish procedures and forms, and to insure the integration of online resources into all information gathering processes. Although online searching is a constituent of the library's information services, the search service is a unique combination of personalized service, technology, and expertise that make a separate management plan important for efficiency and developing a quality service. Significant features of this unit include dependence on an information source outside the library; the individualized nature of the service, with one patron working with one librarian at a time; specialized equipment for communication and delivery of information; staff with expertise that must be continuously developed; the rapidly changing technology and information industry; and widely fluctuating costs that must be accounted for and controlled.

The primary concern of a search service is to provide a responsive information delivery system for the academic community. In addition, since the budgetary investment for a search service is substantial, it is important that the organization be carefully planned. To achieve maximum efficiency, the management tasks and responsibilities for the head of the unit should be clearly defined. The size of the library and amount of searching expected will determine the time requirement and scope of the management position.

The manager's responsibilities are:

selecting and maintaining equipment, supplies and search aids
arranging contracts with vendors, continuing communication
keeping records, statistics, and making reports
coordinating activities of searchers, scheduling searches
arranging for training and continuing education for searchers
managing income and expenditures, budgeting, accounts
monitoring cost-effectiveness of the operation

developing procedures and forms
keeping searchers, equipment, and manuals up-to-date
providing a quality information service
educating patrons, demonstrations
supervising public relations
planning for growth, changing technologies.

The many facets of a search service, combined with the changing environments of technology, the commercial online industry, and library budgets, result in a dynamic situation where dedicated management is required to administer procedures; coordinate staffing; monitor fiscal arrangements; work with the library administration, vendors, and the public; and be concerned for patrons and their needs.

COORDINATOR/MANAGER

Responsibility for the search service and its functions may fall to one of the searchers, the head of the reference department, or to a systems librarian. It is important for someone to be in close touch with everyday operations and to direct the activities. The manager should be a librarian with good organizational skills and a public services background who has an interest in computers or some previous training in online searching. The position may range from a part-time coordinator, with much of the management tasks shared among the searchers, to a full-time manager. The arrangement will be influenced by the size of the institution, the number of searchers, and the type and quantity of clientele served. If searching is performed in more than one library location, there will be a broader scope of activities that must be integrated into a cohesive service. The manager should be someone who participates in searching for patrons and may be selected by the administration, elected by colleagues, or serve on a rotating basis.

The personal characteristics of a good manager include:

leadership potential
concern for patron needs and satisfaction
ability to evaluate priorities
organizational skill for creating procedures and appropriate forms
logical thinking to design and maintain records that adequately
    monitor the service
aptitude for producing and controlling budgets
teaching skills for working with new or inexperienced searchers
writing capability for procedures and reports
interest in keeping up with new developments and incorporating
    them into search service procedures.

It is also essential for the search service manager to have good inter-personal skills to work with the library administrators, members of the library staff, and the academic community. Both library and campus administrations may have to be educated to the many advantages of online information retrieval and its place in the information services of the library. Reports of search activity and evaluations by patrons may be necessary to justify costs. As the advocate for the needs of the search service, the manager must be able to present a knowledgeable and comprehensive picture of search activities and potential. This ability requires an understanding of cost components, trends in the field, and a feeling for what is reasonable and appropriate for the library situation.

In some libraries the search service manager will become the resident expert on the online information field. To carry out this responsibility, it is necessary to keep up with the literature and learn more about computers, databases, and applications of online searching. The manager becomes the resource person for answering questions from staff or patrons. Advising on problems with machines, suitable databases for a particular subject, the cost of a search, or effective search strategy is a part of the everyday workload. The manager will also be the representative of the service to the outside community. Speaking to groups of administrators, department faculty, and organizations, the search service manager will be expected to represent a progressive academic library as he or she describes information services that make worldwide resources immediately available.

FACILITIES MANAGEMENT

The development of an online searching environment that encourages efficiency, expertise, and responsiveness of searchers to patron requests will benefit both searcher and patron. Procedures should be both simple and logical. Clerical duties should not burden searchers, and patrons should be able to schedule searches easily and at convenient times. Enough records must be kept, but should be limited to those that are useful. The manager must be sure that the equipment is reliable and up-to-date, and that vendor contracts provide a source of databases appropriate for the needs of the academic community.

Environment

The manager may not have control over the type or amount of space allotted for searching; however, the room should be adequate for a suitable and comfortable arrangement of equipment, table and chairs, shelving and files. The ambience of the search room or area can be influenced by the placement of the furnishings and machines. An area for planning the search should include enough desk or table surface for manuals, thesauri, and other resource materials needed during the discussion and drafting of the search strategy. Online searching can be centered at a different table with the terminal or microcomputer, and the arrangement should allow the patron to conveniently view the screen and/or the printer as the search is underway. It should be possible to spread a manual out next to the terminal for quick consultation when needed, and a stand to support the search plan and any brief system guides will make them easy to view by the searcher at the keyboard. A logical arrangement of search aids encourages neatness and provides easy access to support materials. The manager's considerations should extend to noise, not only that which could bother searchers and patrons when they are planning and executing a search, but also the effect of the discussion and printing, which may impact on those using facilities outside the search service. The manager may wish to set up accommodations for a small class or group of graduate students with some chairs and an easel and pad for explaining the development of search strategy.

Vendor Contracts and Communication

The manager will be responsible for maintaining liaison with the database vendor(s). Adequate communication with the vendor regarding search problems, questions about new techniques, and availability of databases will be important. Careful reading of the system newsletter, checking the online news for database changes and new additions, and watching the banner when logging on will help to keep system information current. Circulating the vendor's newsletter and announcements to all searchers is important, and posting the latest list of training sessions will alert searchers to these opportunities. System and database manuals must be clearly labeled and maintained in a convenient location. They must also be kept up-to-date. Either the manager or one of the searchers can be responsible for inserting new sections or pages, or writing in changes; it is important that this be done regularly and promptly. The manager should be concerned that all additions and changes have been received from the vendor and that searchers are aware of these developments.

There should be clear responsibility for purchasing additional manuals and search aids. Either the manager can initiate all orders or, if searchers are responsible for a specific database or databases or those in a subject area, they can order materials that are needed. Even if the selection is delegated, the manager should make certain that sufficient resource material is available. Some thesauri, dictionaries, and other recommended search aids may be borrowed from the reference collection when needed, but if they are used very often there should be a copy available in both locations. Extra copies of indexes can be added to the resource collection for illustrating the print form of the database. All supporting materials should be easily available near the search discussion area and terminal.

Equipment and Supplies

The manager must be familiar enough with terminals, microcomputers, modems, printers, and software to know the available choices and the important features for online searching. It is important to be able to discuss the equipment with the staff of the campus computer center or sales representatives. Keeping up with the availability and costs of faster, smarter machines is a continuing challenge. The manager must evaluate the additional capabilities or speedier communications and know when they are cost-effective or provide significant advantages. Any different searching equipment means more training and adjustments for the searchers. There should be enough assistance and practice time for each searcher to learn the potential of new equipment, whether it provides a faster communication speed or an additional capability such as downloading search results on a disk.

Maintenance of equipment must be a continuing concern. The manager should be able to take care of minor problems that may occur when loading paper, changing ribbons, or connecting different components. Serious problems with a printer, a computer, a modem, or other pieces of equipment can result in search results being lost, as well as the inability to respond to patron requests while repairs are made. The manager will need to know the institution's policy on service contracts and the procedure for repairs and maintenance. Arrangements for local assistance and for replacement machines when needed must be in place and ready to implement. Back-up equipment may be available within the library, at the computer center, or from a nearby department or laboratory. These provisions must be convenient and prompt when equipment breaks down. A swift response to machine problems will be important for the reputation of the search service.

In an online search service there are also a number of other links in the computer connections where problems can occur. These include vendor downtime or busy periods of the day, when logon is delayed or response time is very slow; unavailability of the communications network; static on the telephone line, that will garble messages and break communication between computers; and heavy telephone use on campus, when it is difficult or impossible to get an outside line. These problems are difficult to cope with and can be very frustrating for both searchers and patrons. The manager should be able to assist searchers by suggesting alternate techniques, other lines or services, or delaying the search when that is the best solution.

Supplies can be the responsibility of a clerk; however, the manager must be sure that materials have been ordered and are available when needed. Provisions may include writing paper, pencils, forms for various purposes, log books, computer paper, ribbons, extra disks for downloading, and other materials that should be on hand when a searcher sits down with a patron.

Security and Controls

Security of both the equipment and the passwords is a concern of both the search manager and the library administration. Equipment devoted to the search service can be locked up when not in use, securely mounted on a desk, or kept in a controlled location. If the terminal is in an open public area, students may wish to use it for class assignments or word processing. The manager should be certain that there is adequate signage to indicate use by library staff and, if necessary, move the equipment to a closed room at night. If there are any questions about protecting the equipment, the telephone, or supplies, consideration should be given to relocating the search service in a secure room or a location within sight of the reference desk.

Library staff members, campus faculty members, library school students, or computer-literate undergraduates may have had online searching experience and wish to use the search equipment. The manager must anticipate these requests and establish clearly defined policies that authorize whether anyone other than the regular searchers can use the equipment and library password(s). These policies should cover the possibility of graduate students or other library staff performing searches for patrons. In most instances, the answer is "no." This policy must be consistent and enforceable or it will be easy to lose control of the equipment and the quality of the search service. Assistance for patrons should be provided in relation to the amount and type of information needed. All who provide online searching should be well trained in technique and knowledgeable about databases. Since it is relatively easy to log on to a database, type in a few terms and receive a response, beginning searchers, other library staff members, a student or faculty member can perform a database search. Online information retrieval, however, on topics scheduled for the search service should be performed by the most competent searcher, especially if the patron is paying for the search. Providing expert assistance both at the reference desk and the search service should be standard policy and a matter of pride. A separate facility for patrons to do their own searching may be a viable option, but if so, a definite distinction should be made between the objectives of the two facilities.

As the use of online databases is extended to in-house functions such as verifying interlibrary loan citations, consideration should be given to the use of the equipment by support staff, or whether the searchers should be expected to do the actual online searching for verification. The decision will depend on the amount of expected use for this purpose, the number of terminals, the time impact on the searchers, and the capability of the support staff. Searching for library purposes can be assigned to any searcher needing practice or there could be a separate password to assist in keeping accounts.

The manager must also be concerned if the microcomputer used for searching has other uses within the library, such as for word processing, statistics, bibliographies, or keeping library records. If so, equipment scheduling is particularly important to have the machine available when needed for patron searches. Flexibility must be built into the arrangements so the time span allotted for searching can be expanded as the demand increases. Even a printing terminal may have other in-house uses, such as electronic mail, accessing the campus computer, or practicing online search techniques. Firm policies, therefore, must be in place that specify a first priority for patron online searching. Any sharing of the searching terminal or microcomputer should be considered very carefully. One solution is to have the manager approve any other use of the equipment on an individual project basis; otherwise there is a great potential for interruptions, or inconvenience for patrons, by individuals who do not understand the priority for serving the public and the need for concentration on the search process.

Password security is also important. Procedures should be followed that make certain searchers do not expose the password or leave it written down. Vendors often require a security password, a second code the user can easily change online. A new password can be instituted weekly or at regular intervals, and this procedure should be implemented if there is any concern about unauthorized usage. If software on a microcomputer is used for automatic logging on, the password should not be visible. Procedures should permit masking or omitting the password from the screen and printed output.

Passwords may be a special concern when patrons are doing their own searching on library time. There will be great temptation for curious students, who have their own computers, to try searching at home. Having a librarian log on for each patron, changing the passwords every day, and other tactics may have to be devised. Checking the monthly vendor bills against an accurate log of search activity is important to determine if password controls are adequate.

Keeping Records, Writing Reports

Adequate record keeping is very important to form the basis for monitoring costs, providing information for reports and fiscal accounting, and future planning. Data such as the cost of each search; the number of searches for patrons; the numbers of faculty, staff, graduate and undergraduate students, and off-campus patrons using the service; the databases used; the amount of searching by each librarian; and other appropriate information will provide a picture of the amount of activity, the time demands on the searchers, and the costs being generated.

The manager must create forms to collect appropriate data. Statistics sheets should be evaluated carefully to insure that the information collected is useful and yet sufficient to make up reports that characterize search service activity. Writing annual reports and answering survey questions about the average cost of a search, the number of hours online for the year, or the primary databases utilized will help the manager determine the important figures and the amount and type of records that must be kept. Both procedures and forms should define categories and terms on the data sheets so the information is clear for the searcher and subsequently others who read the reports. The definition of a "search" is especially important for uniform figures. Usually a single search is the answer to one question or research topic regardless of the number of databases used. The number of searches for patrons per month and year is a figure that will be used to track the search service activity, indicate increasing activity, and determine the subject areas of highest demand. It is possible that some of the information for reports can be obtained from the vendor bills that list by day the databases used, connect time, number of prints or types, and costs. A brief search log, along with the monthly bills, may provide sufficient information without more extensive records. (Examples of forms can be found in chapter 7.)

There should be a regular review of the data collection procedures and the usefulness of the information. The value of the data can be determined by the objectives of written reports. Annual reports tabulate activities, while some data may be used for evaluation of the service effectiveness by examining the changes in numbers of patrons, the departments served, the utilization of a variety of databases, and average costs. The amount of searcher activity can be used in annual reviews of performance and to support requests for promotion and tenure. Average search charges can be the basis for a grant proposal asking for funds for a particular number of searches. Costs relative to the number of patrons served can suggest the cost effectiveness. Any proposal by the manager for increased personnel, more search equipment, or more online time for practice or demonstrations, will have credibility if accompanied by adequate supporting data.

The most important purpose of keeping records is to provide enough information to the library administration to justify the continuing expenditures, any adjustments in fees, and expansion of the service. There must be enough data collected for a logical and persuasive presentation.

MANAGING SEARCHERS

The manager must be responsible for coordinating the activities of searchers, planning the distribution of search topics, and organizing the scheduling of searches. Search procedures must run as smoothly as possible for searchers who have other library responsibilities and demands on their time. They should not have to cope with an uncomfortable environment or the necessity of finding inconveniently located resource material. The manager must coordinate the search activity so that the tasks are clearly defined and appropriately distributed. Searchers must know what their responsibilities are, when searches are appropriate, and the scheduling process. The development of clear procedures provides a consistent and professional quality of service for patrons and allows searchers to plan schedules, workloads, and other commitments. The manager should monitor the search schedules to keep arrangements flexible enough so patrons can have searches performed at convenient times.

Selecting and Scheduling Searchers

Utilizing terminals and computers for information retrieval may be a new experience for some members of a reference department. It takes a flexible staff to absorb this interaction and to embrace the additional learning that must take place. Nevertheless, all the reference librarians should be trained to participate in online searching. Even if most of the searches are performed primarily by a few individuals, all who provide information services must have enough background and training to know when a search is appropriate and how to access the many online resources. Some librarians will have more interest, background, and personal qualities desirable for searchers. Even mechanical skills among individuals—turning machines on and off, loading disks, learning to type, feeding paper into printers, and other aspects of the interface between people and machines—will vary considerably. It is essential, however, that reference services include online access to information and that all reference librarians are able to participate in this process.

A search service manager must recognize different personal capabilities and organize the searcher's responsibilities to take advantage of expertise. Planning must consider the necessity for each searcher to spend enough time online for adequate practice and yet not so much as to be overloaded with searches. The manager may need to spend more time with some individuals than others as skill is developed, and in some situations may want to recruit individuals in other library positions to help staff the search service. Librarians who do not usually work with the public may have particular skills or interests in subjects or computers that would make a valuable addition to the searching staff. Their participation should depend on their subject expertise, their ability to work with patrons, the flexibility of their schedule so they can be available when necessary, and the need for additional searchers.

The manager must be concerned with scheduling staff to maintain responsiveness to patron requests. An arrangement should be chosen that will provide the best service for patrons. If searchers are generalists working with undergraduates on term paper topics, they can be assigned hours of availability on a regular schedule or for variable periods depending on other commitments. If searching is divided among searchers by subject or database specialties, and searches are primarily on research topics, searchers may wish to make their own appointments for searches. If the librarians' schedules are dependable, the manager or a department secretary could keep a calendar and make appointments. The system selected should be the most appropriate for the searcher and yet provide enough flexibility to meet the needs of patrons, who will often wish to have searches performed as soon as possible.

An important task of a manager is to assist the searchers to achieve a balance between searching responsibilities and other demands on their time and attention. They may be scheduled at the reference desk and also need time for collection development, bibliographic instruction, research, writing, and professional activities. Even before a search service is instituted, public service librarians at an academic library are usually committed to full-time responsibilities that include their library workload, involvement in campus and/or professional groups, and the requirements for research and publication. Adding new service responsibilities will have a decided impact on the time available for these activities.

The searcher's online searching time with each patron may be brief; nevertheless, the need for training and practice time, search preparation time, time to discuss the search with the patron, time for accounting, and follow-up assistance for patrons, plus time for reading to keep up-to-date on the changes in searching techniques and resources, add up to a significant number of hours every week. As the search service reaches more patrons there will be more demands on searchers even as they become more experienced and need less practice and preparation time. Searchers can be burdened by excessive paperwork, complicated charging structures, unchanging priorities, extensive evaluations, and inefficient work flows. The search manager must understand these problems and make sure that procedures and support systems are established to make the searching operation as efficient as possible. The adjustment of the searcher's time schedule and workload will be one of the most difficult aspects for both the individual and the manager to deal with.

If the manager and any of the searchers are unable to schedule searches promptly or if they feel their time is overcommitted, the responsiveness of the search service will suffer as well as the morale of the unit. While the number of search requests will vary according to the time of the semester, a continual overload or periods of time when searches must be delayed could harm the reputation of the service and interfere with the prompt delivery of information. Procedures should be kept simple, as many responsibilities as possible should be delegated to other library staff, and documentation should be provided for the library administration to demonstrate that more help is needed or that service priorities should be changed. Another reference librarian, search specialist, paraprofessional, or clerk can lessen the impact on present staff and adjustments can be made to redistribute responsibilities. If more personnel is not an option, then certainly there must be compromises in priorities, with some other service or responsibility assuming a lesser role.

Whatever choices must be made, it is probable that they will be difficult to determine. Therefore, it is important to examine the full context of services and decide what the essential elements are and how the librarians' time can be utilized to best advantage. Effective management of the search service will be critical to insure its place among other service responsibilities.

Distributing Search Topics

In a small library, deciding who shall conduct a search on a particular topic may not be a problem, since there are only one or two searchers and both may perform any search that is requested of them. When there are several searchers, the manager may be responsible for deciding on the best method of dividing up requests. If expertise is important for searches on specialized research topics, searchers should be encouraged to develop knowledge of subject areas or of major databases. If it is more important to have a searcher available when needed, searchers should have broader experience without as much specialization. Even with limited personnel, however, there is an advantage to having some field of concentration for searches. A plan for assigning searches should result in the most competent assistance for patrons.

Searcher's responsibilities can be general covering any requests, by subject specialty, according to a time schedule, or assigned as needed by the manager. Each method has particular advantages and disadvantages.

Distribution of Searches

General (all searchers share search requests as received)

Advantages: Searchers have wide range of experience with
                databases
                Easy to relate to reference desk questions
                Suitable for a separate unit with full-time search
                staff
                Works well for homogeneous clientele
                Patrons do not have to be referred to another
                person
                Convenient for general topics of undergraduate
                papers
                Distributes search responsibilities evenly.

Disadvantages: Difficult to develop and maintain search skill in
                all subject areas
                Need extensive knowledge of database resources
                Extra training for complex databases will be
                needed by all searchers
                Hard to keep up with changes, new resources
                Some terminology will be difficult
                Research problems will require substantial prepa-
                ration.

By subject (according to searcher's expertise or interest)

Advantages: Training can concentrate on subject area
                Other subject-related job responsibilities rein-
                force expertise
                Knowledge of indexes, databases in subject area
                improved
                Better communication with faculty and staff in
                subject-related departments
                Better knowledge of database choices and re-
                sources in field
                Can develop relationship with graduate and re-
                search programs
                As specialist in subject area, can advise others.

Disadvantages: Probable uneven distribution of searches
Much pressure on searchers in some subject areas
May need backup searchers
Overlapping subjects may be a problem for distribution
Searchers may not be aware of database resources outside subject area
Patrons must be referred to appropriate searcher.

By database (according to interest, related subject responsibilities)

Advantages: Expertise developed on particular files
Searchers can concentrate on most used databases
Can be resource for other searchers using database
Training focused on a few databases
Easier to keep up with changes
Especially good organization for consistent use of complex databases and those with specialized terminology
Good for serving academic units which match major databases.

Disadvantages: Interdisciplinary searches may not fit searcher's database responsibilities
Expertise may not extend to related databases
May limit searching flexibility
May not match subject interests of institution
Patrons must be referred to appropriate searcher.

By time schedule (with searchers assigned to search service for specific periods)

Advantages: Searcher available at all times
Broad exposure to searching topics
Easier to plan daily schedule
Reference responsibilities can be integrated between reference desk and online searching.

Disadvantages: Time assigned even if no searches required
Patrons may not work with most competent searcher for topic
Hard to develop specialization and expertise
Difficult to keep up with database choices
Search distribution may be uneven
May not get enough practice.

Assigned as needed by search service manager

Advantages: One person for patron to contact for search request

                  Can schedule by availability of a searcher

                  May be a way of providing better and quicker service

                  Requests can be screened and other sources suggested before working with searcher

                  Response to patron consistent

                  Can even out searching load

                  May be more convenient for searchers

                  Provides more control over search activities.

Disadvantages: Manager must be available to discuss topic

                  Manager must know searcher's schedules and experience

                  Appointment may not always be convenient for searcher

                  May take more of the patron's time

                  Puts another level into search request process.

The search service manager can work with the searchers to develop the best method of distributing responsibilities. The decision may be dictated by the number of staff, pressure of other work assignments, the number of search requests, the number of terminals and passwords, and the expertise of the searchers. The training and specialties of the librarians and the accessibility for the academic community should be primary considerations in making a decision about the division of search topics.

Scheduling Searches

Scheduling searches by appointment at the convenience of the patron, with searches immediately available for simple topics and with priority given to individuals anxious for the results, is an optimum objective for a responsive service. This concept of providing searches as conveniently as possible for patrons takes advantage of the speed of searching and the up-to-date characteristics of databases. Many researchers look for information when they need it and delays in scheduling searches will cause increasing frustration with library services and the intermediary necessary for literature retrieval. The manager of the service should be sensitive to patron needs, time pressures on both patron and searcher, and the importance of utilizing the best expertise for each topic. Procedures for scheduling searches can assist or delay responsiveness, and patrons must feel that their interests are the primary consideration.

Whether searches can be done as soon as requested or whether appointments will have to be arranged will depend on the experience and expertise of the searchers, their availability, and demand for searches. This decision may also depend on the complexity of the search topic and whether preparation is needed by both the patron and the searcher. Making appointments for searches, when the procedure is to refer patrons to librarians according to subject or database specialty, usually works best when searchers can manage their own arrangements. To work well there must be flexibility in schedules for the reference desk and other commitments. If there is only one terminal, scheduling will be facilitated if there is a calendar nearby to write in appointments. With more than one terminal there may be a calendar for each, or a master schedule can be maintained by a member of the clerical staff or the search manager, who could have the responsibility of making appointments for individual searchers. The calendar should allow approximately an hour for each search with a space for recording appointments with searcher's name, patron's name and telephone number, and search topic. If searches are accepted according to the librarian's subject specialty, it may be advantageous to have secondary subject coverage so when the appropriate searcher is too busy or unavailable the patron can still have some immediate or scheduled assistance. The manager should be able to act as general searcher when others are particularly busy or when necessary to fill in at vacation times.

The manager must guide the search process, balancing the needs of patrons, the schedule and experience of searchers, and the need to maintain a quality information service. Searchers without experience, or without enough requests to keep up their search techniques, can be encouraged to use practice files, perform some in-house searching when needed, and ask for search requests ahead of time in order to consult manuals and thesauri, select databases, and write out search steps. Careful preparation of a topic outlined by the patron or discussed in a consultation ahead of the search appointment can help compensate for lack of knowledge of the subject, lack of expertise, or need to investigate database resources. Complicated search topics or those for patrons desiring comprehensive retrieval on a subject may also require considerable preparation time before the search. Once the search staff is experienced, the time scheduled to perform searches can be adjusted to correspond to the complexity of the topic.

Policies for scheduling searches should include an arrangement for patrons not present when the search is performed. A decision can be made not to accept these requests. Otherwise there should be a system established for telephone requests, for patrons who do not have enough time for appointments, or for searches that may be referred from other libraries. There could be a requirement for the manager to approve these searches on an individual basis, or a special search request form may be used to collect sufficient information on the topic. If other librarians who are not searchers are accepting requests, the manager must be responsible for educating these individuals to be sure that they understand the fundamentals of the search process, know what databases are available, and what subjects are suitable for online searching. Anyone accepting a search request must be able to collect enough information for a satisfactory search and be able to interpret the results for the patron.

The manager must communicate with the library administration to emphasize the importance of flexible schedules for the librarians in order to respond to changing search demands. Each search must be allotted enough time for the patron and searcher to fully discuss the topic, choose the terminology, create a search strategy, and determine that the outcome meets expectations. The search is not complete until the patron understands how the results were obtained and what to do next to secure the documents or data. Procedures must be written to encourage the prompt response to search requests and yet accommodate the many time demands on both patrons and librarians.

FISCAL MANAGEMENT

Whether the search service has a separate budget or is part of the reference or public services budget, the manager will be expected to have accurate figures of expenditures in all appropriate categories, along with any income amounts. These figures will not only be used for calculating the next year's budget, but also for planning future growth and costs. The manager will also be expected to monitor charges, keep control of expenditures, and be able to assess the cost-effectiveness of the service. Adequate records are very important for fiscal management. The vendor's billing, the search log, a file of search requests, or an automated collection of search statistics may provide the data needed.

The variable costs of online searches, which can quickly add up on the monthly bill, are the most uncertain aspect of managing the finances of the search service. While trends can be identified with experience and a cost recovery fee can cover most of these expenses, there is still the potential for unexpected charges due to searcher's inexperience, problem searches, practice time, personal errors, unauthorized use of a password, or simple mechanical problems. Vendor bills may arrive two months after searches were made and if there are large or unusual amounts listed, they may represent problems or misunderstandings of searchers and it is too late to make corrections or adjustments in procedure. In a larger operation with several searchers, who may also be very busy reference librarians, it is often difficult to establish accountability.

Budgets

The manager will be expected to manage the current budget allotment for the search service and to provide funding requests for the next year. In an academic institution where budgets are submitted and approved a year or more ahead of time, there is usually little flexibility in the current year's budget, which should contain a line item for the search service. If most of the online search costs will be recovered by user fees, the budgeted amount will include the investment in new equipment and maintenance, manuals and search aids, supplies, software, and training for new and advanced searchers. If searches are free to patrons, the budget must contain an amount for the number of searches expected to be performed at an approximate average charge.

After a preliminary period of operation, there will be some basis for estimating another year's costs based on an expected increase in activity. Both the amount of advertising and the fees charged to patrons will affect this prediction of growth and expected expenditure. To some extent the expertise, enthusiasm, and time commitment of the searchers, the list of available databases relative to the subject needs of patrons, and the efficiency of the search service will all contribute to the uncertainties of budget prediction.

If patron fees are a necessity, the required tasks of handling money, billing department funds or research grants, giving receipts, and accounting for incoming funds can consume a great deal of time. The manager must be responsible for forms, internal procedures, and arrangements with campus offices for the transfer of funds from other accounts. There may be specific regulations for handling cash. This income must be included in an accurate picture of the finances and must be projected for budget planning.

Records for expenditures and income must be accurate, complete, and clearly organized. They may be kept in a ledger by a clerk, or on the computer on an accounting spreadsheet by the manager. Categories can include vendor charges for patron searches; vendor costs for in-house searching and manuals; searcher training; search aids; equipment and supplies; and income in cash, charged to accounts, and billed to patrons. This organization should be consistent from year to year to allow comparisons for noting changes and trends.

Monitoring Costs

In order to keep finances under control, searching activity should be followed closely and a log of searches and their costs maintained. From this record, monthly totals can be charted for comparison with previous months. When vendor bills arrive, they can be matched against the log of searches, which will help to keep the records accurate and should reveal any discrepancies where problem searches have occurred, searching has not been recorded, and estimated charges differ from the actual cost. If searches are free to patrons, it is even more important to keep an accurate accounting of vendor charges. If these costs are more than the budgeted amounts, the screening process for search requests must be reconsidered. Regular review will help keep costs within acceptable limits and provide the necessary information on which to base requests for additional funding.

Whether the library plans to pay all the search costs or a fee is levied to recover the online expenses, it is important to maintain a continuing awareness of these monthly charges. When the library has planned to recover a percentage of the costs, the income from searching fees should be compared with the monthly vendor charges to see if the goal has been achieved or maintained. Keeping track of the individual search costs will make it possible to calculate an average search cost that can be used in the budget proposal process for estimating figures as activity increases, and projecting the finances at various levels of service. The calculation of an average charge to patrons can be quoted when potential users ask about fees—the range should also be mentioned to indicate the wide variations in search complexity and charges.

If funds for supporting materials, such as thesauri or database manuals, are limited, a search manager can be selective, only ordering items as needed. Costs can be reduced by ordering manuals only for the databases used the most frequently, by using printed subject indexes instead of specialized thesauri as a source of terminology, by getting recommendations for useful material from experienced searchers or online user groups, and by watching for reviews of databases and mention of the value of associated search aids. It may be possible to order them through the book budget or with a special allocation rather than using the search service funding.

The telephone bill can be a problem for some budgets and it may be necessary to examine the various communication networks to balance their charges against the distance from the library to the closest node. In order to operate equipment at a faster speed, it may be necessary to reach a telephone number in a more distant city. Although the telephone charge is higher, it may still be cost-effective to use that source at a higher transmission speed if most searches are for extended periods of time. Trying similar searches through various networks and nodes in different cities and then comparing the costs will give a practical basis of comparison. Even when the communications and connect-time charges can be passed on to patrons, the telephone bill must usually be absorbed by the library's operating budget.

There are many cost components that are part of a search service operation. Some, such as utilities, are hidden or absorbed in other parts of the library's budget. Total personnel costs for online searching may be difficult to separate from those for other responsibilities. Materials, equipment, and search aids can be ordered on a priority basis as funds are available. The direct vendor search cost will be the most critical for the manager to monitor and the vendor bills, along with the search records, can supply details of the variable individual and total search costs.

MANAGING FOR QUALITY SERVICES

The management and organization of an online search service can greatly affect the quality of the service provided by this operation. Procedures must be clear, logical, and efficient. Searchers must be encouraged to maintain and improve their search skills, take advantage of new equipment, try new databases, and give priority to patron requests. Evaluation should be a regular process for reviewing procedures, service provided, and patron satisfaction. The manager must be concerned about efficiency, coordinating staff activities, cost-effectiveness, accessibility for patrons, and keeping current.

Efficiency of Procedures

The manager will wish to examine the efficiency of the search service at a number of steps in the search process. This scrutiny will include a review of procedures to be sure that they are simple and accomplish their purpose. Scheduling of searches, the interaction of the searchers and patrons, the performance of search equipment, the timeliness of the delivery of results, and the flexibility of searchers both in techniques and scope of resources used can be examined. Problems can occur in many different areas. Searchers can accept topics unsuitable for searching, perform searches that are too costly for the purpose, use subject terms that retrieve too much or not enough, have difficulty limiting search results, or need assistance with the software being used for downloading. These potential difficulties must be carefully monitored and enough flexibility built into procedures to allow for adjustments of personnel, procedures, or equipment when necessary.

As difficulties are solved and searchers become more experienced, they will develop confidence and know-how to handle most crises that may materialize. Any time there are changes in the service with new personnel, a new vendor, new procedures, or a new group of patrons, there should be a review of the overall effectiveness of the service. The manager should determine that patrons are being scheduled for searches at their convenience as well as that of the searcher, that the procedures flow smoothly, and that expert assistance is provided.

Inefficiency means unnecessary costs. The manager must be concerned when a searcher has misunderstandings with a patron, gives a wrong message to the computer (perhaps hitting an incorrect key), or does poor planning that consumes time online to think about decisions or to find the correct procedure. Each time the searcher logs off, the tally of time and fee is relentlessly recorded: database connect time in minutes, total cost for the time online, and additional charges for printing citations. Time-consuming operations can make both searcher and patrons very nervous, especially if they must be concerned about charges. If problems occur too often the searcher should have additional training or supervised practice. However, the library must be ready to pay for an irrelevant printout or some extra online time for corrections, and searchers should be assured that some problems can be considered good experience.

A search service could be overwhelmed by requests impeding the efficient delivery of information. An online information service provided without fees has the potential of impacting heavily on reference personnel and the equipment. Guidelines must be formulated that will help direct patrons to indexes, databases, or other reference material depending on the information needed. Screening of proposed searches may be done by the person at the reference desk, a searcher, or the search service manager. Students who must discuss their subject with a librarian may be referred to printed indexes that are more appropriate than an online source, or some preliminary use of indexes may be required to prepare for a search. It may be necessary to limit free searches to a specific amount of online time and number of citations retrieved in order to control costs. Since many requests will come through reference desk inquiries or referrals, all who work at the reference desk should receive enough training to know when a search is most appropriate and when a printed index or reference book can provide the best answer.

Fees for service will have an automatic limiting effect on the number of requests for searches, and this number is usually affected by raising or lowering the charges. The number of searches undertaken will also be restricted if the searchers have full schedules, a single password, or there is only one machine for searching that allows access by one patron and searcher at a time. These limits by cost, personnel, or equipment, however, are often unfair to patrons who need rapid and efficient information delivery. When procedures seem to be too restrictive, or there are extensive delays in scheduling searches, the screening process should be reviewed to insure that guidelines are adequate for directing patrons to the best source of information. Topics that require an online search should be given attention as soon as possible. Providing additional assistance for patrons so they will use indexes more effectively may also relieve some of the pressure for online searches. If there is still greater need for providing searches or they must be delayed longer than a predetermined length of time, perhaps two days, then consideration should be given to securing another terminal, an additional password, or more searchers.

Improving Searcher Expertise

Concern for the quality of searching techniques should start with providing adequate training for searchers. The manager should be sure that each individual has a good grasp of searching fundamentals, usually obtained by online vendor training, in formal classes, or an in-house training program. Informal instruction by one searcher teaching another or by a new searcher sitting in with an experienced searcher may be satisfactory for learning a second vendor's system language, but usually will not provide the necessary basic search skills and strategy development that are essential elements for satisfactory online searching. There are so many alternatives available for searching each database that it is important for every searcher to be exposed to training that provides a solid foundation on which to build the knowledge and flexibility of options that can be utilized when appropriate to retrieve the information needed. It is easy to slip into the habit of searching in the manner learned when first trained or only using subject terms and not taking advantage of other search elements and new procedures or resources.

If the manager's position is full-time, in-house training courses can be developed for new searchers. The manager must have enough time to put together adequate materials, organize and present the instruction, and work with beginning searchers to be sure they have achieved a good level of competence. When a new vendor system is secured for the library, the manager can take the initial training and then teach the new system language and techniques to the already experienced staff.

The manager can also encourage searchers to work together to improve the results of complex searches, where terms are difficult to define, or others where patrons are anxious to keep costs at a minimum. Other techniques that can improve search results include performing a search in steps, with time allowed for study of the preliminary results; doing a limited search on a single database and using those results to plan a more comprehensive strategy; trying out search terms in a practice file; or utilizing cross-file searching to suggest the most appropriate database and an estimate of the costs. Searchers can help each other by consulting on searches ahead of an appointment, by reviewing a search strategy when results have not been satisfactory, and by having an experienced searcher and one who is learning do the same search and compare them; much can be gained by examining different strategies and the resulting bibliography. The manager may wish to encourage searchers to work together on searches that are complicated, those that are on topics that are cross-disciplinary, or searches that have retrieved inadequate results.

The manager should schedule regular meetings for the searchers. These sessions are very important to review problems, new databases, changes in the vendor's system language, and the service procedures. Discussions can include the scheduling of searches and the priority to be given to them. Consideration should be given to limiting the time delay between a search request and performing a search. Searchers can agree that if a search cannot be scheduled within three days, arrangements should be made for an alternate searcher to respond to the request. Delivery of search results when offline printouts are ordered, or a search is performed for individuals who are not present, could be restricted to not more than two days.

The manager should encourage searchers to attend advanced workshops, spend extra time on practice files, and discuss problems with the manager or other searchers. There must be concern for those who may not be receiving enough patron requests to keep up their search techniques. They may be able to act as backup for one of the busier searchers, to sit in on other searches, to do some in-house searching, or to regularly spend some time practicing. While some searchers will confine their efforts to one vendor's system, unless there is a good reason for this, all searchers should be able to access and search the databases of all vendors under contract.

Part of the manager's responsibilities includes working with the administration to be sure that searchers are allowed enough time for practicing; receive funds for workshops, training, and conferences; and secure adequate release from other responsibilities to provide this priority service. The manager must coordinate the activities of searchers and be sure that all are well informed and able to take advantage of group meetings, additional training, and practice of search skills.

Patron Access and Information

The manager must be sensitive to the information needs of students and faculty. Not only the types of questions and the subject areas of interest, but also the time demands of the semester, thesis, or dissertation; publication and grant proposal deadlines; and the necessity to keep up with new developments stress the need for quick answers to questions and the importance of accurate, precise data. To assist these library patrons, adequate information must be made available about the search service and how it can aid research and course work. Enough public relations, demonstrations for faculty and students, an informed library staff, and clear procedures for securing a search are very important. Innovative publicity will include various opportunities for demonstrating searches—library or campus open houses, orientation sessions for new faculty, departmental events, seminars, campus committee meetings, and individual demonstrations for library patrons. Brochures can be mailed to new graduate students and distributed at different campus locations. Signs can be placed on the shelf with an index to indicate that it is available online. The visibility of the search service equipment, searches underway, and adequate signs to describe the process and applications will be a primary method of alerting potential patrons.

The manager can also work with librarians who provide bibliographic instruction to include demonstrations for classes whenever appropriate. Undergraduates may be required to do preliminary work in the indexes before an online search on their term paper project. This exercise can accomplish a number of objectives such as practice using the indexes, working with terminology, and thinking about the emphasis and organization of the assignment. The opportunity for an online search not only stresses careful planning of topics and the increased access to sources of information, but also provides an introduction to electronic information retrieval. When online sources are utilized for questions at the reference desk, there should be discussion and review among the reference desk personnel to be sure that a brief search is considered whenever appropriate. Consistency of service that utilizes all sources of information should be an important element stressed in meetings of searchers, in educating personnel at all the service desks, and in the review of search topics.

If there is concern that some patrons are unable to use the service because cost is a factor, the manager should investigate alternate charging methods or additional funding to be sure that adequate information retrieval is available for everyone who needs it. Fees for specific categories of patrons could be reduced or eliminated. These patrons may be undergraduates or graduate students working on unfunded projects. Other assistance for library patrons could be free searches when permission is obtained from the manager or one of the searchers, special quick searches for undergraduates for a minimum fee, or small grants that could be obtained from a campus source to provide funds for sponsoring searches by particular groups, such as faculty or students in the humanities. There may be research funds available on campus, gift money given to the library, contributions by alumni or friends groups, or departmental funds that can be tapped for these special projects. The manager could also propose canceling a costly index or one used infrequently and using that money for patron searches.

Advisory Committee

The manager may wish to meet regularly with an advisory group. This committee may be composed of searchers only or searchers, patrons, and other library personnel. To be effective there should not be more than three to five members. The primary responsibility of the committee should be the establishment of policies such as charging fees, selecting additional database vendors, considering end-user searching and CD-ROM, and for long-range development as technology changes and more online resources become available. The committee could also conduct surveys to assess patron satisfaction, help write grant proposals for special projects, and seek additional funding to subsidize fees or increase free searching.

Evaluation

The manager must be concerned that searches are meeting the needs of the patrons, that online information is readily accessible, and that searchers are performing effectively. To determine if these objectives are indeed being met, an ongoing plan of evaluation is necessary. Evaluation may be as simple as a meeting of the searchers to discuss their problems, their feelings about the quality of the search results, and comments of patrons. Evaluation procedures will change as the searchers gain more experience and online searching becomes more fully integrated into the information retrieval process, but quality of searches and patron satisfaction should be a continuous concern.

A searcher who examines the completed search with a patron usually has a reasonably good idea of the effectiveness of the search terms and strategy. A more quantitative evaluation can be expressed by the terms "recall" and "precision." Recall is usually defined as the number of relevant citations retrieved compared to the total number of relevant citations in the database. A patron may wish to be sure that all the information on a topic has been found and will request a lengthy bibliography. The search results, then, may have a very high recall but may also include items that are not of interest. The patron, however, will often feel more confident that the literature review is comprehensive because he or she has retrieved more references than needed.

To use the capabilities of computer searching to best advantage, however, a searcher will usually try to achieve search results with a high precision. This search will yield primarily records appropriate for the patron's topic. Precision can be expressed as the percent of relevant records retrieved compared to the total records retrieved. The results may have high precision, but may have a low recall; the bibliography has few references that are not appropriate; however, some relevant material may not have been found. Both high recall and high precision would indicate a highly accurate, efficient search. Finding known literature on the subject, such as the paper that the student brought along as an example of the subject matter, or publications of the student's thesis advisor, are usually good indicators of precision.

Recall and precision are based on the relevance of results to the search topic. The determination of relevance is primarily the opinion of the patron. Sometimes students may need to confer with their professor to decide if the references are appropriate, and the researcher may have to read the article to determine its relevance. In addition, some patrons will know exactly what they need, while others will not be sure; some topics are easy to define, while others are more complex. The manager can assist searchers to determine recall and precision, but must also recognize that other factors affect the quality of search results. The important consideration is the satisfaction of patrons, who may need only a few relevant citations, or just enough literature to get started on the research. They may also be concerned about cost and be satisfied with a brief search, realizing that it is just a sampling of recent literature.

To monitor quality, the manager should consider which aspects of the search service should be evaluated and then decide on the best method(s) to use. Evaluation of patron satisfaction can be accomplished with a survey form distributed as the search is completed. A few questions to be answered immediately will give some instant feedback. Some patrons will not be able to judge the value of their printout until they have time to study it. The results of the quick survey can be compared to those from a more thoughtful questionnaire to be returned later, probably reducing the percentage response. Questions should be carefully thought out to bring forth comments that can be used to assess and improve the operation. A questionnaire mailed out to past users can also solicit suggestions, or a telephone survey can be a more informal contact with the clientele. (For examples of forms see chapter 7, figures 14, 15, and 16.) Questions in a patron evaluation form can be used to determine:

If patrons were satisfied with the results.
If search results were received promptly.
If the searcher's explanations were clear and complete.
If the citations were relevant to the topic.
If the citations were new to the patron.
If the searcher understood the topic and was helpful in selecting terms.
If the choice and selection of databases were appropriate.
If the organization and execution of the search were understandable and efficient.
If the charge seemed fair.
Suggestions for improving the search service.

Some objective evaluation can be done from data collected as searches are performed. The amount of time between the request and the actual search, the length of time devoted to the search and its preparation, how soon the printout was actually delivered to the patron, and the number of repeat searches or increased use by a department can provide some statistics about the service, and trends can be noted. The number of interlibrary loan requests generated from searches can be used to show the impact on that library function and will also be one indication of the increased amount of information retrieval made available to patrons.

Searchers may comment on their own performance, and regular discussions that review search strategy, discuss choices of databases, and analyze procedures are opportunities for evaluation of individual searches and success of the service from this viewpoint. Copies of searches can be circulated among the group for comments to help improve quality. The mechanical aspects of the search, as well as the intellectual content, should be noted. Review and discussion by the searchers may reveal different techniques such as simpler methods of combining groups, methods of limiting retrieval to major emphasis, advantages of improvements in the vendor's system language, and the use of different record formats. A list of topics that have been selected from search requests can be used for discussion to help determine the appropriateness for computer-assisted research or if a printed index search would have been better. The manager can also sit in on searches or monitor them from time to time to evaluate the quality of the search interview and the apparent user satisfaction with the results.

Any type of patron-assisted evaluation will tell individuals that the librarians are concerned about the quality of service. Survey documents should be brief and should recognize that the value of the results will vary according to the patron's needs. Even a search that retrieved no literature on the topic may be a success when the patron hopes they are investigating a new phenomenon or trying a new approach. However, it may be difficult for the librarian to judge the adequacy of a search yielding no literature. The manager must act as a guide for this process, to see that searchers become familiar with their clientele, the type of research or projects they work on, their approach to the subject, and the breadth and depth of information usually needed for that discipline. In some fields finding the information needed and receiving it quickly may be much more important than cost when there are fees for service. On the other hand, for some patrons, cost is a great concern and it is important for these searches to be as efficient as possible, perhaps retrieving the minimum amount of information on the subject.

A manager should have the authority to authorize that a search be rerun for a patron unsatisfied with the results. The manager can review the strategy with the searcher to determine if there was a problem and how to improve the results. If there are typing errors, very slow response time, or static on the line, the searcher could repeat the search, or the charge to the patron could be reduced. If there has been a lack of understanding of the search topic, the manager could work with the searcher, or someone else could repeat the search. The manager should be ready to examine a search with a patron to provide another interpretation of the results when someone is not happy or does not understand the search procedure. In some cases dissatisfaction may be due to the patron's unrealistic expectations, and the manager can offer support for the searcher's results.

Evaluation from the points of view of the patron, the searcher, and the manager can be used to determine the patron satisfaction with the search service, the adequacy of the scheduling, the effectiveness of searches, and the efficiency of product delivery. These review procedures should be repeated regularly and should include a means of follow-through to correct any deficiencies. The manager should strive to use evaluative methods to improve the quality of searches and to effect more efficient methods of operation.

Keeping Up-to-date

The manager must be concerned about keeping the searchers informed of new developments in vendor system language, new databases, and opportunities for additional training. The changing marketplace requires constant attention, and interest and involvement in the information field will be required in order to follow trends in the online industry that will help anticipate and plan future developments in the search service.

Some of this information can be obtained by reading current journals such as *Online, Database* and *Online Review*; vendor newsletters such as the *Dialog Chronolog* and *BRS Bulletin*; newspapers such as *Information Today*; and proceedings of conferences such as the MARS programs at the ALA Annual Conference or the National Online Meeting. The manager should make certain that the library subscribes to as many of these major sources of online news and developments as possible. Searchers should be encouraged to go to workshops, meetings, and conferences. Experts from other libraries can be brought in to discuss procedures, equipment, or techniques. An online users group provides a good forum for comparing problems and successes.

Free time offered by the vendor on new databases can be shared and utilized. Improvements in search language or other vendor changes should be practiced by all the searchers in order to feel comfortable with the more efficient options. Update sessions sponsored by the vendors are well worth the time to attend because of the emphasis on newer techniques.

Advances in technology must be monitored and new equipment examined to determine the advantages and cost-effectiveness. Faster speeds, a better connection to the telephone line, or an improved keyboard may be very important. The manager must also be aware of new vendors, new databases, and new contract opportunities. The present vendor contract must be continually compared with other options and opportunities as they become available. A list of potential vendors can be maintained with a file of literature on their databases and contract choices. Information from displays at conferences, advertisements in journals, and articles in newsletters can contribute to the file. The manager will then be ready, when additional databases are needed or when the library administration asks about a different vendor or new service, to provide information and a comparison of resources and costs. Evaluations of other vendors must include an awareness of different types of databases such as data files, full-text journals, and books, and statistical sources. There may even be some files maintained in departments on campus or available through government agencies that can be utilized by the search service.

Regular meetings of the searchers are opportunities to discuss more than problems and procedures. Demonstrations of new databases, discussions of techniques or strategies, reports from meetings and workshops, and other brief segments of in-house training can take place at these times. Newsletters, articles of interest, and information on new technical developments can be circulated. If departmental or branch libraries offer search services, it is important to maintain communications with the searchers in these locations. They should be included in all meetings and kept informed of any changes in policies or procedures.

Keeping up-to-date also includes investigating potential new clientele and services, such as providing facilities for patrons to do their own searching. Setting up an "end-user" service can help reduce the searching load for the search service as well as increasing the opportunities of information retrieval for patrons.

MANAGING PUBLIC RELATIONS

The amount of promotion of online services should be considered carefully. Too much publicity at first can overload the searchers before they have enough experience and will disappoint patrons. It is then very difficult to reestablish credibility. Phasing in a search service without any significant publicity should allow slow growth of the operation, although word-of-mouth communication will usually keep the search requests on a steady increase. A planned program of promotion as the searchers have more experience will then reach other patrons and expand the user community.

One of the manager's responsibilities is the development of a professional looking brochure that describes the service, the resources available, and the procedure for scheduling a search. The advantages of this computer-assisted search service to extend traditional reference sources and to retrieve specific information can be stressed. Care must be taken to make the publicity free of jargon and clearly written, with any fees mentioned. Searchers' names and telephone numbers can be included, or just the name of the manager and a telephone number for questions and appointments. If possible, these brochures should be printed and given out at service desks in the library. They can also be distributed to groups, mailed to faculty, or made available next to the printed indexes. The brochures can also be part of a more extensive packet that may include a sample search, a list of appropriate databases, and a form for requesting a search.

As public relations materials are developed, emphasis should be placed on the interests of the audience and the appropriate applications and benefits of this fast retrieval of information. Literature, combined with demonstrations, is usually a very effective approach. Starting with deans and department chairs, then faculty, and finally student groups and classes, informing them of this literature service and the value for their research and projects will build a solid core of interest and support of the service.

When a department or research unit is identified that is not taking advantage of this service despite good database resources, a special presentation can be made to the faculty to attract their interest and demonstrate the value for supporting their research. A representative search on their funded research topics could be sent to them along with a brochure that would alert them to the relevant databases. This procedure can also be followed when new databases become available.

The manager can be innovative in finding groups of potential patrons—individuals seeking grants, faculty who have just received funds for research, graduate students beginning their thesis work, new faculty to the institution, or library patrons with special interests that can be identified. These groups or individuals can be offered a free search, receive a special mailing of literature, or be invited to an online demonstration.

Public relations efforts by the manager can include posters, advertisements in the student newspaper, presentations to groups, open online demonstrations, and written material for campus publications. However, the best public relations will come from referrals from the reference desk as questions are being answered. The use of an online database is then geared to the immediate need of the patron. With all reference librarians trained as searchers, they will be able to recognize when a search is appropriate and be able to describe this option. This integration into the regular reference process is very important and the manager must make sure that enough printed information is available at all service desks and that questions about online information retrieval can be answered accurately and promptly.

Part of the responsibility of the person in charge of an online search service is to keep all the library staff informed. This process can include distribution of public relations materials and status reports on the number and types of searches being performed. A yearly demonstration, a brief free search for each staff person, and a discussion of sample searches can stress its value to the public and the increased service for patrons. If there are branch librarians expected to refer patrons to a central search service, it is essential to increase their awareness of available resources and to encourage these staff to acquaint their patrons with the search service and the procedures.

MANAGING DEVELOPMENT

Regular review of potential improvements of the search service can include the examination of new vendors, new equipment, new databases, additional uses for database searching, systems for end-users, and software. New and different resources are continually becoming available and the search service manager should investigate each opportunity. These developments must be considered and evaluated in light of the interests of the library patrons. As new trends in technology become apparent, the manager must be familiar enough with them to recognize the ones that will be cost-effective. It is also important to be alert to opportunities for funding assistance and alternatives to or different methods of implementing fees for service. Additional funds can be pursued in the form of grants for new equipment, persuading companies to donate or test new products on the local site, or providing service to an outside group as a profit-making experiment. Being able to present these new options, applications, and opportunities authoritatively to the library administration is a considerable challenge for the search manager.

The tasks of budgeting, contracting with new vendors, and updating equipment and software all require skill in planning. Collecting enough statistics to substantiate requests to the administration, knowing enough about developments in computers to select appropriate hardware, and educating searchers to anticipate and accept new procedures are important aspects of a dynamic operation. Besides the technical developments, knowledge of the clientele and their interests, and the potential use of online searches for research, graduate student problems, term papers, and other applications are important for any projection of search activity.

The manager must also determine the best procedures for integrating online information into reference desk service, finding new searchers, and developing space for expansion. When it becomes appropriate to change the emphasis from a librarian-mediated operation to a patron-oriented, end-user service, this development will require additional patron education programs and the role of librarians and searchers will broaden to cover additional responsibilities. There may be a need for the manager to act as consultant to other departments within the library to advise on the value of online searching for assistance in their operations and to apply the experience gained from the online search service to the development of an online catalog or other projects where computer systems and patrons come together.

Keeping up with changing interests on campus is as important as keeping up with the online field. The needs of a particular department or group of faculty may make the selection of a specific additional vendor or database very important. New faculty may bring different research interests to a department, or a new Ph.D. program may require the addition of specialized resources. Changes within the library may also affect the online service. As the online catalog is developed, patrons will become more accustomed to finding material electronically with quick response and retrieval, and will expect the online search service to complement this efficient delivery of information. Providing a quality service in a time of continual change is a great challenge for the capable search service manager.

Bibliography

Atherton, Pauline, and Roger W. Christian. *Librarians and Online Services.* White Plains, N.Y.: Knowledge Industry, 1977.

Blair, John C. "Measurement and Evaluation of Online Services." In *The Library and Manager's Guide to Online Services,* pp. 127–59. Edited by Ryan E. Hoover. White Plains, N.Y.: Knowledge Industry, 1980.

Blood, Richard W. "Evaluation of Online Searches." *RQ* 22:266–77 (1983).

Parker, M.D. "Password Protection: Some Dos and Don'ts." *Database* 8:107–10 (1985).

Reynolds, Dennis. "Organizing and Administering the Search Service." In his *Library Automation: Issues and Applications,* pp. 546–600. New York: Bowker, 1985.

5

BUDGETING *117*
    Operating Expenses *118*
    Variable Search Costs *120*
    Overhead and Management Costs *121*
PATRON FEES—YES OR NO *122*
    No Fee Charged *124*
    Fee for Service *125*
FEE STRUCTURE. *127*
    Fees to Recover Direct Search Costs *128*
    Fees to Subsidize Direct Search Costs *128*
    Standard Search Fee *130*
    Recovering More Than the Direct Search Costs *131*
FUNDING FOR ONLINE SERVICES *132*
    Support from within the Library *132*
    Support from the Institution *133*
    Outside Support *134*
ACCOUNTING RECORDS AND PROCEDURES *135*

Financial Arrangements

Budgeting, financing online services, deciding on fees for service, and keeping accounts are all responsibilities included in the fiscal management of the search service. Costs related to online services can be easily isolated and identified, making it practical to have a separate segment of the library for this operation. It is then the responsibility of the search service manager or head of reference to keep very careful records and to continually monitor costs.

Because each online search generates a charge that can range from a few dollars to a hundred or more, the total costs are uncertain from week to week and greatly depend on the demand for the service. Library administrators must decide whether they can absorb this variable cost and control the maximum outlay, or recover some of the expenditures by charging a fee or finding an alternative source of funding. In practice, the arrangement for each institution is tailored to the library budget, the clientele, and the objectives of the search service. Consideration of these factors results in extremely diverse policies, from free online searching to a profit-making operation. If some portion of the costs is recovered by charging a fee for service, this arrangement is a new responsibility for most academic librarians and will mean additional procedures and paper work. Handling cash or billing patrons requires accurate records for accountability. If the service is funded from the overall library budget, considerable planning will be necessary to prevent a negative impact on other library operations. Regardless of the financing arrangement, it is important to have sufficient records to maintain an awareness of the current financial status and collect enough data for budgetary and planning purposes.

BUDGETING

Budgeting for online services must begin with an examination of the components of searching costs. These costs will include equipment, vendor contracts, search fees, search support materials, promotion, personnel salaries and training, overhead, and document delivery. Expenses generated by the everyday activities of providing information services must be budgeted for yearly, and will include operating costs, which are relatively fixed and can be predicted according to the level or amount of anticipated online searching, and variable costs, which are search-dependent and unpredictable. Operating costs include equipment, manuals and search aids, supplies, personnel, and public relations. These expenses will increase along with the amount of searching, but most of this growth will be at a relatively steady rate and can be projected for budgetary purposes. Variable search costs include online time and citation fees. These direct search costs will vary from day to day depending on demand, the type of searches performed, and the output. While these expenditures are variable and difficult to predict, they are at least easy to identify. Less obvious are the overhead and management costs, often absorbed into the overall library budget.

Operating Expenses

Regularly occurring elements of the search service budget include costs directly related to the functioning of a facility that provides online database searching for patrons.

Components of Operating Costs

Equipment: purchase, rental, lease or depreciation/replacement of microcomputer or terminal
additional equipment such as printer(s)
maintenance, repairs or service contracts.

Search system
access fees: vendor contract charges and advance payments
library network memberships to reduce online charges
start-up fees for new vendor systems
additional password costs
account maintenance fees.

Search aids: additional database chapters
updates to vendor manuals
new thesauri, journal lists
database producer search manuals
database directories
software.

Supplies: printer paper and ribbons
log books, ledgers
binders for manuals

	forms for requests, billing, records, statistics microcomputer disks.
Public relations:	brochures advertising materials database charges for demonstrations.
Personnel support:	training, both new and advanced travel for training professional meetings, conferences practice time on vendor systems subscriptions to professional journals membership in online user groups.

These operating expenses include all the equipment and support material required for effective online searching. Predictable vendor costs will include fees for additional passwords, advance payments for contracts to reduce the hourly online charges, and various maintenance or service fees. A network membership may replace the need for advance contract payments, but may incur a network service charge. Manuals, computer software, and supplies are materials that support everyday searching activities. Training and practice time to develop the competency of searchers is a continuous investment. Brochures, advertising, and demonstrations are necessary for patron awareness and education.

The commitment for these costs can vary considerably. The total investment in operating costs is not directly affected by the number of and charges for individual searches, but is maintained at a level appropriate for the overall amount and type of activity expected. An analysis of the range of patrons, from researchers to undergraduates; the scope of subject interests, from concentrating on a few significant databases to covering a broad range of resources; combined with the number of potential patrons will form a reliable basis for this estimate.

Controls can be established to maintain an established level of expenditure for these operating expenses without impacting on quality. Searchers may be limited to one or two training sessions a year to keep their skills current; the manager or one searcher can attend conferences and report back to the other searchers; additional manuals can be restricted to those for the most frequently used databases; and the investment in new search aids kept to a specific amount. Public relations can be maintained at a conservative level and demonstrations only given for groups or classes. Careful planning for these expenditures is important, as an appropriate amount of support is necessary to maintain a viable service. In addition, more searchers, terminals, and passwords, new software, or new vendors must always be under consideration as needs change and new technologies become available.

Variable Search Costs

Direct costs for online database searching are usually disparate. Each search is unique with differing characteristics of subject, database used, and information retrieved.

Elements of Variable Search Costs

online connect time with the vendor's computer
telecommunications charges
vendor record type and display fees
vendor off-line print and mailing fees
database royalty charges for connect time and citations
stored search strategies
current awareness (SDI) charges
telephone costs to network node
special print fees for reports, labels
document ordering.

The vendor's monthly charges will vary with the number of searches; the databases used; the telecommunications network(s); and display, type, and printing fees. Vendor charges can be affected by the type of contract; a reduction can be achieved with a prepaid commitment or with a volume discount; a reduced rate to subscribers of the print form of the database; academic discounts; or by using some systems at off-peak hours. The charge for the same database from different vendors will vary and is affected by the vendor's pricing policies. The institution's telephone costs correlate with the searching charges and will depend on the distance to the nearest communications node.

These search-related charges will often differ substantially from month to month, with the possibility of little activity during summer months to a major impact during the busiest part of the academic year. The number of scheduled searches will be affected by the time of the semester when new graduate students begin and start their research, due dates of term papers, class vacations when there is time for faculty research, final reports before graduation, and deadlines for research projects, grant proposals, and theses or dissertations. Besides the number of searches performed, the types of searches—whether short and concise for term paper topics or reference questions, or more exhaustive searches for research work, review articles, or surveys of the literature—will influence the total search charges. The subject areas utilized are also important; e.g., databases in the humanities and education are usually much less costly than most business or science databases. The importance of these factors will be influenced by the amount of research work on campus, the number of graduate programs, the size of the student body, and the major areas of study.

In addition, variable costs are influenced by the type of service established and its objectives—whether searches are performed strictly by appointment for in-depth research, on demand for undergraduates, utilized for reference questions, or a combination of these. The amount of in-house database searching utilized for interlibrary loan verification, research by librarians and bibliographic instruction, will contribute to the total variable vendor charges. The amount of advertising can also increase the amount of activity. Negative influences on the total search costs generated include fees for service, limits to clientele served, and restrictions such as screening by reference librarians. The number of searchers, the responsiveness to patron requests, and the efficiency of searching techniques all enter into the complexity of the factors affecting the monthly costs incurred. These variable charges are the most difficult of the financial aspects to deal with in a planned logical manner. Since the charges may be $25 or $100 to as much as $1,500 or more in a month, matching income or budget allotment to direct search expenses is usually very difficult.

Overhead and Management Costs

Building and personnel costs are most often included in the overall library budget. However, if it is important to calculate the total financial impact of an online search service, these cost components must be included.

Institutional expenditures are often difficult to break down into segments for individual services or operations. In addition, building upkeep may be controlled by another unit on campus, and furniture and utilities are shared with other library operations. Most staff have a variety of responsibilities included in their daily activities. Personnel costs for online searching will include time for training, practice, search preparation, search time with the patron, and follow-up time to complete searches, deliver printouts, and make reports. The search manager may be full-time, or there may be a part-time coordinator. Support personnel, such as a clerical assistant or an accounting clerk, may take care of appointments, keep records, and make financial reports. If these costs are not absorbed by the general library budget, they are probably part of the budget for public services. Total amounts will be affected by space occupied, energy costs, salary adjustments, and activity level of the search service.

Most search service operating budgets are primarily funded as a subsection of the public services budget. Some costs may also be supported by patron fees, other institutional sources such as a percentage of campus research overhead funds, a student library fee, or a reallocation from the overall library budget to reflect a change in library policies or priorities. Online searching can be substituted for print material, such as an index that is very expensive or rarely used, or funded from an increase in the materials budget. If patron fees are being used to offset the cost of operation, care must be taken to be sure that the funds generated can be used to pay vendor bills. In some state institutions all income may go to the state's general fund unless otherwise arranged. Procedures established for managing income from copy machines and book fines may offer a model for search fees.

Estimated costs for budgeting purposes will be much easier to assemble after the service has passed an initial period of operation. Experience with patrons and the development of a pattern of searches will indicate the significant cost elements. Although the continuing costs will gradually increase as the amount of searching grows, the direct vendor search charges will always be a variable and unpredictable amount. However, experience will provide some basis for the projection of even this component of cost. If there is no patron fee, an average cost per search can be calculated and multiplied by the number of searches expected, and that amount used for budget proposals. Knowledge of the clientele's interests and research needs will help evaluate the potential for expansion of the service. Budgeting for searching that patrons can do themselves will have the same limitations and problems as that for a librarian-intermediary search service. The costs that depend on demand will always add an element of uncertainty.

The budgeting procedure provides a clear process for determining the ability of the library to fund the total costs of an online search service. The continuing expenses for equipment, materials, and development of search skills, and the variable costs of each online search must be balanced against the library's income from all sources and the priorities for various library services. Many newly established search services have been able to offer free searching through grants or special allocations that provided funding for equipment and training searchers. Often search fees have been instituted after this initial period of operation. Now, after a number of years and the acceptance of online searching as a necessary component of information services, budgets are often being adjusted to include more of the costs of providing this service. The factors of clientele, library resources, and academic environment will help determine the necessity and justification for any charges to the patron.

PATRON FEES—YES OR NO

The common practice of charging a fee for online searching in academic and other libraries has caused extended discussions. Some characteristics of searching online databases that have made charging for this service a convenient and workable option include:

An online search usually produces a bibliography, a product tailored to the specifications of an individual patron.

The results of an online search are used by one individual and are usually not available for another patron.

Most of the search-related costs can be easily identified and assigned to the patron receiving the results of the search.

The cost of a specific topic search is so variable that it is usually impossible to predict.

Some searches can be very expensive. A researcher can easily need a search costing $100 or more.

A library may not be able to offer online searching without recovering some of the costs.

A search for information is not available without a librarian-intermediary or equipment and a password made available for individuals to use.

Individualized information services for patrons and appropriate bibliographies on research topics cannot usually be provided without the computer-assisted information retrieval process.

Patrons may consider the fast, comprehensive retrieval of information more important than cost, or else very cost-effective.

Funded research in an academic institution may provide moneys allocated for information services.

Department accounts can often supply funding for searches for faculty, graduate, or honor students on their research projects.

The variability of each search cost and its link to an individual request are probably the key elements to charging for online services. In addition, the fact that the information is not available without the intervention of a librarian and the use of specialized equipment keep access under control and patron fees relatively easy to implement.

Many methods have been devised to calculate fees for an online search. The critical elements in the decision are the amount of cost recovery that a library feels is necessary and the primary clientele to be served. The most common system of fees is to use the vendor's estimated cost of the search and have the patron pay all or a portion. Other schemes include a standard basic charge, a surcharge, paying for parts of the search results, or receiving a subsidy according to the type of search or category of patron.

The controversy over fees revolves primarily around the tradition that libraries provide information services without charge to the consumer and the worry that information will be supplied according to the ability to pay rather than on the basis of need. Some of the arguments on each side of the issue of charging fees are discussed in the following paragraphs.

No Fee Charged

Arguments for free online services for patrons emphasize that online searching of remote databases is one of the library resources available for information retrieval. Since there are no fees for consulting even expensive materials, no fee should be charged for using an online source. Database searching provides an extension of reference use of printed indexes, and information on some topics can often be found much more efficiently online. Databases greatly increase the resources available to even the smallest library or unit, and costs should be handled in the same manner as those for any other resource utilized to provide information.

Advantages of Offering Free Searching

Information resources are available when needed, rather than limited to those who can pay for them.

Even though individual search results benefit the single patron, the search service provides greater resources for all who need information.

The reference staff can often find information more efficiently online than in a printed source.

Additional access points become available for highly used printed indexes.

Accounting and paperwork can be kept to a minimum with only enough records for monitoring costs.

Online information retrieval results in an enhancement of the library's image in relation to available resources and computer technologies.

Disadvantages of Free Online Searching

The possibility of too many requests to handle, including some that may be improper or trivial.

There may be a large impact on the library's budget that may affect other services or materials and that is difficult to estimate with a dollar amount.

Searching may tend to be inefficient if there is no need to justify charges.

There may be a significant impact on the workload of the librarians to provide free searching.

Search requests will probably have to be screened to decide on those appropriate for online retrieval or limited in some other way, such as by output or unit cost. Therefore, the service will still not be available to everyone.

Fee for Service

Judith Turner reported in the *Chronicle of Higher Education* in 1984 the end of free library service, since charges have become common for database searching.[1] It was estimated that more than $100,000 a year had been spent by the University of California at Berkeley for this purpose. It may be difficult for most academic libraries to think of absorbing even a much lower figure into already tight budgets. Patron fees can bring in income to offset these searching charges.

Advantages of Charging Fees

There is more concern with efficient searching when the patron must pay.

Search topics are scrutinized more carefully by both patrons and librarians.

There is less likelihood of casual or frivolous searches.

Patrons have more leverage in having searches performed because they are paying.

Charges can be limited to those directly associated with an individual's request.

Since many libraries already charge for copying and interlibrary loan services, charging for another service is not a new policy.

Disadvantages of a Fee for Service

Patrons are limited to those who can afford to pay.

Fees may provide a precedence that could lead to charging for other services.

Fees may result in poor public relations.

Searchers may take more time to prepare for paid searches.

Searchers may feel the need for more training when the patron is watching the search and must pay for errors or inefficiency.

Searches may be performed on inappropriate topics if the patron is paying and wants the search.

Additional accounting and administrative procedures are needed when money is handled.

There may be an increasing expectation for the library to own journals or acquire material by interlibrary loan when a bibliography from a database search has been paid for.

1. Judith Axler Turner, "Computerized Data-Base Services for Research Bringing Era of 'Free' Library Service to End," *Chronicle of Higher Education*, 19 Sept., 1984, p. 23.

While the library budget may be the major influence in the fee for service, the type and size of the academic institution will play a role. A small college with a primarily undergraduate clientele and a limited library collection will find online searching a cost-effective way of expanding the resources available to students rather than purchasing additional material. Searches can support reference assistance when printed indexes are unavailable or the topic is difficult to find under the subject index terms. If facilities are available for students to do their own searching, this procedure can supplement their use of indexes and can familiarize them with computer searching procedures.

A library with a larger and more diversified clientele may find it more difficult to allot enough funds to satisfy the needs of the student looking for a few references for a term paper topic and the researcher who needs in-depth information and sophisticated assistance to determine publications on a special field of investigation. With millions of dollars in funding for research on campus, the use of a small portion of these moneys to find information when needed may justify a library search fee. Many of these research faculty feel that a fee is acceptable, especially if it implies a priority service. They often cannot find time to use the library and must rely on graduate students and librarians to assist them. The quick flow of search topic to printout to finding documents is a very critical process for those working in the frontier areas of science and needing up-to-date information.

Graduate students are often working on problems that require access to the more sophisticated methods of literature retrieval. They are often supported by funded research projects, but even for those individuals who must pay personally for the search, the saving of time spent with printed indexes, the ability to merge subject aspects, and the confidence of a comprehensive search, may well be a cost-effective choice. If the library chooses to subsidize the direct search cost, the positive public relations may foster an image of service for library patrons. Considering the librarian's traditional philosophy of offering no-fee services to everyone on an equal basis, it may be hard to justify a fee schedule, just as it is difficult to find a scheme that will offer searches to those who need them and not only to those who can pay for them. Nevertheless, most fees for online services recover only a part of the total costs. Overhead and personnel expenditures are usually not included in any calculation of fees, as they are difficult to separate from the costs of other library operations, but they do impact on the overall library budget.

All decisions about fees may be strongly influenced by the attitude of the director and that of the administration of the academic institution. Availability of funds, opinions about charging students and faculty for services, an appreciation of the value and the additional resources provided by computer-assisted information retrieval—all play a role. Priorities for purchasing books or serials, online catalogs, salaries or additional personnel can be overriding forces that will influence the judgment on fees for service.

Some libraries may feel a commitment to provide information services to a wider constituency—state residents, local businesses, area hospitals or nearby firms with government contracts. In a few instances a separate unit within the library has been established to supply fee-based services. This organization prevents outside demands from impacting on the library's primary clientele—faculty and students. Besides online searching, copies of articles, manual searching, and other services can be provided for these patrons. An information service, based on the ability to provide online searches by trained library personnel, can be offered by contract or an on-demand basis. Operated on either a nonprofit or profit-making basis, the unit would probably seek to recover the personnel, capital investment, and overhead costs as well as the variable searching fees. Budgeting for this type of service unit would be totally separate from the library budget and could operate in competition to or instead of a commercial information company.

FEE STRUCTURE

Academic online search services vary widely in the implementation of fees for service. Methods used to recover some of the costs include charging a fee related to the information received; charging a standard fee for all searches; providing a minimum search with the patron paying above that amount; charging at different rates for faculty, graduate students, undergraduates, and off-campus users; and charging for lengthy or expensive database searches and absorbing the costs of reference questions and brief searches. While there are many differences in the application of these examples, the most common practice is to have the patron pay the vendor search fees that are the variable charges, and for the library to absorb other costs.

Managing a fee service requires more planning than just developing a list of charges. It is important to first decide on the necessary amount of cost recovery. Then a method of calculating the fee must be devised to meet that goal. The system should be rational, appropriate for the clientele, and easily understood by patrons, who will be paying for searches even if they are inefficient or produce no relevant results. Calculating the final bill should be logical and uncomplicated. Libraries have used many different plans to recover various percentages of costs. Examples of some fee structures follow.

Fees to Recover Direct Search Costs

Fees, based on the vendor charge per search, can be set to recover this variable portion of the costs of individual searches. The income from this arrangement will increase as the amount of searching grows and more funds will be recovered for extensive and expensive searches. Search costs will vary with each database, the time online, and the output. Since these figures result in an income that is very close to the actual database search costs, budgeting for the varying monthly vendor charges is eliminated and efforts to monitor these charges can be minimal.

Estimated Search Cost · The most common custom of charging patrons is to pass along the vendor's charge for the search. Usually the estimated cost is printed at the end of the online session. There is no calculation to be done, the patron can see the charge immediately, and the searcher is not required to make any adjustments. The patron usually pays in relation to the amount and value of the information received.

Time, Citation Calculation · Calculating a per-minute connect-time fee and adding the costs of typing, displaying, and printing the records will give an approximate cost that will reflect the length and complexity of the search and the amount of information retrieved. This fee structure is calculated from the vendor's database hourly rate and citation charges that vary with each database; calculations may be extensive if a number of databases are used for a single search. A list by database of charges per minute of connect-time, plus the cost of typing or printing various formats, must be developed. While complex, these calculations can be used when a vendor or producer does not print an estimated cost at the end of the search or if the library subscribes to several different vendors and wishes to keep the charges the same, regardless of the source of a database available on several systems. The fees can also be adjusted to bring in a little more or a little less than the vendor's charge. It is important, however, to keep up with changing vendor fees, so adjustments must be made frequently.

Fees to Subsidize Direct Search Costs

In order to assist the student or other patrons, the library may choose to pay some of the vendor's individual search charges. A subsidy can be calculated to insure that a percentage of the variable costs are recovered. Although some of the variable charges for searches will be part of the library's budgeted funds, the impact will be minimized. The calculation of subsidy, however, must be clearly specified to insure a uniform policy followed by all searchers.

Any subsidy can be used for public relations efforts to advertise the service and to show the library's concern for patron fees. It also eases stress on the searcher, since most typographical errors or slow response times can be covered by the subsidy. In some cases the purpose is to provide free or low cost basic searches with the patron paying for a more substantial investment. Costs and patron charges must be monitored carefully if the library wishes to maintain a certain percentage return and if the total expenditure is to be kept within a budgetary limit. Subsidies can be provided by a number of different methods that can result in free searches for simple topics, a limited monetary impact, or assistance for particular groups of patrons.

Subsidizing Direct Search Costs · Reducing the vendor's estimated charge by a percentage commits the library to supporting some of the patron's cost. The amount of subsidy may be fairly small, but the total dollar amount absorbed by the library will increase as the service grows. The patron's charge is relatively easy to calculate from the estimated vendor's charge. The percentage of subsidy could be adjusted at intervals to control the library's costs. Records must be accurate and charges monitored to determine the budgetary impact.

Subsidized Time and/or Citations · A system can be developed for free searches utilizing five minutes online and generating twenty-five citations or less, the patron paying for any additional time or output. A variation of this type of subsidy would be to provide free connect time, with the patron charged for the citations retrieved. The patron could choose to extend the search with an additional cost commitment, or a short search would be available free. The cost to the library for each search would vary with the database and would be difficult to estimate, but the expenditure per search would be limited and the patron would pay for expensive searches. Some assistance would be provided for all patrons and an estimate of total costs could be determined by projecting the number of requests and knowing the databases most likely to be used.

Standard Cost Subsidy per Search · The first five or ten dollars for each search would be paid by the library. This will give some individuals a free search; others with more complex subject material or needing more information could choose to pay an additional amount. It would also cover a preliminary search at library expense to help estimate the cost of full retrieval of information for the patron's topic. This method of subsidy limits the cost to the library and budget projections could be made from estimated use. The choice of database would not affect the total commitment.

Subsidized by Categories of Patrons · Undergraduates could have free searches or all graduate students a free search on their thesis problems. Another plan could provide for nonfunded research to be charged a lower rate than searches for individuals with research grants. These systems could be used to favor some patrons, perhaps those who can least afford to pay, while others would pay a larger amount. Librarians could also be allotted some free searching for their own research or on library-related problems. This type of system could be initiated to encourage use by a selected group, but it would be difficult to estimate the impact on the budget.

Database Subsidy · Certain low-cost databases could be used for free searches and charges for more expensive databases passed along to the patron, or a search of any one database could be provided free, with charges for additional databases. In another variation, the patron could pay for the first database searched and subsequent databases used for the topic charged at a reduced rate. These systems might be difficult to explain to patrons and in some cases limit a subsidy to those with more complex problems. It would be difficult to estimate the impact of any of these charging methods.

Subsidizing Additional Resources · Free or subsidized searching of databases for which the library has no print counterpart would provide a database search when the library has canceled an index or when the reference collection is small. Free searches could also be provided in other cases for those files that have no print counterpart. A variation on this scheme, to encourage use of printed indexes, would be to make the charge greater when the database represents an index owned by the library. The budgetary impact could only be roughly estimated.

Subsidized by Need · Searchers could choose to reduce a charge if patrons were unable to pay or needed assistance with difficult topics. While the motivation is admirable, this process could be difficult to control and provide uniform judgments by different searchers. It would also be difficult to justify to patrons. Reduction in search charges at the discretion of the searcher when technical problems occur or errors creep in could, however, be a logical subsidy.

Standard Search Fee

A fixed fee for a search is the simplest charging system to describe to patrons and to administer. It does mean, however, that the library must be prepared to pay a variable amount that could, theoretically, either mean a large cost item or some income generation. A standard fee usually implies a certain maximum amount of connect-time and number of citations. This system would be difficult to budget for until some experience has been gained. It is possible that a standard fee offers no encouragement for efficiency and careful planning, since the charge to the patron will be the same regardless of the library's cost. This system, however, could be used to reduce stress on the searcher and inform the patron of the search charge before the search is underway. It may be difficult to calculate a standard fee that would bring in a desired percentage of the vendor costs.

Single Searching Charge · A specified charge would cover any search, regardless of length or complexity. This system is best for a uniform clientele with similar needs. An average charge must be calculated and the set patron fee could be adjusted to subsidize the search costs or to bring in some extra funds. If the patrons do not use the same database or have problems of different complexities, those with brief simple searches will help pay for the longer, more complex searches.

Classified Fees · A standard fee could be available for different categories of user groups, with undergraduates paying one price and faculty another. Databases could also be grouped into charge categories with a search of science files at one fee, humanities another. The search fee would probably cover a maximum amount of connect time and citations. This system would be easy for patrons to understand and remember but could be complex to calculate. It would be difficult to project yearly costs.

Brief Search · A quick search at a standard low price, such as three or five dollars, could be limited by time online, by number of citations, and to a selection of less expensive databases. Brief, simple searches could be offered as a special service for undergraduates or for anyone requiring specific information.

Recovering More Than the Direct Search Costs

Fees above the direct search costs may be necessary to cover some of the operating expenses. This additional income can be accomplished by a surcharge that would be an extra fee added to each search bill, or could be added to the fees for certain categories of patrons. Usually, even a substantial surcharge will not cover all the library costs of providing the search service, but may help defray some of the overall costs necessary for efficient information delivery. Strategies for additional fees can include:

Standard Surcharge · A search fee of twenty-five to thirty-five dollars or more may be added to the fee for the search. This system is often used when searches arc performed for individuals not part of the academic community. There may be a differential between business or industrial users, nonprofit groups, and the general public. More could be charged if document delivery were part of the service.

Percentage Surcharge · There may be a 10 to 50 percent charge added to the search fee for some categories of patrons. These individuals, usually from off campus, may represent local industries, private contractors or consultants, or other groups that could impact heavily on the library search service.

Handling Fee · A small charge, significantly less than a surcharge, could pay for the delivery of search results or provide any special handling of printout or data.

When the patron is paying for a search, it is important to have a policy to cover the occasion when there are problems. Consideration must be made for poor searches, those with unsuitable results, difficulties of inexperienced searchers, machine and vendor problems, and searches that may be inappropriate due to misunderstandings. Funds to pay for some of these searches or to apply a larger subsidy to be used at the discretion of the searcher may be important to back up the fee service.

FUNDING FOR ONLINE SERVICES

Besides search fees, other methods of funding an online search service should be explored. Sources for the initial outlay to establish the operation could include the library gift account; a special institutional appropriation; a grant from a campus research office, development or alumni program; or an outside funding agency. While these special funds can often be tapped for specific projects, they are usually not available for continuing expenditures. If the library budget can absorb the overhead, the salaries, the equipment servicing, and other operating costs, the varying monthly vendor charges for connect-time and citations must be the major consideration for funding. To eliminate patron fees or to provide money for a subsidy, creative ideas are needed to find funds not already absorbed into the library budget. Sometimes it is possible to change the priorities for use of established income; otherwise additional money must be found.

Support from within the Library

An increase or adjustment in the public services budget could be used to support online searching as one among many information services available for patrons. The search service could compete with other services for the available funds and priorities adjusted as their value for patrons is determined. Funds provided could be in the form of a monetary amount or a percentage increase in the total allotment for reference services. The potential for a budget increase will depend on the financial status of the library and the costs of other services. The materials budget could also be a source of funds if a percentage were set aside for online searching as a means of extending library resources.

Canceling index subscriptions or reducing the acquisition of new serials could release funds to apply to database searching. Expensive indexes could be identified and those with infrequent use replaced by searches of the equivalent database. Several year cumulations of indexes may not be as important when the online version is available. Duplicate subscriptions for indexes in departmental libraries can be examined for possible replacement by the online version, with the printed indexes retained in only one location. Online access to full-text journals or the ability to order individual articles online could be considered instead of some journal subscriptions. The amount of use of these journals and the way they are read—for browsing or just for relevant articles—will help determine the value of the print copy.

Copy machine and fine money are fees already in place, which may provide income that can be used to subsidize online searches. They provide a steady source of income although the funds may already be utilized to offset other expenses.

Reducing other services to release funds for subsidizing online searching will have to be considered carefully. However, a current awareness service provided for faculty by distributing copies of tables of contents of journals might be better served by an online SDI service, and manual preparation of bibliographies for classes or individual faculty members can be much easier, faster, and more efficiently prepared online. It is important to evaluate all special services for costs in relation to the effectiveness of the service provided.

Support from the Institution

A small percentage of the overhead from funded research projects on campus could fund a considerable amount of searching for researchers. A search service can provide active support for research activities, with current information for reports, retrieval of laboratory procedures, and reviews of developments in fields of interest. Income generated by research funding would then increase along with a greater need for online search support.

Library fees added to students' registration charges could be applied to undergraduate searches for all who need assistance for a term paper or project. It would be important to make certain that searches are available to all students who need them, and that the search service could handle the increased search load. These funds could also be used to install microcomputers for students to learn to do their own searching.

Special grants to support searches for selected groups can often be secured from a faculty development fund or campus committees such as those promoting the humanities or summer research projects. Participants of summer school institutes, faculty beginning research work, or part-time graduate students could be selected as targets for special assistance. A development or grants office could supply funds for individuals to do literature surveys for writing grant proposals and to retrieve background information on potential research topics. Searches of the grants and foundations databases can assist a development office by providing lists of possible funding sources. Department or instructional budgets can sometimes be tapped to provide searches for seniors writing up projects, classes with research papers, an upperclass seminar, honors projects, or for graduate students starting their thesis work.

Outside Support

Services provided for off-campus constituencies might be utilized as a profit-making effort to bring in additional funds. Charges could be set at a rate that could subsidize on-campus searching. A network of small public libraries might help pay for a centralized service at a nearby academic library to provide searching for local residents. Establishing a search service as a resource center for a group of hospital libraries, or contracting for information services for a business association or council, are services that can be organized on either a nonprofit or profit-making basis.

An active friends or alumni group could provide continuing funds for undergraduate searches. Local industries may be willing to support searching for students majoring in business fields. Any local group that could benefit from the expertise developed by online searchers is a potential funding source. Unfortunately, this strategy may be limited by the number of library personnel available to provide information services.

There is usually no easy answer to finding money for online searching other than user fees. Most in-house sources have already been utilized for regular budgeted items. Other efforts may be limited by personnel and facilities. The only real solution may be in the evaluation of priorities and the balancing of online services against another service or internal operation. This can be a decided challenge for the library administration and those responsible for providing the best possible information services.

ACCOUNTING RECORDS AND PROCEDURES

In order to establish an adequate level of record keeping, it is necessary to determine what information is needed for planning, budgeting, and accounting of income and expenditures. If online searching is a free information service and there is little concern about costs, it may be only necessary to monitor the vendor bills to maintain awareness of these variable charges, and any other costs can be incorporated into the public services budgeting process.

However, when library funds must be carefully allocated and accounted for, it will be essential to assemble data that will provide justification for expenditures, and procedures that will accurately track costs and income.

Records for Adequately Monitoring Finances
At the terminal—

Costs generated for each search:

connect-time
telecommunications
display, type and print fees.

Costs for any other use of databases:

practice time
answering reference questions
interlibrary loan verification
library research
problems with patron searches.

Income from patrons:

cash or checks
charges to institutional accounts
charges to be billed
fees deducted from a deposit account.

From vendor bills—

Total costs per month and items such as:

usage and charge by database
offline print charges
mailing fees
use of free time
SDI
document orders
additional manual chapters for databases

training
special services, such as mailing labels
additional passwords
monthly maintenance fee
printed material about the vendor's service.

From purchase orders for operating expenses—

supplies such as computer paper, ribbons, diskettes
individual database manuals
search aids, such as thesauri, word or journal lists
forms printed for the search service
brochures and other public relations materials
training costs (other than listed on vendor's bill)
software
subscriptions to professional journals
membership in library networks which coordinate vendor contracts
membership in online user groups.

Search logs and monthly vendor bills provide data on the number of searches, individual search costs, and total database charges. Operating expenses can be recorded as funds are committed. Overhead and management costs are less obvious figures that usually must be calculated, if needed, from the overall library expenditures. These items include personnel costs and those for space, furnishing, and utilities.

Log entries of searches should be correlated with vendor billings to check the accuracy of the data recorded and to note any charges that may not be included in the log, such as fees for stored searches, mailing offline printouts, database chapters, training, and other items. Vendor bills can be used to determine the monthly or yearly costs generated for connect-time and printing citations. If a patron fee is charged for searches, it is necessary to keep accurate records of the income. If the search service is being subsidized, these monthly totals can be compared to the amount from patron fees to calculate the percentage of the search costs being paid by the library. It may also be of interest to separate out and record the charges for in-house use by reference desk activities and for supporting other department and personnel uses. A different password for each library unit can assist in determining the vendor searching costs for different activities or locations.

In order to maintain accounts when patrons pay for service, a standard billing form is needed for each search. (See chapter 7, figure 8.) These printed forms should have space for the patron's name, affiliation and status; the date and time of the search; the vendor and the database(s); the connect-time and number of records printed, typed or displayed; method of payment and figures on which the charge is based; any reduction or surcharge; and the total. The method used to calculate the fee will determine the amount of information needed on the form. Copies of the statement should be made for the patron and for the person handling the accounts. The type of clientele and the constraints on the library budget may indicate whether or not the patron should be asked to sign a statement ahead of time that they will pay for the search.

If cash is accepted from the patron for the search, the billing statement may be marked paid and signed by the searcher or a separate receipt provided. Clerical assistance and policies of the institution and library may determine if cash, checks, or charge cards can be used. If the search is to be charged to a department or institutional account the procedure should be established in conjunction with the campus accounting office to follow the necessary steps for transferring funds from another unit's account to the library. Deposit accounts can also be established for patrons or departments if there is clerical assistance to manage the bookkeeping. The amount of assistance available may also determine whether or not patrons can be billed for searches. If delinquent accounts are a problem, it may be necessary to require patrons to pay before receiving the results of the search. A department secretary or a fiscal clerk could take care of collecting the money and keeping track of patron accounts. Clear procedures for handling cash income must provide for security of the money and follow established rules for recording and depositing funds.

Budgeting and recording expenditures and income are necessary components of search service management. Since the costs of individual searches are unpredictable and the totals dependent on demand, it is especially important to maintain an ongoing awareness of these expenses, especially if they are to be kept within a budget allotment. If some of the costs are recovered by patron fees, records must be sufficient to provide accountability for these funds. (See chapter 7, figure 18.) The decision of whether or not to charge patron fees requires consideration of the library's income and budget, the type of searches performed, the needs of patrons, and the availability of other information resources. Free searching as a component of the information retrieval process is the ideal arrangement, but the demands not only on the budget, but also on available personnel and equipment, must be appraised.

Free searching probably means screening or restricting search requests to eliminate inappropriate and expensive searches. While patrons will be directed to other sources, it still may mean denying a search that could be as unjust as a fee that limits searches to those who can pay. Either procedure can reduce the productivity and efficiency of the search service, unless there has been very careful planning. The best arrangement is likely to be free searches for some categories of patrons and topics, and charges for others depending on complexity, application, and cost. A just, equitable, and practical resolution will call for many compromises. Flexibility in any system is essential for coping with the changing factors of the fiscal environment.

Bibliography

Boyce, Bert R. "A Cost Accounting Model for Online Computerized Literature Searching." *Journal of Library Administration* 4:43–49 (1983).

Cannell, Sheila E., and Ian R. M. Mowat. "Charges for On-line Searches in University Libraries: A Report on a Survey." *Journal of Librarianship* 14:176–203 (1982).

Dowd, Sheila, John H. Whaley, and Marcia Pankake. "Reactions to 'Funding Online Services from the Materials Budget.'" *College and Research Libraries* 47:230–37 (1986).

Evans, John Edward. "Methods of Funding." In *Online Searching Technique and Management*, pp. 135–48. Edited by James J. Maloney. Chicago: American Library Assn., 1983.

Linford, John. "To Charge or Not to Charge: A Rationale." *Library Journal* 102:2009–10 (1977).

Poole, Jay Martin, and Gloriana St. Clair. "Funding Online Services from the Materials Budget." *College and Research Libraries* 47: 225–29 (1986).

Revill, D. H. "Charging for Online Services: The Questions and Arguments from an Academic Library Point of View." *Program* 17: 58–67 (1983).

Rouse, Sandra H. "Charging Policies for On-Line Services in the Big Ten Universities." In *User Fees: A Practical Perspective*, pp. 97–107. Edited by Miriam A. Drake. Littleton, Colo.: Libraries Unlimited, 1981.

Saffady, William. "Cost of Online Searching." Pt. 2 of "Availability and Cost of Online Search Services." *Library Technology Reports* 21: 37–111 (1985).

6

POLICIES AND PROCEDURES MANUAL *142*
MISSION STATEMENT OR PURPOSE *144*
I. SEARCH SERVICE *144*

    Goals *144*
    Clientele *145*
    Staffing *145*
    Equipment *151*
    Database Resources *151*
    Service Guidelines *152*
    Search Procedures *153*
    Finances *155*
    Statistics and Records *156*
    Evaluation *157*

II. READY-REFERENCE SEARCHING *158*

    Goals *158*
    Clientele *158*
    Searchers *158*
    Management *158*
    Equipment *158*
    Guidelines for Questions to be Answered Online *159*
    Search Procedures *160*
    Online Restrictions *160*
    Record Keeping *160*
    Evaluation *161*

III. DATABASE SEARCHING FACILITY FOR PATRONS *161*

    Goals *161*
    Clientele *161*
    Management *161*
    Equipment *162*
    Location *162*
    Training Patrons *163*
    Finances and Fees *163*
    Evaluation *163*

The Procedure Manual

An online search service, whether integrated into reference activities or established as a completely separate information service, is a unique unit with specific objectives and procedures. Activities are carried on by a number of searchers who usually have additional responsibilities. The searchers must learn to use the computerized database systems, work with patrons, apply mechanical and subject skills, and set aside time for providing an effective personalized service. Guidelines are needed for managing this information service in order to secure optimum efficiency, consistent response to demand, and control of expenditures. Other applications of online database searching should also be included. Searching equipment at the reference desk to broaden resources for answering questions and helping patrons, and the increasing availability of facilities for end-user searching—both should have policies and guidelines for management.

Written policies and procedures describe otherwise informal arrangements and form a framework for the development of a successful and responsive search service. All procedures should be focused on developing a quality and efficient service for patrons who expect that priority attention be given to their requests and that the search results be delivered immediately or within a short length of time. With a written manual, searchers will have guidelines for performance that can be referred to when questions arise. Procedures are especially important to insure a uniform search process when there are several searchers and/or if searches are done infrequently. Guidelines also include those established for keeping records and the collection of data on search activities. Authority can be given to these organizational and public service policies by having them approved by the library administration. New staff members will find a procedure manual valuable for learning established routines, and continuity of the search procedures can be maintained despite changes in personnel.

Searchers are often busy covering hours at the reference desk, teaching library research skills, responding to patron questions, working at collection development, and participating in professional activities. In addition, staffing hours in the library may vary, and the combination of these factors often makes it difficult for a group of searchers to meet often enough to discuss questions and everyday problems. Nevertheless, written guidelines should be developed by those responsible for providing the search service. This approach will insure that the philosophy of service is agreed upon and that the procedures are clear and understandable. The manual must be drafted carefully so it is concise, relevant, and well organized. Reviewing the procedures on a regular basis will help maintain the flexibility necessary to cope with changing technology and resources.

Procedures will not only include the conduct of daily work with patrons, training of searchers, and management of the search service, ready-reference, and end-user facilities, but will also guide the collection of data for making reports, projecting expenditures, and future planning. All procedures·are created to help searchers provide effective and efficient service and to assist patrons seeking information to use the most appropriate source for their needs.

POLICIES AND PROCEDURES MANUAL

An online services procedure manual should begin with the purpose or goals of the service. A goals or mission statement may include integrating online searching into the information services of the library, providing expert and efficient personal assistance for patrons, and providing extended or additional resources. The manual can be divided into parts according to the type of service being described: a search service, reference assistance, and patron searching.

Sections of the manual can be devoted to describing categories of patrons; the responsibilities of the manager and searchers; the priority given to search requests and keeping up search skills; the procedure for patrons to request a search, have it performed, and the results delivered; screening search topics; monitoring finances and (if necessary) collecting fees; and keeping records. Not only must normal situations be considered, but also the occasions when patrons are dissatisfied or the equipment does not perform to expectation.

The formulation of a procedure manual can be accomplished by having the search service manager, the head of public services or the reference department, or one of the searchers produce a draft document. Then each section in turn can be discussed by the searchers to reach general agreement on the philosophy of service and the best procedures to provide efficient systems that enhance the strengths of computer-assisted retrieval of information.

Outline

Mission Statement or Purpose

I. Search Service
   A. Goals
   B. Clientele
   C. Staffing
       1. Manager or coordinator
       2. Searchers
       3. Support personnel
   D. Equipment
   E. Database resources
   F. Service guidelines
       1. Hours of operation
       2. Appointment or on-demand
       3. Priorities for service
       4. Other use of search equipment
   G. Search procedures
       1. Requesting a search
       2. Screening requests
       3. Presence of the patron
       4. Performing the search
       5. SDI (Selective Dissemination of Information)
       6. Downloading
       7. Other uses of database searching
   H. Finances
       1. Fee schedule or cost recovery
       2. Payment for searches
       3. Backup funding and in-house searching
   I. Statistics and records
       1. Record of activity
       2. Financial records
   J. Evaluation
       1. Internal evaluation
       2. External evaluation
       3. Review of evaluation information.
II. Ready-Reference Searching
   A. Goals
   B. Clientele
   C. Searchers
   D. Management
   E. Equipment
       1. Type and location
       2. Security
       3. Availability for other uses

      F. Guidelines for questions to be answered online
      G. Search procedures
      H. Online restrictions
      I. Record keeping
      J. Evaluation
  III. Database Searching Facility for Patrons
      A. Goals
      B. Clientele
      C. Management
      D. Equipment
      E. Location
      F. Training patrons
      G. Finances and fees
      H. Evaluation

Procedures must be precise and yet flexible enough to serve as guidelines for both the experienced and the new searcher and to establish a range of online services provided. Clarity and enough detail to understand each section without making the document too lengthy are both important considerations. Procedures should cover everyday situations, answer questions that arise, and provide justification, when necessary, for the mode of operation. More detailed information is now introduced.

Expanded Outline

Mission Statement or Purpose
    This general statement of mission or purpose should reflect the dedication of the library to provide information services for the academic community and the integration of online database searching into this process. A few sentences will indicate that information resources include databases available from commercial, government, or campus sources and that these are utilized by expert searchers for providing individual assistance to researchers and scholars by means of a search service, for brief questions at the reference desk, and/or by patrons who are provided the means of searching databases themselves.

I. Search Service
    The name or acronym for the service as used on a brochure or for any advertising should be included. The place of this unit in the overall library organization, its physical location, and a general description of services provided can be listed.

      A. Goals ☐ Goals may include the acquisition of a broad expanse of scientific, business, and humanities databases for access by the research community, databases that represent resources not available in the library, or the online form of heavily used indexes. The search service provides a means of working with individual patrons on special problems and specific topics in narrow fields of interest, and helping them keep up with the latest information on their research interests. An effective online service furnishes expert assistance for researchers who need to quickly secure recent literature on specific information.

B. Clientele □ The primary library patrons are the faculty, students, and staff of the institution. Online services may be restricted to this group alone. If online searching is available for additional categories of patrons, these should be identified. Alumni, high school students, patrons referred from public libraries, students and faculty from other colleges, employees of local or state government, and researchers and business men and women from profit-making companies are all potential clientele. Any limitations and restrictions of service for particular groups should be clearly outlined.

C. Staffing □ The selection of a search service manager, searchers, and other personnel responsible for the operation of the online search service may be made by the head of the library or the head of public services. The staff may be composed of all the members of the reference department and also include selected individuals according to expertise and interest. Any qualifications such as subject specialty, reference experience, or previous work with computers should be identified.

1. *Manager or coordinator* · The person responsible for the service may be appointed or elected. A manager may be a full-time or a part-time coordinator, depending on the demands of the service and the number of searchers. In a small library the head of reference may be the person responsible for the search service management. The percent of the individual's time to be expended on management duties should be specified, and the person to whom the manager reports listed. The manager will keep the library administration informed of search activities and will work to accomplish the goals of the information services of the library. Responsibilities include:

a) *Space, equipment, and furniture* · The physical environment is a continuing concern of the manager. New furniture and equipment such as additional terminals, printers, or microcomputers will be needed from time to time. The selection process and the procedure for requesting them can be included. Maintenance of equipment is very important and a system for finding a backup machine when necessary is critical to a well-functioning unit. The manager must be alert to changing technology and have the authority to introduce faster terminals or microcomputers with software to assist the search process and to automate the record keeping. Cabinets, files, bookshelves, ergonomic furniture, and other office components must be obtained as needed.

The manager shall be responsible for arranging the security of the equipment and passwords.

b) Arranging contracts and communicating with vendors · The manager is the intermediary between the searchers and the online database vendors, and communications should be established to take care of any problems. Various types of contracts must be continuously evaluated as new options become available. The manager will prepare proposals to the library administration for contracting with new services and canceling those not judged effective.

c) Training searchers · The manager has the responsibility for encouraging the development and maintenance of expertise among searchers. Arranging for training, developing an in-house training program, coordinating up-date sessions, encouraging searchers to work together, and developing tutorial programs may be appropriate. The manager should alert searchers to online workshops, conferences, and related meetings. There could be special guidelines for new searchers to receive vendor training, to work with experienced searchers, and to have extra practice time.

The amount of training to be given to staff members who are not primary searchers should be mentioned here. It may be important to instruct some potential backup searchers, or all library staff members could be trained so they understand more about online services.

If searching is performed for any other groups such as patrons of a branch library or a group of public libraries, any reference staff in these locations should receive enough orientation so they can alert their patrons to the potential of online resources and provide realistic expectations of results.

d) Coordinating or assigning searches · A system for assigning search requests to the individual searcher is important. Responsiveness to patron requests must be a primary concern. Searching may be done by librarians according to their subject responsibilities in reference work or collection development. Or specific databases, such as PSYCINFO, BIOSIS, or MEDLARS, may be the responsibility of particular individuals, especially if there is heavy use of these large files, which have specific terminology and complex or precise organization. Depending on the clientele, staffing, and amount of searching performed, searches may also be assigned according to a time schedule with searchers taking a certain number of hours per week to perform searches, according to who happens to make the appointment or arrangement, or by rotation with the next available person taking the requests as they are received.

With a small staff there may need to be a combination of these arrangements, with most searches divided among the searchers and individuals specifically assigned to science or business or other subject areas, where searches are not as frequent and/or there is a need for more specialized training and experience. A list of backup searchers may be important as the service becomes busier. Secondary subject areas or a system of referring searches to an available librarian may be devised. Another alternative is to make the subject or database divisions broad enough for two people to share an area of responsibility.

e) Keeping manuals up-to-date and alerting searchers to system changes · Specific tasks may be listed, such as filing new information and replacing outdated procedures in vendor manuals, regularly monitoring online messages about downtime of the vendor's computer, new databases, and particular functions that are (or are not) available, and circulating vendor's newsletters or articles on search techniques. Any additional methods of helping searchers keep up with changing procedures, databases, and equipment can be included, such as the organization of regular review sessions, workshops, and meetings of searchers.

f) Purchasing search aids, manuals, and supplies · Securing additional search aids and manuals published by database producers may be the responsibility of the manager, or this material may be ordered on the request of the searchers. The acquisition procedure should be outlined along with any budgetary guidelines or restrictions. Supplemental material could be limited to the most used databases and subject areas with priority given to those databases that have no printed counterpart in the library.

Supplies, such as paper for the printers, ribbons, printed forms, extra disks, and log books are the responsibility of the manager, but a clerk may be assigned the task of making sure that they are available in the search service area.

g) Devising forms and keeping records · Forms to request a search, charge the patron, record the search activity, and compile statistics must be composed and distributed. The number of different forms may depend on the amount of business, whether or not patrons are charged, and the necessity for keeping records and collecting data for reports and planning. A list of required forms should be included and copies appended to the procedure manual. Regular review of the forms should be mandated so they are kept up-to-date and so that only the most necessary data are gathered to eliminate any unnecessary record keeping.

> Selective List of Forms:
> Online Search Service Log
> Online Literature Search Request
> Online Search Request for Undergraduates
> Interdepartmental Authorization Form
> Calendar for Search Appointments
> Online Search Service Billing
> Online Search Service Evaluation(s)
> Statistics Sheet
> Financial Summary Sheet

Forms for collecting data must provide enough information for writing annual reports and supplying statistics to justify budget requests. The manager must be informed about the type of information needed by the administration so that searchers are not burdened unnecessarily. Reports may be issued quarterly, or an annual summary of activity may be sufficient.

h) Managing finances · Budgeting is a responsibility of the search service manager or a joint responsibility with the head of the reference or public services department. This process will require keeping track of search costs and other expenses. Sufficient data will be needed to evaluate these expenditures and project figures for the next library budget. Consistent data collection will provide information that will identify trends and show when there are abrupt changes in the service offered or the patrons who utilize it.

The manager will check the monthly vendor bills with the search service records to insure accuracy and to monitor any unauthorized use of passwords.

The manager will be responsible for devising a fee schedule, if appropriate, to recover an adequate amount of funds for any costs that cannot be supplied by the library. If fees are not charged, the manager must be responsible for maintaining control over expenditures. Efficient accounting systems and adequate documentation of vendor search charges and income generated are essential. The duties of each searcher and any support personnel in regard to the handling of funds and keeping records should be clearly specified.

i) Coordinating public relations · A brochure and other explanatory material will be developed and kept up-to-date. All public relations, such as advertising in the student newspaper, articles in the library newsletter, fliers distributed to the faculty, and posters in prominent locations will be the responsibility of the manager, who will also coordinate with the searchers any demonstrations for colleges, classes, or individuals.

j) An advisory committee · The manager may wish to have the assistance of a committee of searchers, patrons, or other library personnel. There should be three to five members and the criteria and method of selecting them should be clear and the duties outlined. Responsibilities of the committee may be limited to advising on policies, long-range planning, and general arrangements such as charging fees, expanding the service, or adding additional searchers. Other concerns may deal with fund raising, evaluation, and public relations. Regular meetings may be planned or scheduled as needed.

k) Maintaining quality of service and an efficient search process · The manager will monitor the interaction between patrons and searchers and will recommend procedures, when needed, to make searches more easily available to faculty and students, to increase their awareness of the service, and to make searches more cost-effective. The quality of the search service and the efficiency of the operation are primary considerations. Regular meetings of the searchers should be held to discuss problems and search techniques, review procedures, and plan additional training.

A regular system for evaluation will be devised and carried out. This can include surveys of patrons, examining statistics, and reviewing individual searches.

A procedure for complaints by patrons should refer them to the search service manager, who can authorize a search to be repeated or may make the decision not to charge for a search when there has been a problem with a machine, a vendor, or other difficulties. The manager will attempt to resolve any questions between searchers and patrons, and will review procedures when clarification or adjustment is needed.

The manager should monitor established procedures regularly and recommend changes when they become cumbersome or outdated. A procedure for formal review by the search group and the authority to make changes should be determined. A procedure for securing clerical support should make it possible to have a secretary take appointments and a clerk accept and process payments or bill patrons when appropriate.

2. *Searchers* · The searching staff are those individuals who work with patrons to perform searches on specific topics.

a) *Selection and requirements* · All reference librarians are searchers and will participate in providing this service for patrons. Other staff members may be included as needed if they have had training and public service experience. Searchers must have had training by an online vendor or a library school course and a certain amount of previous experience or a number of hours of practice. In addition, previous or current reference work is expected. An internship period may be available to beginners so they can work with experienced searchers, or they may perform the simpler searches for the unit until some experience is gained. Subject expertise developed through education, training, or experience and reflected in work responsibilities such as a reference specialty or as a subject bibliographer for collection development may influence the division of work loads.

b) *Responsibilities* · Searchers work with patrons to perform searches that will be assigned by subject, database, time period, or as they are requested. Search skills must be maintained and individuals are expected to be responsive to patron needs. Keeping up with changes in search techniques and the availability of databases appropriate to searching assignments is the responsibility of the searchers.

The amount of time to be allotted for searching tasks may be noted in the manual if this is a separate responsibility from providing other reference and information services. Adjustments necessary in schedules, the maximum number of searches assigned per day, and individual work loads may be considerations when the amount of time each individual can expect to spend on online searching is discussed. Some statement should be made regarding the priority for online searches among the other responsibilities that are part of the librarians' work loads. It is necessary for all work assignment schedules to be maintained with enough flexibility to allow for adjusting to periods of peak use.

c) *Continuing education* · As experience is gained, searchers may be expected to attend update or advanced training sessions on individual databases or system techniques. Guidelines may include recommendations of attending one or two workshops per year. There may be an allowance of funds for practice or unlimited use may be made of the learning files when they are available. Searchers are encouraged to attend appropriate conferences and meetings and to keep up with the current literature.

3. *Support personnel* · A clerk or secretary may be assigned to certain tasks for the search service. These include: maintaining supplies of computer paper, ribbons, forms, and brochures; making search appointments; billing patrons and keeping accounts of cash; billing to college accounts; paying vendor bills; and keeping accounts for income and expenditures.

D. Equipment □ Selection of equipment is the responsibility of the manager, who will work with the library systems analyst, other library personnel who have an interest in computers, or a campus computer center. Some of the criteria for the terminal or microcomputer, modem, and printer include:

1. *Standard operating system,* compatible with other machines in the library, on campus if appropriate, and with online database vendor systems. If a microcomputer is used, there should be a good selection of software available.
2. *Comfortable to use* with convenient keyboard and clearly marked function keys
3. *Quietness of operation*
4. *Capability* of as fast a communication speed as possible
5. *All possible memory* and information storage capacity
6. *Reliability and support* by manufacturer.

E. Database Resources

1. *Selection* · Database vendors will be chosen primarily for their resources to meet the needs of the library clientele. Other considerations include:

   a) Costs and choice of payment plans

   b) Search language and procedures that are clear, logical, easy to learn and remember with clear and current search manuals

   c) A reliable system with little downtime, lengthy hours of operation, and assistance available

   d) Training provided in many locations at frequent intervals; several levels of expertise available.

2. *Selecting additional online services* · Qualifications for changing or adding vendors can include:

a) Providing access to an important database, full-text, or data files

b) Securing more cost-effective access to heavily used databases

c) Adding additional resources requested by faculty or expanding resources for departments in which faculty are active online patrons

d) Committing funds to acquire and maintain these resources.

F. Service Guidelines

1. *Hours of operation* · Searches are available during the week from 9:00 A.M. to 5:00 P.M. Arrangements can be made for appointments at other hours at the availability of a searcher.

2. *Appointment or on-demand* · Searches will be performed with the patron present at a time convenient for both the individual and the searcher. Searches can be performed without appointment if a searcher and the equipment are free from other scheduled activity.

3. *Priorities for service* · Search requests can be accepted on a first-come, first-served basis, but it is important to have priorities stated for instances when requests impact heavily on the time or equipment available. Service priorities may indicate that faculty requests come first, information services at the reference desk have second priority, and service for students third. There may be some other sequence depending on the type of institution and the goals that have been established. If searches are available to a wider group of patrons, the academic community must have the priority for scheduling searches. There is a potential for any online operation to result in an overload for the searchers and the machines. Measures to control this situation can include a calendar for appointments with an hour allotted for each search or a sign-up sheet to space out the scheduled searches. Searches by appointment should have priority over requests for immediate service.

4. *Other use of search equipment* · Searches for patrons will always have first priority for the search equipment. Any searching that is permitted by personnel other than the regular searchers should be mentioned and the limits clearly established. These could include interlibrary loan staff or other librarians with some training. If the equipment is to be used either occasionally or regularly for other library operations, it is especially important to have precise guidelines for scheduling and the priority to be given the

search service when more terminal time is needed to satisfy patron requests. Searches for other units within the library may be performed by trained searchers as time allows. Passwords shall not be used by anyone other than authorized searchers.

G. Search Procedures □ The steps taken by a patron to request and receive a literature search should be outlined. This process should be as simple and efficient as possible.

1. *Requesting a search* · Patrons may request a search by filling out a search request form. If searches are performed by appointment, the patron must contact the appropriate searcher or a secretary who maintains the calendar. The selection of a searcher will depend on how the searches are assigned to individuals. Searches on demand can be accepted as often as possible, not made available, or left to the discretion of the searchers. If searches are performed without the patron present, a different request form may be required; or if searching is to be done for mail and telephone requests a procedure can be included for this type of service.

A maximum length of time should be recommended between the scheduling and the actual search and between the search and delivery of results. It might be stated that appointments are made as soon as possible and the search completed within two days of the request.

A presearch interview may be especially important when searches are free of charge, when most patrons are inexperienced, or whenever there is a need to screen out requests for searches on topics inappropriate for an online search. Undergraduates may be asked to show evidence of preliminary work to identify some key words or the use of an index. The search request procedure should be flexible enough to encourage searchers to help patrons find the most appropriate source of information for their problem.

2. *Screening requests* · Some topics are not suitable for an online search. Searchers should be ready to recommend other sources when they seem more appropriate. If the patron is paying for the search, he or she should be warned that the charge is in effect even if no results are obtained.

3. *Presence of the patron* · The patron will be present during the search whenever possible. Searchers can perform other searches at their own discretion for telephone and mail requests or when patrons cannot be present.

4. *Performing the search* · Searching by appointment allows time for preparation by both patron and searcher. At the scheduled time they review and refine the terms, select the database(s), create

the search strategy, and prepare for any decisions that must be made during the search. These results may be printed immediately, printed offline, or downloaded on a disk. The procedure to be used may depend on the wishes of the patron, the speed and sophistication of the equipment being used, and a comparison of the costs. The procedure manual can include a section on the responsibility of the searcher to assist the patron in understanding each step of the search process, in reading the printout, and in finding the cited journals and additional material on the topic if needed.

Information on each search should be entered into a search log and as a minimum should include the patron and status, vendor, databases, and costs. Copies of searches can be maintained in a file. This procedure may depend on the amount of searching being done and whether it is helpful to refer back to searches previously done for individuals. If the library is paying the search costs, some printouts may be duplicated when there are popular topics used by students for term papers or a class assignment. A file of searches could be maintained by patron or by subject. Any request for confidentiality should be observed and if a patron pays for a search the results should be considered the individual's property and not distributed to anyone else.

5. *Selective dissemination of information* · Since arrangements can be made with many vendors to mail regular searches of a stored profile on the newest database update, the handling of this service must be the responsibility of the individual searcher who arranges it, or that of the manager or coordinator. Since this service is continued indefinitely until canceled, there must be a method of billing the patron when the charges are passed on. Printouts mailed regularly to the library must be sorted out and delivered to the patron. The procedure could specify that a clerk manage this responsibility.

An alternative procedure is for the searcher to run the stored strategy against the latest segment(s) of a database or databases at prescribed intervals. Responsibility for this regular service must be assigned, and the delivery of results and treatment of costs described.

A list of patrons and their subject interests could be maintained so they can be alerted to new databases in their field of interest.

Stored search profiles must be reviewed by the manager at regular intervals to be certain that they are still needed.

6. *Downloading* · Search results may be transferred to a disk provided by the patron. Any other copy will be erased. The patron will be informed of copyright regulations.

7. *Other uses of database searching* · Free searches for the president's or dean's offices or demonstrations for classes, publicity, departments, or new faculty may be part of the public relations and educational function of the search service. These extended uses of online searching should be noted and any limits to patrons or costs established.

Using an online database for verifying an interlibrary loan request or for searching on a subject of interest to a library committee may depend on the searchers' time and the amount of internal funding available. These uses should be identified and listed with cost restrictions, if any, specified. Each professional in the library may be allowed an amount of searching each semester or for the year on a research or publication topic. Searchers, especially new or inexperienced individuals, may be allotted a specified amount of funding for practice time or to maintain search skills when the number of search requests are insufficient for this purpose.

H.   Finances □ The policy of the library regarding the charging of fees for online services should be clearly stated. If searches are provided without charge to the patrons, any limits of clientele, subjects, amount of search time, or number of records should be mentioned. An accurate log sheet of searches and costs may be especially important when there is a limit to the total funds available for this service.

1. *Fee schedule or cost recovery* · Patron fees should be listed along with the method of calculating them. When a certain amount of cost recovery must be accomplished, this arrangement should be mentioned with any subsidy or surcharge indicated. All searchers will be expected to follow this procedure. Any special arrangements for particular groups of patrons (undergraduates, off-campus users, class projects, thesis or grant searching) must be included. All literature on the search service and any advertising should state that a fee is charged.

2. *Payment for searches* · Cash, checks, charge-cards or authorization to charge campus accounts may be accepted. Payment should be arranged before the search is carried out. Money and forms may be turned in to the searcher, a secretary, or a library employee responsible for other accounts. If there is a concern about payment for searches or making certain that the procedure is understood, the patron can be asked to sign a release stating that the fee will be paid even if the search yields no results. Arrangements for patron deposit accounts or billing for searches should have procedures to specify who is responsible for keeping track of and collecting these payments.

3. *Backup funding and in-house searching* · Problems encountered when performing searches with patrons may require the search to be repeated or subsidized. Difficulties can include response time, misunderstandings, human error, or machine difficulties. Guidelines for charging a search to the library should indicate if the searcher can make the decision or if approval by the search service manager is needed.

Online practice time for searchers may be restricted to specific databases or expenditures. Searching for in-house purposes may be limited to certain applications such as interlibrary loan verification, ready-reference questions, bibliographic instruction, demonstrations, or professional support. Any limits of time or cost should be outlined and all searching for these activities should be included in the search log.

I. Statistics and Records □ Statistics are collected for annual reports, budget planning, and reporting monthly data on the amount and cost of searches. Figures can be tabulated from a log, from a file of search bills, from the vendor's billing, by accounting software available with a microcomputer, or from copies of searches. Data collection may include:

1. *Record of activity*

   a) The number of searches for patrons. (The definition of a search is needed here. A search may be one subject for one patron regardless of number of databases, the number of questions searched, or the number of database searches accomplished.)

   b) The number of patrons for whom searches were performed

   c) The number and names of departments these patrons represented

   d) The number of searches performed by each searcher

   e) The number of searches from each database vendor

   f) The status of patrons: faculty, graduate students, undergrads, staff, in-house, or individuals from off-campus

   g) The number of searches of each database

   h) The number of in-house searches by purpose or use of results

   i) The number of hours searched by vendor, database, and searcher.

2. *Financial records*

   a) Online and citation charges per month for each database vendor

   b) Income from patron fees and the average charge for a search. If there is no search fee, the average cost for each search may be determined.

   c) Other special charges for SDI, mailing fees, etc.

   d) Expenses for training

   e) Expenses for manuals, supplies, and equipment

   f) Expenses for other operating costs

   g) Cost of in-house searching

   h) The total expenditures, total income, and percent cost recovery.

J. Evaluation ☐ The effectiveness of the online search service must be reviewed at regular intervals. The results will be used to discuss adjustments in procedures or other changes needed to improve services for patrons.

1. *Internal evaluation*

   a) Regular meetings of the searchers to discuss problems, strategies, and techniques

   b) Review of data on number of searches, departments served, and status of patrons

   c) Evaluation form for searchers to record their impressions about the success or failure of each search.

2. *External evaluation*

   a) Brief questionnaire for patrons to be completed as search is concluded

   b) Longer questionnaire for patrons to be returned after review of search results

   c) Questionnaire sent to patrons who had a search performed sometime in the past to ask for the value of the search results and the reasons for following (or not following) up with another search.

3. *Review of evaluation information* · Comments and conclusions from the various methods of evaluation should be utilized to

examine the search procedures, the effectiveness of the searchers and the responsiveness of the service to the needs of the clientele. This regular review should insure the most effective service for the academic community.

The procedure manual should be a guide to better, more efficient service and should assist the individual searchers to work with patrons in a rational, logical system organized to make the best use of their time and expertise. Regular review of performance and procedures is essential as new equipment, systems, techniques, and technologies are acquired. The procedure manual itself must be reviewed regularly, probably annually.

II. Ready-Reference Searching

A. Goals □ Goals for online searching at the reference desk include providing better information services, increasing the resources available to the reference librarian, improving the efficiency of the librarian, providing additional access to heavily used printed indexes, and updating reference sources with very recent information.

B. Clientele □ Patrons are those who come to the library or call on the telephone. They are faculty, staff, and students of the academic institution and may include the general public or special library users such as alumni, visiting scholars, or local residents.

C. Searchers □ All reference librarians will be trained to use the systems available at the reference desk and utilized to answer questions.

D. Management □ The head of the reference department will be responsible for searching at the reference desk, but will work with the manager of the search service to work out the best procedures, equipment, and to determine the support materials needed. The head of reference is responsible for monitoring costs, keeping records, and evaluating the quality of service.

E. Equipment

1. *Type and location* · Equipment should be compact, quiet, and simple to maintain and refill (paper and ribbons). The terminal should have an easy to read keyboard. Searching equipment must be located at the reference desk or very close to it. It should not interfere with the regular use of the telephone or with the interaction between reference librarian and patron. A position behind the desk, slightly away from the center of activity, will allow the refer-

ence librarian to maintain contact with the patron as the search results are secured.

2. *Security* · Equipment should preferably be anchored to a desk or be a portable machine that can be locked in a drawer; otherwise it should be removed to a secure room at night. All passwords, extra disks, and accessories should be kept in a locked cabinet. The last person at the reference desk each night should secure the terminal and the first one each morning should be sure it is ready for use.

3. *Availability for other uses* · Reference search equipment should be dedicated to answering questions at the reference desk and not used for any other purpose.

F. Guidelines for Questions to Be Answered Online □ An online database is used at the discretion of the reference librarian. An online search is an appropriate response when:

1. *The information* cannot be found in a printed source.

2. *Very specific information* is needed such as dates, events, or data.

3. *A database* will provide a quick answer to a question that would take a long time to research in a printed source.

4. *The most recent information* is requested or a span of years must be searched.

5. *The printed index* does not yield satisfactory subject access.

6. *The patron's information* is incomplete and a search will quickly provide an answer.

7. *Printed sources* are unavailable—in use, at the bindery, or not owned by the library.

8. *A more comprehensive source* of addresses, telephone numbers of companies, associations, or individuals is needed.

9. *A citation* must be verified or completed.

10. *New, colloquial, very specific terms or acronyms* cannot be found under standard indexing.

11. *A database* represents a source for which there is no print version available.

12. *Students need help* finding relevant citations.

13. *Concepts must be combined* that are treated separately in the indexes.

14. *Subjects are interdisciplinary* and it is difficult to find good coverage in standard indexes.

G. Search Procedures

1. *Log on and off quickly*

2. *Questions requiring lengthy interviews,* complex strategies, or more extensive results should be referred to the search service

3. *Usually use free-text searching*

4. *Note restrictions* of time online, output, and cost.

H. Online Restrictions ☐ If funds are limited, the ready-reference search may need to be closely monitored and controls established. These restrictions will have to be determined by the needs of patrons, resources of the library, and the philosophy of reference service that may determine the amount of assistance to be provided. Possible qualifications to be specified:

1. *Citations only are provided,* no abstracts. Certain formats are used.

2. *Maximum number of citations* (five or ten) are provided.

3. *Only online use* is provided; there are no offline printouts.

4. *Maximum amount of time* to be spent online (three to five minutes) is set.

5. *Access is limited to specified databases.* (For example, use only ERIC, SOCIAL SCIENCES INDEX, MAGAZINE INDEX and ENVIROLINE).

6. *Costs per search* should not exceed a certain amount (five to eight dollars).

I. Record Keeping ☐ The monthly vendor bill may provide sufficient data to track reference desk activity, especially if there is a separate password for this purpose. If not, or if more information is needed, a brief log may be maintained to record:

1. *Initials of reference librarian*

2. *Vendor and database used*

3. *Patron category* (faculty, staff, graduate, undergraduate)

4. *Question topic* (brief narrative) and/or type (directory, data, citation, subject)

5. *Time online* and time spent with patron

6. *Vendor charge.* The log should be checked monthly with the vendor bills for accuracy and to determine any unauthorized use of the equipment or passwords.

J. Evaluation ☐ Evaluation should be part of the overall assessment of reference desk activities or information services of the library. Review of the number and types of questions, the costs, and the success of finding answers should be an ongoing process among the reference librarians.

III. Database Searching Facility for Patrons

A. Goals ☐ This service may be a means of offering free searching, primarily for undergraduates; helping library patrons use resources independently; providing another vehicle for teaching about library research; relieving the search service of simple, routine searches; and/or giving patrons the opportunity to extend their interest and expertise in using computers.

B. Clientele ☐ Patrons will be the academic community, although emphasis could be placed on making the service primarily for undergraduates. If this end-user service is tied into a campus network, clientele may include those who search databases from other locations on campus.

C. Management ☐ An end-user facility will be directed by the search service manager or another searcher who will coordinate the systems, equipment, and procedures with those of the search service. Records will be maintained and evaluation of the service carried out regularly. Specific duties of the manager of end-user searching include:

1. *Selection of equipment* coordinated with similar computer equipment in the building and with concern for simplicity and ease of use, security, and the environment in which it is placed

2. *Selection of database systems,* chosen in cooperation with the reference librarians and the search service manager

3. *Preparation of brief manuals,* charts of directions, and handouts to assist the patrons to use the systems independently. This may include the development of work sheets, examples, and forms to assist searchers formulate search strategies

4. *Maintenance of a schedule,* if necessary, for patrons to sign up for time on the computer

5. *Staffing, if necessary,* with librarians and/or students depending on the amount of assistance needed and the location in relation to the reference desk

6. *Integration with reference activities* including bibliographic instruction

7. *Cost monitoring,* arranging for collection of fees if necessary, keeping accounts

8. *Evaluation and records.* Keeping a log for patrons to add comments, putting out surveys, and determining the impact on other library services.

D. Equipment □ Terminals, microcomputers, and software should be chosen with regard for standard specifications, features advantageous for searching, and compatibility with other library/campus equipment. Important features include:

1. *All equipment* should be reliable and sturdy. The fewer disconnected parts the better. Keys should be well marked. Servicing should be convenient, and backup equipment available. Security is important.

2. *Printers* should be quiet, easy to load with paper, and make changing ribbons simple. They may need special consideration to stand up to heavy use and to limit wastage of paper.

3. *Software* will be kept in a master file with a single copy made for the microcomputer it was purchased for. Only authorized personnel should be able to change operating parameters of the equipment and software. An inventory will be maintained of all library software utilized to support end-user searching.

4. *Machine and software manuals* and directions will be kept in a designated location.

5. *Equipment* is only for online database searching, unless other uses are approved by the manager of the service.

E. Location □ A facility with several pieces of equipment may be established in a separate search room, as part of a microcomputer facility, or with several machines near the reference desk, the printed indexes, or the search service. Location may depend on the amount of assistance needed by patrons, the location of telephone lines, and the space in the building. If possible, end-user facilities should be near the other indexes and the reference desk.

F. Training Patrons □ Some training may be advisable for most end-user systems. It may be provided by:

1. *Search counseling* before going online to advise on terms, databases, and procedures. May include work in the printed indexes. (May be required.)

2. *Manuals or handouts* prepared by the manager or reference librarians to provide brief, clear directions.

3. *Brief instruction sessions* for first time users. (May be required.)

4. *Tutorials,* either online or on an individual basis with reference librarians.

5. *Introduction to the system(s)* and some training may be included in regular bibliographic instruction sessions.

6. *Special classes* on the use of online information systems will include more advanced procedures and relate online systems to other methods of information retrieval.

G. Finances and Fees □ Database searching by patrons should be free if at all possible and considered another method of information retrieval along with printed indexes. Any fees should be minimal or for searching beyond a basic limit of online time and/or citations. Start-up costs may be a special appropriation or grant, but continuing funding will be by budget appropriation.

H. Evaluation □ A log will be maintained to record patron comments. Brief surveys from time to time will be carried out to determine the value of the service, problems encountered, relevancy of the information found, the value of training received, and any suggestions. Data on the number of patrons, departments represented, databases searched, and costs per search may be collected to analyze the patterns of usage.

The procedure manual provides important support for all aspects of online services. It should encourage efficiency, supply continuity, help establish priorities, and help personnel provide an effective information service. Creation of the manual will require a careful examination of casual procedures and the assigning of responsibilities. It must be firm, yet flexible, and reviewed annually to be certain that procedures have kept up with changing technology, costs, and expectations of patrons and the library administration.

Bibliography

Carlson, David, and P. Grady Morein. "Online Bibliographic Database Searching in College Libraries." *Clip-Note* No. 4–83. Chicago: Assn. of College and Research Libraries, American Library Assn., 1983.

Katz, Bill, and Anne Clifford. *Reference and Online Services Handbook: Guidelines, Policies and Procedures for Libraries.* New York: Neal-Schuman, 1982.

Pensyl, Mary E. "The Online Policy Manual." *Online* 6:46–49 (1982).

7

RECORD KEEPING *168*
   Sources of Data *168*
   Tabulating Data *170*
PREPARING FORMS *172*
   Online Literature Search Request *173*
   Online Literature Search Request Form for
      Undergraduates *175*
   Interdepartmental Authorization for Online Literature
      Search *175*
   Online Literature Search Authorization *176*
   Calendar for Search Appointments *177*
   Online Search Service Billing *178*
   Online Search Service Log *179*
   Reference Desk Search Log *180*
   Search Log for Public Terminal/Microcomputer *180*
   Planning Your Search *180*
   Search Form for Printed and Online Sources *183*
   Evaluation Forms *184*
STATISTICS AND REPORTS *188*
   Statistics Sheet for Online Searching *188*
   Financial Summary of Direct Search Costs and
      Income *189*
   Summary of Ready-reference Searches and Costs *190*
   Summary for Patron Searching and Finances *190*

Records, Forms, and Reports

The consistent collection of data on the activities of the library's search service can be very important when accounting for current expenditures, formulating the following year's budget, proposing the addition of a new online database service, and justifying the need for more staff or equipment. The manager must be responsible for organizing and collecting these data, making certain they are accurate and kept current. Forms are helpful to guide the data collection process, especially when they are convenient to use and can be filled out quickly. Care must be taken that terms and categories on the forms are clearly defined so that everyone who uses them will supply the same information. The data should provide useful figures that can be analyzed to determine past activities, current status of the budget, some conclusions on effectiveness of the service, and future projections of demand, costs, and staffing.

Different figures will be gathered for a search service where individual searches may run over $100 and fees are collected, the reference desk with short and frequent queries, and the end-user service, which may show longer sessions on less expensive systems or on a CD-ROM database. Search service activities may involve handling a good deal of money, and result in very large monthly statements from the online vendor. Keeping accounts will require exacting records, while it may only be necessary to monitor the cost of the services at the reference desk and/or by end-users to keep within a budget allocation.

Forms, however, can also be as important as brochures for advertising search services, helping explain the search process, and encouraging patrons to think about their research topic and to gather required information and terms that are needed for a satisfactory online search. These search request forms must be carefully written so they are understood by inexperienced patrons. Evaluation forms are also important and must be thoughtfully phrased to secure responses that will help to improve procedures and services.

Whenever possible, data should be collected automatically by the microcomputer. Transferring the figures from forms to the computer for storage and analysis is a second alternative, especially if statistical analysis is desired, but any extra handling of the data increases chances for error and means additional time must be spent to secure meaningful information. The most important consideration is to collect only the data necessary for proper management of online searching and needed for reports to the library administration.

RECORD KEEPING

Most of the accounts will be for the search service, since it is the online service most demanding on staff, costs can be greater and more variable, and it more often includes the handling of money. Records of the search service must be adequate for documenting activity, monitoring costs, and producing reports, but should not be burdensome for the searchers. These figures will be used for annual reports, budgeting, accounting for income, reconciling vendor bills, justifying expenditures, and planning for future activities and needs. An analysis of these activities will serve as a guide for determining the records that must be organized, the number of forms that must be arranged, the individual figures needed for compiling statistics, and some of the procedures that must be drawn up to insure the uniform collection of these data.

Sources of Data

Consistent records in a search log or journal can be used to track search activity. The search service, reference desk, and end-user service can each use a search log to tally individual searches. For the search service, data is usually recorded by the searcher at the beginning of a search or when it is completed and a fee collected. Reference librarians can log in each online answer to a reference question and patrons can sign a record book next to the computer or terminal.

The search log may be as simple as a lined sheet with columns to check for characteristics of the patron, the searcher, the vendor, the databases used, the vendor charge, and the amount and method of payment. The log can also be in a narrative style like a diary with additional details that include information about the topic searched; the time online; the number of citations displayed, typed, or printed; the date when the offline print arrived; and fee calculations. A column or space for comments can record any difficulties encountered such as slow response time or line noise. Other notes may include statements by the patron regarding the value of the search or the searcher's opinion of the success of the search results.

The simple log can yield quite a bit of information—the number of searches per month or per year; the number of patrons—faculty, graduate students, undergraduates, staff, and those from off campus; the departments served; the databases used most frequently; and the average cost of a search. These figures can be used to show increases or decreases in search activity, heavy use by certain patron categories or departments, peak request periods of the semester, characteristics of search topics, and the distribution of workloads among the searchers. If searches are primarily by graduate students, perhaps the faculty needs to be better informed about the capabilities of an online search service. If few undergraduates are asking for searches, the fee schedule should be examined and a method of quick searches, a subsidy of search fees, advertising or promotion by the reference librarians, or bibliographic instruction that includes a literature search as a component of library resources should be considered. A tabulation of departments these patrons represent will show where the activity is heaviest and which units need better information or a demonstration to illustrate the potential results of online searching, especially when there are databases appropriate for the interests of that department. If there are few relevant databases, this information can be used to back up a request for an additional database vendor.

A log that provides a record of searches and the approximate costs can be used to check against the billing by the database vendor. There is an obvious value in determining that the records agree, and this also provides a check against the unauthorized use of a password or any unexpected additional charges, such as those for storing search strategies not needed again. The total costs can be compared with a budgeted amount or the funds recovered through fees. Institutions with a number of active searchers can use the vendor's billing statement to be sure all searches are recorded, to verify charges, and to track the costs of problems, slow response time, and interrupted searches.

The number of searches performed during a year shows the level of activity of the online search service and the impact on individual librarians. The method of counting searches undoubtedly varies from institution to institution despite efforts to standardize the collection of statistics. One of the problems is the many variables encountered in performing online searching. A patron may ask for several questions to be searched in the same database, or a single topic may be searched in several different databases. A single database may be divided into several parts with different vocabularies. A preliminary search may be done on a subject and a follow-up search on the same topic performed at a later date with a different structured search. In general, however, a search should be considered a response to a patron's request for information regardless of the number of databases used. A follow-up search at a later date would then be another search. The total number of searches can include both those for patrons and those for library purposes.

The vendor bills alone can be used to determine the number of database searches, the amount of time and the cost for each search, and the total hours online per month. Most billings will also provide a list of the databases accessed; the number of citations displayed, typed, or printed; the telecommunications network charges; charges for stored searches and special print formats; and the costs of training and search aids charged to the account. Separate passwords for each location where searches are performed will provide comparative data and relative costs for different purposes. Information can also be tabulated from a file of search request forms or copies of the patron billing statements.

Instead of using a log to record information on searches, part of the search itself on a microcomputer may involve the entering of details about the patrons, their status, the searcher, and the purpose of the search. Commercial software or some programmed in-house will collect the data automatically and keep track of search time and costs. All searchers must consistently enter the information into the accounting file and this automation of data collection will simplify the production of weekly or monthly reports. A variety of data tabulations can be produced, such as a list of search times and costs by patron or an account number, searches by each searcher, searches by database, and a total list of searches with costs for each online vendor.

If there is a need to account for staff time or to calculate personnel costs, figures can be kept for time spent at training programs and workshops, time needed to prepare for searches, practice time, and other search-related demands on personnel.

Tabulating Data

Search Service · Statistics to collect for management and planning:

number of searches for patrons
number of in-house searches
number and status of patrons
number and list of databases searched
departments served
time spent online
number of citations displayed, typed, printed offline, or downloaded
average cost of a search
number of searches by vendor

number of searches by database
number of searches per searcher
number of total searches per month and year.

It may be of interest to look at the range of costs or charges for scheduled searches. Many low cost searches may back up a proposal that patrons could do their own searching with adequate facilities and the trained searcher be better utilized for the more demanding, complex searches. The proportion of search time on one vendor system may indicate that more training is needed on an alternative vendor's system, or perhaps the second system could be dropped if there is a subscription charge or a monthly minimum fee and no significant additional resources are represented.

These figures certainly do not tell much about the quality of searching. Only the frequency of searches, the use by many patrons from the same department, and repeat searches for the same faculty member may indicate satisfaction.

Reference Desk · Data on search activity at the reference desk:

number of searches to answer reference questions
number of searches performed by each librarian
number of patrons by status: faculty, graduate students, undergrad-
    uates, other
number of times each database was used
average cost/search
total costs/week/month
types of questions: directory, citation, subject, data
perceived success rate.

If more than one online database system is utilized, there can be a separate tabulation for each. If there is enough backup at the reference desk, further details on the types of questions, the patrons' departments, or the class they are doing work for can be included.

Patron Searching · Collecting information on end-user searching may depend on observation, relying on patrons to record their own activity, or requiring presearch training or scheduling of search time when statistics on patrons can be collected. The more formal the arrangements—such as requiring work in the indexes, consultation with a librarian, or collecting a fee—the easier it will be to record interest. However, the more independence of the patron and the more informal the system is, the more difficult it will be to secure accurate information on usage. The amount of online connect-time used each month and the number of citations printed can be determined from the vendor's billing, or a menu system may include the registering of each patron searcher and this information can be printed out regularly. If possible, data should supply:

number of patrons doing their own searching
status of patrons: faculty, freshmen, sophomores, juniors, seniors, graduate students
success at finding helpful information
repeat usage
costs per search.

Records must be accurate, consistent, and as brief as possible. Every survey or vehicle for collecting information should provide an opportunity for comments. The data gathered should be examined for trends and conclusions about the adequacy of procedures and services, and the demand for more databases, more equipment, and more assistance by librarians.

PREPARING FORMS

Forms are usually necessary to assist the smooth flow of activities from patron request to delivery of search results. An individual who does all the online searching might have an informal system that could work effectively, but if there are several librarians who share this responsibility, the availability of forms will help systematize search procedures, encourage patrons to supply appropriate information, and make sure that necessary data is collected from each search session. One purpose of forms is to limit the amount of time spent on recording activities and yet to secure enough information for monitoring and justifying budgeted funds, staff time, and service priorities. When a fee is charged, it means that there must be more records to account for cash and the handling of accounts. Consistent collection of the same categories of data will allow comparisons over various time periods to provide information for detecting trends and making projections of future activity.

Few forms should be needed at the reference desk where trained searchers do brief, unscheduled searches. However, a record of the number of times a reference librarian used an online source will indicate if all patrons are receiving equal access to information. A regular examination of reference questions and the database consulted will encourage the discussion of appropriate usage of these resources. When patrons are doing their own searching, besides recording activity, forms can be devised to help students plan the approach to their search topic and organize concepts of a subject into a search strategy. The use of a system with Boolean logic capability will be different from one that guides the searcher with menus and will require more planning and understanding of searching principles.

Online Literature Search Request

A patron requesting a search can use a form such as the *Online Literature Search Request* in figure 2 to provide a title for the search to help
focus on the specific information needed. Additional questions ask for a
description of the subject and a listing of some key words or phrases and
synonyms. The patron may wish to request particular databases and can
indicate whether the search is to be comprehensive, or only for some
recent references. Citations can be limited to the English language or to a
specific time period. This basic information is often enough preparation
for a search when the patron sits down with the searcher and they dis-

---

Online Literature Search Request

Appointment Date: _____ Time: _____
Librarian: _____ Telephone: _____

Problem Statement
Name _____ Telephone _____
Academic department _____
Status ___ Faculty ___ Grad. Student ___ Undergraduate ___ Staff ___ Other
Title of search _____

Please give a short narrative description of the problem to be searched.
BE SPECIFIC. Cover all aspects of the problem but underline particular phrases
that are more important to you. LIST THESAURUS TERMS IF KNOWN, KEY-
WORDS, SYNONYMS AND ALTERNATE SPELLINGS. Use scientific and technical as well as common vocabulary. Please indicate if any words or phrases
have a special use that you wish to exclude.

_____
_____
_____
_____
_____
_____
_____
_____

Databases requested: _____
Material needed: _____ A few recent citations _____ All relevant citations
Years to be searched: _____
Language: _____ English only _____ Other languages

Figure 2. Sample request form

cuss the topic in more detail. If the searcher is inexperienced or the subject requires some study and preparation, the form can be turned in ahead of the search. As long as the patron is present when the search is performed, most additional information can be secured when the search strategy is formulated. Discussing the search terms, determining emphasis of the topic, and preparing for decision points online help insure that the results match the patron's expectations.

If the patron is not going to be present for the search, it is necessary to ask more questions, and a second page can be added to the *Online*

Online Literature Search Request • Page 2

Please list any authors and/or titles of articles you already have that are relevant to this search.

_____

_____

_____

_____

_____

Are there any journals that you are particularly interested in?
_____

Have you already done some searching on this topic? Where have you looked?
_____

Would you like to have references to any particular kind of material or would you like any of it excluded? Books _____; articles _____; reports _____; dissertations ____; patents ____.

If a great many references are found, would you like just the most recent printed? If so, what is the maximum number you would like to have?
_____

How would you like the citations delivered? Printed online ____; printed offline ____; downloaded on a disk ____.
Would you like abstracts if they are available _____; or just citations? _____.
Is there a deadline for receipt of this information?

_____

_____

Is there a maximum amount you wish to pay? _____
Would you like this search updated monthly or at regular intervals? _____

Figure 3. Sample request form (cont.)

Literature Search Request forms as illustrated in figure 3. Further questions about the search topic can ask for authors and titles of relevant publications already found on the subject, and any previous searching online or in printed indexes. Specific directions for the search results can include whether or not abstracts are desired; the type of material needed: books, articles, reports, or dissertations; and the format of the citations: printed online, printed offline, or downloaded on a disk. If there is a charge for the search, the patron can indicate a maximum amount and any deadlines for receipt of the search results.

Completed search request forms can be filed to collect information on topics that have been searched for review of strategy preparation and for information on previous searches by returning patrons.

Online Literature Search Request Form for Undergraduates

If searching is performed for undergraduates, the experience can be used to reinforce bibliographic instruction. In this case a search request form for a brief free search such as figure 4 may ask for some preliminary work in the indexes to demonstrate that the student understands how to do library research. She or he can be asked to find and identify an appropriate citation and to determine whether or not the library owns the periodical as a preparation for finding additional references online.

Interdepartmental Authorization for Online Literature Search

When fees are charged, the cost can often be billed to institutional accounts. These sources may include departmental funds or those for research grants. Both undergraduates and graduate students may be working on funded projects or may be doing searches for a professor. An authorization form that is signed by the department head, the principal investigator, or someone else with authority can be used for this transaction. If there is a centralized accounting office, the form should be approved there so the transfer of funds from the department to the library account can be accomplished smoothly. Figure 5 illustrates a sample authorization form. The signed form, along with a copy of the detailed bill, can be turned into the library fiscal clerk or sent directly to the campus accounting office. This form also serves the function of requiring an authorizing signature before a student can charge to an institutional account. The professor can also indicate any limits to the expenditure. Securing this information ahead of time can keep some problems or misunderstandings from developing.

Online Literature Search Request Form for Undergraduates

Appointment Date: _____   Time: _____
Librarian: _____   Telephone: _____

Problem Statement
Name: _____ Telephone Number: _____
Major or class: _____
Title of search topic: _____
_____

Is this for: _____ Speech or brief paper?   _____ Longer term paper?
            _____ Specific information?   _____ Seminar report?
            _____ Personal interest?   _____ Item at bindery?
What indexes have you used already: _____
_____
_____

What subject terms did you search under: _____
_____
_____

List at least one reference you have found already: _____
_____
_____
Does the library own this periodical: _____
When you have completed this form, a librarian will do a computer literature search with you. This free service will be limited to a single database search and a printout of up to 20 recent citations. We will do our best to find relevant English-language articles, but cannot guarantee that the source journals will be held by the library.

    If you would like a more extensive search (for a fee), interlibrary loan service, or suggestions for printed indexes suitable for your topic, please consult the librarian at the reference desk.
Database: _____ Number of references: _____

Figure 4. Sample request form for undergraduates

Online Literature Search Authorization

If it is necessary to recover the search costs and there is any concern about receiving the payment for service, patrons can be asked to sign a release stating that they will pay for the search as illustrated in figure 6. In addition, there can be a sentence noting that the search may not result in any citations of interest to the patron. This form will emphasize the necessity of payment and the uncertainty of the results.

Interdepartmental Authorization for Online Literature Search

Name of user _____

Academic department _____

Appointment date _____

Expenditure maximum _____

Account number _____

Signature _____

                               Department Head or Principal Grant Investigator

Date _____

Figure 5. Sample authorization form

Online Literature Search Authorization

I agree to pay the charges for an online literature search. I understand that every effort will be made to retrieve appropriate and relevant material at a modest cost; however, results are difficult to predict. Search fees cannot be refunded.
    The maximum amount that I wish to pay is $ _____. This maximum will be adhered to as closely as possible.

(Signed) _____ Date _____

Payment by: _____ Check   _____ Deposit Account
                 _____ Cash   _____ Please Send Bill

Searcher: _____

Figure 6. Sample search authorization form

Calendar for Search Appointments

Appointments can be scheduled on a master calendar. There may be separate calendars for additional terminals, passwords, or vendors. Figure 7 illustrates a simple system where each appointment is allotted an hour's time and there are spaces for the searcher's initials and the patron's name.

Calendar for Search Appointments

Week Beginning _____

	Monday	Tuesday	Wednesday	Thursday	Friday
8–9					
9–10					
10–11					
11–12					
12–1					
1–2					
2–3					
3–4					
4–5					

Figure 7. Sample search appointment calendar

Online Search Service Billing

When fees are charged, the billing form should list the particulars of the search: date, time, name of patron, status, and department as well as vendor, database(s), number of types or prints, and any additional charges. Figure 8 is a sample billing form showing a 20 percent subsidy and space for a surcharge for noninstitutional patrons. The original bill can be given to the patron and a copy can be sent to the accounting office with the cash, check, or fund authorization form. The basic charge reported on this sheet can come from the vendor's estimated charge, which is printed at the end of the search, or it can be calculated from the cost per connect minute plus telecommunication charges and citation fees. Modifications can be made for standard search fees or other methods of calculating a patron fee.

Online Search Service Billing

Name of user _____
Status ___ Faculty ___ Grad. Student ___ Undergraduate ___ Staff ___ Other
Academic department address _____
Telephone number _____

Date of search _____ Log in time _____
System _____ Dialog _____ BRS _____ SDC _____ Wilsonline _____ Vu-Text

Data Base	Number of Types/Prints	Charge
		$
		$
		$
		$
		$
		$

	Net Charge	$ _____
	Other Charges	$ _____
	User subsidy (less %)	$ _____
	Non-Institution fee	$ _____
Search Saved? _____	Total Charge	$ _____

Payment: _____ Check _____ Cash _____ Billed to Account No.: _____

Make checks payable to Institution Library

Searcher: _____

Figure 8. Sample billing form

Online Search Service Log

The search log should be a diary of the search activity. It should include consistent and careful entries by all the searchers to provide enough information on patrons, databases, search results, and costs.

The more categories that can be checked off rather than writing in an entry, the quicker the search can be recorded. These records can be used for a considerable amount of reporting and analysis. Other information that could be requested on this form includes: date the search was scheduled, the searcher's preparation time, log on time, the time online, communications network, components of costs, date the search was paid for, and session number if available. This type of record can be kept for each terminal or microcomputer, each password, and/or each vendor. An example of an online searching log is shown in figure 9. If the equipment is available for other purposes than online searching, the form could be adjusted to record these activities. A portion of this form can also be used for recording the use of the computer to answer ready-reference questions at the reference desk. Only a few columns may be needed to check off the reference tally. There can also be separate logs kept for training or the use of practice time.

Reference Desk Search Log

Figures 10 and 11 provide records specifically for activities at the reference desk and for patrons doing their own searching. Both collect the number of searches, information about the patron, the databases, and the success of the search process. It may be of interest to know the types of questions answered by an online source. The online activity will change as new databases become available and librarians become more accustomed to using online resources. The categories in figure 10 may need to be adjusted as experience is gained. These figures will be most helpful if they indicate the types of questions for which a database provides a successful response.

Search Log for Public Terminal/Microcomputer

Figure 11 encourages patrons to record their problems and suggestions when they are doing their own searching. Many problems may indicate the necessity for more assistance near the searching equipment, better manuals or signs, or more training for patrons.

Planning Your Search

Another form can be used to help students decide on keywords and concepts and then formulate a search strategy before going online. This form (figure 12) could be used in conjunction with a brief training course or kept near the search terminal to assist patrons who wish to work independently. It is designed to assist with the use of Boolean operators and to stress the concepts of a search topic.

Online Search Service Log

Month _____

Date	Searcher	Patron							LIBRARY/REF					Vendor*	Data-base(s)	Prints/Types	Charge	Payment**	Notes . . .
		Faculty	Grad	UG	Staff	Dept.	Other		Ref Q	Lib	Demo	ILL	Misc. (explain)						

*D = Dialog; B = BRS; W = Wilsonline; **a = account; c = cash

Figure 9. Sample search log

Reference Desk Search Log   Month _____

Patrons: F = Faculty, G = Graduate students, U = Undergraduates, O = Other
Questions: 1 = Citation, 2 = Directory, 3 = Subject, 4 = Current information,
5 = Data
Successful search? Y = Yes, N = No

Date	Librn	Patron				Data-base	Cost	Type of Question	Success		Notes
		F	G	U	O				Y	N	

Figure 10. Sample search log (reference desk)

Search Log for Public Terminal/Microcomputer   Date _____

Please help us evaluate the usefulness of this facility which allows you to do
your own searching. Make an entry each time you use the machine. Thank you.

Patron Status	Data-base(s) Used	Have you used the service before?	Did you find helpful information? Problems? Please comment.

Figure 11. Sample search log (terminal)

Planning Your Search   Date _____

1. Title of search topic (For example: Does salting the roads in winter harm the environment?) _____

_____

_____

2. Decide on the number of concepts to the problem and list keywords for each aspect. These should include synonyms and different spellings. Use a thesaurus for additional terms.

Use *or* between each keyword in a concept. Concepts are joined by *and*. For example: (salt *or* sodium chloride) *and* (roads *or* highways *or* streets) *and* environment.

Concept A _____ or _____

or _____ or _____

or _____ or _____

and Concept B _____ or _____

or _____ or _____

_____

and Concept C _____ or _____

or _____ or _____

_____

Using *OR* expands the citation pool to include additional words with the same meaning. *AND* between terms or groups of words narrows the search to records that interrelate the two or three different ideas.

PLEASE HAVE YOUR STRATEGY CHECKED BY A LIBRARIAN BEFORE PROCEEDING ONLINE.

Librarian's initials _____

Figure 12. Sample search plan form

Search Form for Printed and Online Sources

If the classroom professor or the librarians feel that students must learn about the traditional forms of indexes before they use electronic access, a form such as figure 13 can be used to require preliminary use of indexes or abstracts before students are permitted to use the online system. It also illustrates the contrast and the similarities between the two methods of searching for literature on a subject.

Search Form for Printed and Online Sources

                                   Date _____

Name _____

Major or Class _____

Search topic _____

_____

Print Sources
Indexes/Abstracts consulted _____

_____

What subject headings did you use _____

_____

List one reference found:
    Title _____
    Author(s) _____
    Source Publication _____
    Index Used _____
    Does the library own this item? _____

_____

Online Search
Keywords to be used: _____

_____

_____

_____

Database selected: _____
List one reference found online:
    Title _____
    Author(s) _____
    Source Publication _____
    Does the library own this item? _____

Figure 13. Sample search form

Evaluation Forms

A brief evaluation form for the search service can be attached to the search results or the patron can be asked to fill one out before leaving the library. Figure 14 illustrates a few questions that can be asked at the time of the search that deal with information received before the search is begun, the helpfulness of the librarian, and the value of the search results.

    A longer evaluation, illustrated by figure 15, could be distributed with the search and returned at a later date or sent out once or twice a year to patrons who have utilized the service. This form asks questions that include longer-term effects of the search. It requires more thoughtful answers to estimate the percent of relevant citations retrieved, the cost-effectiveness, whether or not the search helped with the research, and if the articles were found in the library. This type of form can also be a vehicle to survey patrons about their interest in end-user searching or to alert them to the availability of continuing updates.

Evaluation of reference desk activity is the responsibility of the reference librarians and should be part of the overall assessment of reference services. However, collecting data on the perceived success rate of answering questions with online resources, the distribution of searches among the reference librarians, and the enthusiasm for using databases to answer reference questions will provide an indication of the availability of appropriate databases, the convenience of the physical arrangement of the equipment, and the capabilities of the librarians at the reference desk.

Patron searching can be evaluated by observing students using the systems and noting their interest and success in producing results helpful for their research or term papers. A log on the desk next to the com-

---

Online Search Service Evaluation (Attach to search results)

In order to improve our search service, we would appreciate your response to the following questions:
1. How much time did you spend with the librarian on this search?

2. Did you receive enough introductory information?

3. What subject did you search and what databases were used?

4. Do you feel that this search was ＿＿ of great value, ＿＿ valuable, ＿＿ useful, or ＿＿ not helpful.

5. Comments or suggestions for improving the service:

Figure 14. Sample search evaluation form

Online Search Service Evaluation (Mail separately)

You recently did a computer literature search with us. We would appreciate your taking time to answer these questions and giving us your comments and suggestions.

1. Did you find this system of obtaining information productive and responsive to your needs?
2. How did you learn about the search service? _____ friend, _____ librarian, _____ class presentation, _____ professor, _____ poster in library, other: _____.
3. Was the librarian able to develop your topic into a successful search strategy?
4. How much time was there between scheduling the appointment and the actual search? _____ immediate or quick, _____ 1–2 days, _____ a week, _____ too long.
5. Do you consider this service to be cost-effective?
6. Did you become aware of other library services and resources through this process?
7. Could you estimate the percent of citations that you received that were relevant to your topic? _____ approximately 100%, _____ approximately 75%, _____ approximately 50%, _____ approximately 25% or less.
8. Were any known citations not in the results?
9. Were you able to find most of the articles listed in your search?
10. Would you consider using the search service again for another topic?
11. Do you think that this service is a valuable addition to the library services?
12. Would you be interested in updating your search periodically?
13. Would you be interested in doing your own searching if equipment and passwords were available in the library?
14. Can you suggest ways we can improve this search service?

Please return to the library Online Literature Search Service. Thank you.

Figure 15. Sample search evaluation form

puter search station can invite comments and suggestions (figure 11). Term papers from classes introduced to online searching can be compared to those produced by a class before this service was available. Worth noting are the number of references, the dates of the material used, and the relevancy of the bibliography.

If there is close control over the search equipment (near to the reference desk, much personnel help available, logging on and off by staff), patrons can be asked to fill out a brief evaluation form (figure 16)

Self-Search Evaluation   Date _____

Status: _____
Department or class: _____
Would you please help us by filling out this brief questionnaire?

1. Have you used a computer before? ____Yes ____No
2. Did you find the system easy to use? ____Yes ____No
3. Did the introduction to the system by the librarian provide enough information so you could use the equipment easily? ____Yes ____No
4. Did you consult the manual? ____Yes ____No
5. What was your subject? _____
6. What database did you use? _____
7. Were you satisfied with the results? _____
8. Did you find this _____ more/ _____ less satisfactory than using a printed
   index?
9. How can we improve this service? _____
   _____
   _____
   _____

Thank you!

Figure 16. Sample search evaluation form

at the end of the search. If a CD-ROM unit is used or another system that has little intervention on the part of the librarians, a survey of the students at the end of the semester in a class that had end-user searching introduced in a bibliographic instruction session, or were given assignments that relied on this equipment, can assess their understanding of the process, its usefulness, and their enthusiasm.

Other forms can be devised as needed. They must always have a date and feature the logo of the search service or library letterhead. Forms can act as a guide to the search process by helping patrons proceed with one step at a time in a logical and thoughtful manner. Forms can be valuable collectors of data and information, but should be planned to minimize the amount of time necessary to record appropriate information. It is important to review these forms regularly to be sure that they serve the purpose intended and that the time required to read and fill them out is justified. They should be useful and not a burden for either the patron or the searcher.

STATISTICS AND REPORTS

Interesting tables of data can be collected monthly on the search service activity, databases accessed, the types of patrons, the amount of online time used, numbers of citations printed, and other details. This basic information may be all that is needed for annual reports of the reference department or of the library. The total number of searches for patrons, the status of patrons, the number of paid searches, and the average charge for a search will help profile use of the service and confirm the costs and any income from fees. Other summaries, such as lists of departments represented by patrons, will show where use is the heaviest and help identify areas where more aggressive public relations is needed.

Statistics Sheet for Online Searching

Figure 17 shows a representative sheet for summarizing the collection of data for a month. Although it may be only necessary to report quar-

Statistics Sheet for Online Searching
Month _____

	Number	Percent
Searches for: Faculty Graduate students Undergraduates Staff Off-campus patrons		
Searches performed by: Searcher #1 Searcher #2 Searcher #3 Searcher #4		
In-House Searches: Reference questions Demonstrations Interlibrary loan Librarians research Practice time Other		
Databases searched: (list by name) Departments served: (list)		

Figure 17. Sample statistics summary sheet

terly or annual summaries, monthly data will keep the figures up-to-date and there is less chance that information will be lost.

Financial Summary of Direct Search Costs and Income

Figures that tally the vendor charges and income from searching should be current to monitor the status of search-related expenditures. Figure 18 compiles the direct searching costs paid to database vendors,

Financial Summary of Search Service Costs and Income
Month _____

	Dialog	BRS	SDC	Wilsonline
Connect Time in Hours				
Online connect-time charge Citation charges Telecommunications SDI costs Saved searches Search manuals and aids Training Special charges Account maintenance Additional passwords Other				
Gross vendor charges Less credits Net charges by vendor				

Income from searching

Total expenditures _____
Total income _____
Percent recovery of direct search costs _____

Figure 18. Sample financial summary sheet

along with the income generated. These data, collected monthly, provide a financial picture of the variable search charges. The summaries can be used to chart the growth of an online search service and, with some experience, trends can be identified and projections made for planning future search service needs.

Summary of Ready-reference Searches and Costs

Figures for ready-reference searching can be compiled primarily from online vendor bills if the desk terminal has its own password. Further information from the reference desk log can supply additional details. The average cost of a reference search can be computed as shown in figure 19 from the number of searches listed on the vendor's bill and the total costs.

Summary for Patron Searching and Finances

Similar data can be compiled for an end-user service such as BRS After Dark. If fees are charged, it is important to keep track of the income and expenditures to determine the amount of cost recovery (figure 20).

The online search service, ready-reference searching, and end-user searching should be organized with enough forms to make procedures

Summary of Ready-Reference Searches and Costs
Month _____

	Dialog	BRS	Wilsonline
Connect time in hours			
Number of searches			
Total costs			
Average cost/search			

Figure 19. Sample search summary sheet

Summary for Patron Searching and Finances   Month _____

	BRS/After Dark	Knowledge Index	Wilsonline
Connect time in hours			
Number of searches			
Total costs			
Fees collected			
Average cost/search			
Percent recovery			

Figure 20. Sample patron-search costs summary

flow smoothly. Data collection on online searching activities should be prepared so a minimum of paperwork is required. This process should be automated whenever possible. Forms for evaluation are used to survey patrons at intervals to indicate user satisfaction and any problems that could interfere with efficient information delivery. Forms and data collection should be as simple as possible, convenient to use and apply to necessary reports, and should require a minimum of staff time. Current data should be available to assess the financial impacts and project future activity. Forms and statistics should be used to assist the efficiency of the operation, guide the patron, and evaluate the success of the service.

Bibliography

Carlson, David, and P. Grady Morein. "Online Bibliographic Database Searching in College Libraries." *Clip-Note* No. 4–83. Chicago: Assn. of College and Research Libraries, American Library Assn., 1983.

Futas, Elizabeth. *The Library Forms Illustrated Handbook.* New York: Neal-Schuman, 1984.

Hawkins, Donald T., and Carolyn P. Brown. "What Is an Online Search?" *Online* 4:12–18 (1980).

McKinney, Gayle. "Forms and Record Keeping for Online Searching." In *Online Searching Technique and Management,* pp. 107–22. Edited by James J. Maloney. Chicago: American Library Assn., 1983.

8

TASKS PERFORMED BY SEARCHERS *197*
    Presearch Interview *198*
    Developing Search Strategy *199*
    Searching the Database *200*
    Completing the Search *201*
THE SEARCHER'S QUALIFICATIONS *201*
    Working with Patrons *202*
    Evaluating Job Performance *203*
EDUCATION FOR ONLINE SEARCHING *205*
    Vendor Training *206*
    Schools of Library and Information Science *207*
    Other Sponsors of Training *207*
    In-house and Self-instruction *207*
    Practicing Techniques *209*
    Advanced Training *209*
IMPROVING SEARCH SKILLS *211*
KEEPING UP WITH CHANGE *212*
    Continuing Education *212*
    Practicing to Maintain Skills *213*
    Attending Conferences and Meetings *213*
    Reading the Literature *214*

The Searcher

The most important component of a search service is the searcher. The need for enthusiastic, efficient, knowledgeable, and capable individuals cannot be overemphasized. The ability of these librarians to provide responsive and high quality online searching is a valuable component of the information retrieval services of the academic library. The challenge of providing access to the rapidly increasing body of knowledge that may be located either inside or outside the library structure has resulted in the need for librarians to become more directly involved in the information retrieval process. The librarian's interaction with the patron involves identifying the information needed, determining a source or sources that may supply the information, and either going to a printed source or probing a distant database with the patron to retrieve the data or a list of pertinent articles.

Computer-assisted searching adds the stored information in a distant database to the available library resources and provides a fast, efficient method of accessing it. It is essential, therefore, that all librarians involved in helping patrons find information should be capable of accessing the online resources. Online database searching in the academic library follows the pattern of increasing computer literacy of faculty and students who use similar equipment to augment laboratory equipment, statistically analyze their data, and word process their papers and reports. Using a computer for information retrieval adds an extra dimension to the responsibilities of the reference librarian, who must remember that there are many resources available outside the reference collection, feel competent working at the computer, and be able to work closely with patrons to satisfy very specific information needs.

Increasingly, advertisements for reference positions in academic libraries include the requirement for training and experience in online searching. Library schools have supported this trend by offering courses in information retrieval or online searching and by including online components in many basic library and information science classes. In addition, individuals seeking academic positions are investing in their own training with an online vendor to enhance their qualifications. As a result, more candidates for jobs as public services librarians have some exposure to online searching. Within the library, experience with online catalogs and the automated processes in other segments of the library organization have increased the possibilities for librarians already on the staff to become familiar with computer-assisted operations. While computers continue to be an increasing part of the library environment, their use in online searching has become a critical aspect of reference service. The patron often cannot have this information without making an appointment, explaining the problem, and depending on the searcher's expertise and knowledge to successfully retrieve the desired results from an appropriate database.

The selection of individuals to be online searchers can, therefore, be a significant element that affects the quality and efficiency of the search service that must provide this expert, comprehensive literature retrieval for the academic community. The searcher's personality, intelligence, and mechanical skills are all-important, along with reference experience and subject knowledge. Depending on the size and organization of the public services staff, one person may do all the searching or every professional staff member may share the responsibility. A librarian responsible for a significant branch library in a subject discipline such as biology or physics may be that single professional who is providing online services, or searching may be done by the staff in a centralized location. While reference librarians are the logical participants in this information service, other members of the professional library staff may also have computer experience, the interest, and the subject specialization to be potential candidates to augment the public services staff as searchers.

All reference librarians should have some training in online searching even if they never expect to work on an in-depth search with a patron. It is difficult, if not impossible, to recognize when online resources are appropriate unless there is a good understanding of the search process. Just knowing what resources are available online is not enough, as many times a choice must be made between a print or online source. The increased access to material offered by the computer may be critical for retrieval of certain types of information; however, in other instances the printed source is a better choice. Using the computer as one more method of finding answers or as a way of extending the resources traditionally used in an academic library should be goals for each information professional.

When setting up an online search service, training of current staff members is often an important part of the integration of online database searching. The education of the searchers occurs on several levels: introduction to basic techniques and fundamental principles, the improvement and advancement of skills, and specialization in subjects and/or databases. Training must be reinforced with practice, and assistance from other searchers can facilitate the learning process. This education must be continued as additional or advanced skills are developed. Experienced searchers as well as beginners will need some amount of continuing education to maintain competency and cope with the changing electronic environment. Sometimes, even before a searcher feels comfortable with one system, a second or third database system must be learned.

The type and quantity of searching required of individuals will vary widely. The qualifications necessary for the librarian who does a great deal of searching in highly specific subject areas will differ from those of individuals who may do brief searches to answer questions at the reference desk and only occasional searching on a limited range of research topics. Both need basic skill and training, but much more education and subject knowledge will be needed by a searcher working with faculty members doing research in medicinal chemistry or clinical psychology. The selection of searchers, then, should begin with a review of the tasks that must be performed. Next, the training best suited for these responsibilities should be selected.

Online searchers must not only be trained, but must also maintain a current awareness to keep up with developments in the information field and in changing search languages and techniques. Information on new databases, older databases that have been reloaded on a vendor's system to increase the access points, and new procedures that speed up the search process or make it more efficient must be assimilated and put to use quickly. A system for receiving and managing this flow of information is very important. Searching education and current awareness must be fitted into the workload of public services librarians, who usually must also spend time at the reference desk, answer complex questions, participate in collection development, serve on committees, and participate in professional activities.

TASKS PERFORMED BY SEARCHERS

Since online databases are not always obvious information sources to the casual library user, reference librarians are responsible for making patrons aware of this potential for information retrieval. This process of educating patrons is most likely to occur at the reference desk, next to the indexes, in the classroom, or in printed material produced as part of the library's public relations. Faculty writing research proposals, working in the laboratory, evaluating results of research, or advising students need to know that an online literature search is possible and that a skilled librarian will consult with them on their research topic, help define search terms, assist in selecting the best sources of information, and produce a bibliography tailored to their interests. The searcher must have enough training and experience to meet these demands.

Presearch Interview

When a literature search is requested by the patron or suggested by a librarian, a reference interview is necessary to determine the search topic, the appropriateness for an online search, the specific aspects of the subject, and the amount of information desired. This discussion should take place in a quiet environment where there are few interruptions. Skills of interviewing and communication, refined at the reference desk, are needed for this process. The searcher must be able to understand enough of the patron's topic to be able to discuss it intelligently and help select appropriate terminology. It is extremely important to be able to recognize when subjects are too broad, poorly defined, in need of historical information, or can easily be found in a printed source. Usually in these cases a computer search would not yield the results needed and other reference assistance must be provided. The searcher must know enough about the subject coverage of individual databases to suggest those that have strengths in the emphasis needed or provide access to particular material. More than one database may be needed to adequately cover the subject and the searcher must work with the patron to prioritize these database resources.

Communication with the patron may include an informational session to provide a description of the search process for the person who wonders where the database is located, what is covered, and what can be expected. The searcher must advise the patron that not all items identified in a search will be owned by the library, that interlibrary loan services can borrow articles the library does not own, and that databases are only part of the information sources available. The search options for each database, such as language of articles, time span to be covered, and types of material included, such as books, articles, and patents, must be explained and choices made. The patron may have very decided ideas about what is needed and where to search for it. Other patrons will be undecided and will depend on the suggestions of the searcher to make the best selection. Some of the discussion must cover the intended usage of the information, whether it is background for a grant proposal, a survey to be sure that the research has not already been done, or a few references on the most recent developments.

If the patron is to be charged for the search, the fees must also be mentioned with an explanation of how the charges are calculated. Patrons may be nervous about the cost, since it is often very difficult to estimate the probable fee. If an average charge for a search is available, this figure is often reassuring, or the experienced searcher may be able to suggest an approximate cost after examining the topic. The searcher must appear confident and be able to provide assurance that costs are being controlled by efficient and capable search techniques. If the search is extensive or has some uncertain aspects, such as nebulous or general terms, the searcher must know how to do a preliminary search, how to look at titles or sample citations to be sure the terminology is effective, or how to get a better estimate of costs before printing an extensive list of citations. Experienced searchers also use other techniques for handling complex search topics such as preliminary work in equivalent indexes, cross-file searching of a few important terms, or breaking a search into components that can be done in separate steps.

Developing Search Strategy

Competent searching for faculty or students conducting research or on thesis problems for graduate students will require some knowledge of the subject area. Even undergraduates may be writing a term paper and need a *Psychological Abstracts* or *Chemical Abstracts* search, where the subject terms are often difficult for the nonspecialist to manage. A subject background through education or personal interest in the field is a valuable asset to the searcher working in the more sophisticated research areas. It is important to have an awareness of different spellings, abbreviations, or colloquial terms likely to be used in the field. Both scientific and common words can be part of a search record and may be necessary for accurate retrieval. Basing a search strategy on thesaurus terms is very important in the social sciences, while the physical and biological sciences often use precise enough language to eliminate this step. Codes for geographic areas, broad subjects, or other categories are additional access points in some databases, and it is important to know which database records have these components, how to enter them in a database search, when it is appropriate to use them, and where to find a list of the codes and what they signify.

The searcher has a responsibility to know enough about the subject, search techniques, and appropriate databases to be alert to alternatives in deciding on the best approach for a search. A search for information on nutrition of the elderly, for instance, can be done in the medical literature using terms from *MESH*, the *Index Medicus* thesaurus; in the psychological literature to study attitudes, eating habits, and intervention techniques; in the educational literature for teaching about good nutrition; or in the social sciences for feeding programs at community centers or for the homebound. Each approach will require different terms, consideration of different databases, and procedures that may vary greatly among databases and systems.

After choosing the database and selecting the terms, the searcher must work with the patron to establish the major concepts of the problem and combine them into a logical sequence to formulate a search strategy. The reasoning behind this strategy development must usually be discussed with the patron and some broader and narrower alternatives decided on before going online. The versatility of the computer presents many decision points for the searcher. To prepare for these adequately, considerable planning is necessary ahead of time until enough experience is gained to know how to judge where these choices must be made and how to be ready to make a quick decision. Some of the options will have to be decided quickly, while online, and it is important that the patron has understood the process if he or she must make choices under pressure. It is probable that many times the procedure must be explained in terms that the patron, who may have had little or no experience with either computers or library research, can comprehend.

The knowledge of very specialized research topics may not be a concern in an undergraduate library where most searching is done on topics of current and general interest. Some results can be found with little training and a minimum skill in manipulating concepts. It is primarily for research programs and working with graduate students that depth of knowledge about databases and subject areas is essential. The generalist searcher can help compensate for lack of subject background by knowing how to use dictionaries, indexes, and search aids to assist the planning when patrons need information in specialized subject areas. If these searches are asked for infrequently, the searcher must know where to find and how to use database search aids and must understand the vocabulary well enough to use appropriate thesauri, terms in a printed index, or words used in significant articles already found on the subject. Even quick searches on subjects such as acid rain, teaching effectiveness, jazz, or business management require using language of the field that is focused on the point of view to be studied, and a search strategy that will retrieve the type and amount of information needed.

Searching the Database

Logging on to the system and selecting databases are relatively simple procedures once some practice has been gained. Searchers must, however, have enough experience to know what to do when the lines are busy, static is garbling the message, or the paper jams in the printer. When the preliminaries go well, the results may be received so quickly that decisions must suddenly be made about adding more terms or qualifying those already selected. This is the time to consider the alternative strategies that have already been discussed. The searcher must recognize the appropriate point to look at the titles of some of the documents retrieved, or the first five or ten citations. When the patron is present to review these preliminary results, he or she can decide if the information is suitable or if further manipulation of terms is necessary. Decisions should have already been made about printing, typing, or downloading the results and whether citations, abstracts, or other parts of the record are needed.

To be efficient, the searcher must be able to think ahead, quickly recognize the value of a response, and make fast decisions about alternative procedures. Some typing skill allows more attention to be placed on the search process. Online practice is important to provide the searcher with enough familiarity of the command language so the choice of formats and the techniques for printing or typing citations can be executed without taking time to refer back to the manual.

Completing the Search

When the results are examined with the patron, the searcher should be able to answer any questions about the use of search terms and strategy or any components of the printout. The searcher must often advise the patron that the results seem inadequate and that further review of search terminology and procedure is necessary, or that a search of a different database should be tried for supplementary information. When there is a fee charged, the calculation must be clear and logical. Following up the search requires an understanding of the patron's needs, knowledge of other sources, and availability of materials identified in the search. Instructions on finding library holdings, using interlibrary loan, and the availability of additional print sources of information must also be communicated to the patron.

It is important that searchers feel confident about developing and executing the search and about their mechanical facility with the computer. They must have adequate time for searches—about one hour each—and have the administrative support of some funding for continuing education and practice time. Enough equipment and manuals must be available and searchers should have the option of reducing the charge for a search that is unsatisfactory because of factors that the patron was not responsible for. This type of support will greatly affect the morale and success of a searching staff.

THE SEARCHER'S QUALIFICATIONS

The library's online database searching may be carried out by only one or two people, or by a group of ten or more. When the service is new or there is great diversity of skills and interest among the reference librarians, a few of them may be designated as searchers with the others referring appropriate questions or in-depth searches to them. When selecting from present staff or hiring new personnel, some personal characteristics may be used to describe good searchers, characteristics necessary to accomplish effective online searching. These include:

Good interpersonal skills. The ability to work with students and faculty both at the reference desk and over the computer terminal.

Capability of listening carefully to patrons and discussing search topics objectively to determine what information is needed.

Creativity and imaginative thinking for working out solutions to problems. These characteristics are important for considering alternatives to strategies, terms and methods of approaching a search.

Ability to think logically and analytically. These are significant attributes for analyzing a subject, organizing terms, and for producing a search strategy to derive the optimum results.

Persistence and patience to keep trying when the telephone line is busy, to wait a few moments for the computer to respond, and to explain again to the patron the elements of Boolean logic.

Ability to perform under pressure when time, cost, and delivery of results are important and the patron is waiting.

Intelligence, resourcefulness and enthusiasm to add quality to the challenge of successful online searching.

Self-confidence to assure the patron that the search will be carried out competently.

Flexibility and willingness to try new techniques, new approaches for developing strategies, and new vendor systems.

Interest in continuing education to maintain competency and effectiveness in a field where the methods and procedures are constantly changing.

Other factors to consider when looking for an online searcher are the accredited masters degree in library and information science, online search training, experience in reference work and online searching, some typing skills, interest in computers, and subject expertise. Many of these characteristics are the same as those used to describe competent reference librarians. The expertise of online searching adds another dimension to the skills cultivated by these information professionals.

Working with Patrons

As librarians work more closely with researchers, it is extremely important to understand the needs of research work and the investigators' methods of approach. Despite the complexity of many questions from active scientists, some may only want a few appropriate references and may worry about the charges. Others are more interested in comprehension than cost and wish to read every relevant citation on their subject. A background of working in these scientific fields, an undergraduate or advanced degree in an area of specialization, or even a few courses where research projects are accomplished will familiarize the librarian with some of the attitudes of these patrons. The expertise of the searcher and experience in finding information is a major contribution to a literature search, but must not overweigh the patron's need for a specific amount of data or approach to a research problem.

Continuing interaction with academic departments, such as meeting new faculty, attending department meetings, conducting bibliographic instruction for students, and assisting researchers with literature needs are a means of learning more about emphasis of courses, subject interests of faculty, and research projects underway. Student seminars that report on thesis work and research projects, visiting speakers in the departments, and faculty presentations to student or public audiences provide opportunities to learn more about the interests of the department and the use of the literature to support and direct research work. Searching for students and faculty in the department will reinforce this knowledge of subject interests.

When patrons are able to do their own searching in the library, there will still be an important role for the librarian as more instruction is needed, more questions are asked about computer equipment and software, more machine problems must be dealt with, and patrons— who may be searching in their homes or offices as well as the library— need to know more about the range of online resources, how to improve search techniques, and how to find the documents they have identified.

Evaluating Job Performance

With an increasing number of computer-literate patrons, reference librarians will be expected to have a knowledge of computer techniques and languages, new developments in online access, and the efficient utilization of online resources. Many libraries have already set the stage in other departments with the online catalog, computerized circulation systems, and online cataloging. When all reference librarians are trained searchers, they may not be equally enthusiastic about this portion of their position responsibilities. The manager must be aware of the attitudes passed along to patrons and the need to monitor the responsiveness of the searchers to be sure that priority is given to this task. Some individuals may need more support than others with additional training or by working closely with other searchers until they become more confident. If new searchers have had no previous experience of working with computers, learning to use word processing programs or statistical packages will be valuable for practicing on the keyboard and responding to computer prompts.

Besides the personal qualities of a searcher, an important consideration when selecting individuals to provide online services is their responsibility for other reference services, for technical services, or management that may need priority. Planning schedules in reference departments already recognize the need for flexibility and that the demands of the public may come at irregular and unpredictable times. A searcher either has to be available at specific times whether or not searches are being requested, or else must have an easily adjustable schedule so that priority can be given to arranging search appointments for times when the patron is available. On other occasions patrons will want searches carried out as soon as possible and searchers should accommodate these requests whenever they can without compromising search quality, which requires sufficient time to give adequate attention and preparation for the topic.

Evaluation of a searcher's effectiveness may be a portion of an annual review process or job performance examinations, but should also be considered as part of the ongoing evaluation of online information services. This process may be difficult, since each individual will approach searches and reference questions differently and it is often hard to determine the correct or most productive methods. In addition, each search is an individual effort with various requirements and simple or complex subjects. There is probably even more of a problem to distinguish between good and poor searches, since the searcher works closely with an individual patron and the varying factors such as determining exactly what information the patron needs and how much material is appropriate may be as critical as the most effective techniques of online retrieval.

Searchers can assess their own search performance and the apparent satisfaction of the patron as they complete each search. Other searchers can sit in on scheduled searches, examine copies of completed searches, while recall and precision can be discussed. Surveys of patron satisfaction usually include a few questions about the perceived capability of the searcher. The search service manager should be responsible for monitoring performance, encouraging practice, and working with searchers to improve techniques. Because this service becomes part of the workload of librarians, who must often balance information services at the reference desk and the terminal with collection development, bibliographic instruction, and professional and collegiate activities, evaluation of performance means weighing many complex factors.

EDUCATION FOR ONLINE SEARCHING

To provide a competent information service, searchers must receive adequate training for all search systems available to the institution. A cycle of training, practice, more training and more practice is usually required. Not all libraries and search services require searchers with a great deal of experience or subject expertise. A librarian with enough training to log on, select a database, and enter terms will certainly get some results. This may be adequate for the patron who needs only ten references on zoo management, and it may be sufficient for most of a small academic or undergraduate library's clientele. To be effective, however, librarians must have enough training and practice to develop the necessary background and skill to know the many alternatives offered by online systems and to search them efficiently. Education for online searching takes place at many levels, as discussed below.

Introduction to online searching for all the library staff. Sessions that explain and demonstrate the value and limitations of this computer-assisted information retrieval, the results obtained, the need for specialized training, the costs and potential impact on the library are valuable for all library personnel.

Basic training for public services staff. This training, geared to a particular database system, should include the scope of online resources, system commands, techniques of the search process, limitations of searching, and how to handle the patron-searcher interaction.

Advanced training in search techniques for all searchers who participate in a search service. Learning new system procedures, methods of increasing precision and recall, utilization of additional capabilities of the system and access points of the databases, and reinforcing efficient techniques will help improve the quality of searches.

Specialized workshops on individual databases, or groups of databases on subject concentrations for all searchers who access the more complex databases or who are responsible for searching within a subject area.

Continuing education through reading, attending conferences and workshops, and talking to other searchers to keep up with developments in the field.

All of these aspects of education for online searching are important in varying degrees, depending on the library environment and the clientele. A library beginning a search service will probably expect the present reference staff to participate in formal training in online searching skills. However, it is just as important that all the public service librarians, if not all the staff, receive some introduction to the search process, learn the advantages and limitations and what results can be obtained. This staff introduction can be done by the search service manager, an experienced searcher on the staff or from another library, a representative of an online vendor, or an outside consultant. It can include an overview of vendor systems, a discussion of some sample databases and the type of information they provide, and the need for training for optimum searching skills. An online demonstration can compare a database printout to a manual search and a brief bibliography can be produced on a medical topic or an answer to a recent reference question.

Librarians who make up the searching staff will need more formal training in the mechanics of searching, the development of search strategy, the structure and content of databases, and techniques for efficient searching. This must be followed up with enough practice to become comfortable with the search process. Various options are available for securing training:

Vendor Training

Online vendors offer introductory training on their systems that may take a full day or more. The content will include a discussion of the general principles of online searching, the vendor's system commands, contents and access points of a few databases, and special features of the system. This training is effective, professional, and offered regularly at locations around the country. It may be very difficult for a totally inexperienced person to adequately absorb the material in the length of time allowed for the training course. Usually manuals are provided for these workshops so they can be used for additional study and review. In addition, some free time is often granted for practice when the searcher goes back to his or her library, and this also reinforces the training received.

Vendors will also send an instructor to the library to put on a workshop for the staff. While fairly expensive, this is a convenient method for instructing a group of prospective searchers. Vendor training emphasizes the system language and some of the important databases, but is not likely to bring in the overall view of information retrieval that compares various options between systems and resources beyond the vendor's holdings. However, since the searchers will be using the system they are training for, the practical aspects are well served and the techniques learned will be up-to-date.

Schools of Library and Information Science

Semester-length courses are taught in library schools on online searching and students receive a good foundation in theory and basic procedures. Sometimes online searching is incorporated into other courses such as reference, information science, or library automation. It is important that there be a laboratory component for either of these approaches so students can have some hands-on experience. There are a number of textbooks for these courses that offer a good basic introduction; however, it is difficult, if not impossible, for books to keep up with the rapidly changing techniques and resources. It is important for the instructors to maintain knowledge of current practices and trends in the online field. These courses are usually excellent as a broader introduction that includes some history of information science, the development of the online industry, fundamental search techniques, and the opportunity to work on search topics used to illustrate specific applications. The interaction with other class participants is also valuable.

Courses usually take a semester to cover the material and can provide important discussions of the broader aspects; they may include managing a search service, comparing database vendors, working with patrons, and the ethics of downloading, but could be lacking in the practical applications and everyday search requests that could be helpful for librarians who must return to the front line of service in their libraries. Students who do not follow up with on-the-job experience will probably need refresher courses when they are ready to work with library patrons.

Other Sponsors of Training

Online user groups, professional organizations, networks, and consortia may offer training as part of their service component for individuals or member institutions. These workshops are usually taught by experienced searchers or by representatives from vendors or database producers. Some may be more informal and may not offer the documentation or the practice time available from the commercial vendors; however, good contacts can be made with other searchers and links may be established to provide backup support when needed.

In-house and Self-instruction

A search service manager or coordinator with experience and expertise may be expected to train librarians for searching. Developing an in-house course will take a considerable amount of the individual's time and may not include the professional handouts or other aids, but training can be offered when needed and can be geared to demands of the

patrons of that specific library. The instructor is also always available
for support and assistance. Published textbooks or workbooks may be
available that can be adapted to the situation. Instruction can also proceed at a pace appropriate for those who are learning. Low cost files of
the online vendors can be utilized for hands-on practice and there are
no travel or registration costs. It is also possible for the manager to
share the teaching with experienced searchers who can each cover a
portion of the course. Searching techniques can progress from a few
bibliographic databases on one system to other types of databases and
then other systems.

Individuals can teach themselves online searching with a manual
and some practice time. Even with previous computer training, it may
be very difficult to learn some of the concepts of search strategy and
some of the practical techniques that seem very clear in a manual, but
are difficult to apply correctly. These individuals may miss some critical information about searching that could be learned from a more
structured course. Textbooks are available that can be read to learn
some of the fundamental concepts, but it is important for self-trained
individuals to have someone they can work with or can call on when
there are problems until they have enough practice to develop confidence in their searching skill. Following the search steps in a manual
may be a satisfactory method of learning a second vendor's system.

Workbooks are another approach to learning. SDC, for example,
provides a workbook, three hours of connect time to practice, and appropriate manuals for $125. There are also computer-assisted instruc-
tion programs (CAI) that provide an interactive learning situation.
Search emulators have been devised at various institutions to act as
model databases to make learning as close to the actual library search
situation as possible, and video is the newest training package that can
be obtained from database vendors. Dialog's package contains a 45-
minute tape of basic commands, choosing a database, the organization
of the database and individual records, and typing results. The video is
accompanied by an instruction booklet, practice exercises for ONTAP
files, and worksheets for planning search strategies. BRS has a three-
part course that includes a videotape and a workbook. The first part is
the basic procedure for logging on, choosing a database, doing a simple
search, and printing the results. Part two covers planning for a search,
formulating search strategy, using some of the system features such as
truncating, paragraph qualification, and printing in various formats,
while part three is the advanced section on vocabulary, saving searches
and executing them in additional databases, language and date restrictions, and searching by author's name. Any section can be ordered
from the set. These various approaches should be effective methods of
reinforcing formal training or utilized to teach new searchers when
other opportunities are not available.

There are probably many variations on these in-house learning experiences that can be used to improve search performance or to provide a refresher for someone who has not done any searching for a while. User-friendly systems developed for the personal microcomputer such as CompuServe, Knowledge Index or BRS After Dark may be available for beginners to get some elementary online searching practice. Since the process is assisted by menus and questions to aid the searcher, it can be very helpful for the novice who needs to have some experience with online terminology and with manipulating a computer terminal. After practicing these guided procedures the searcher can move up to learning the more efficient unassisted search system. Working with experienced searchers is another method of learning, although it is probably better to use this procedure as a supplement to other training as it may be difficult to insure that all the basic techniques have been learned and that a broad enough perspective can be achieved.

Practicing Techniques

Any training is only effective when the individual can actually use the system to try out examples and different strategies. One value of vendor training is the practice time usually provided. Training files such as Dialog's ONTAP serve this same purpose. These portions of major databases are available at reduced prices and they can be utilized to test a search strategy, to practice various search procedures, or to try a different database for the first time. Microcomputer software is also available that is intended to assist untrained individuals to search standard databases and, although the connect time is paid at the regular rate, the new searcher will receive guidance at each step.

Advanced Training

Advanced training or update sessions supplement the basic courses. Here again, vendors offer a variety of experiences from the latest developments on their systems to techniques for more efficient searching. Business, chemistry, social sciences, company information, or patents are examples of some of the subject-oriented half- to full-day advanced sessions. This training is particularly helpful when several databases are compared for content and access points.

Individual database producers also offer workshops on their products. These sessions may be geared to a particular vendor or can be more generic if the database is loaded on several vendors. Much of the time is spent on the content of the database, and will often include the use of codes for products, geographic areas, general subject categories, or specific substances. Searchers who specialize in the subject area or use the database(s) frequently receive excellent training. An advantage of these sessions is the time that is usually spent on the indexing and organization of the equivalent printed index. Comparisons between print and electronic versions provide valuable information that can help increase the precision and recall from the database and can also improve access from and use of the printed index for the reference librarian.

Another type of advanced training may be the in-house or group-sponsored seminar where librarians compare experiences and speak about techniques they have learned from using the systems. Online user groups may bring in speakers, library schools may put on workshops for the working professional, and library organizations may sponsor programs related to searching or managing online services. Individuals can report back to their colleagues on the latest training they received or programs at conferences that provided helpful information. Other support for the searcher includes help from the online database vendor. Toll-free telephone numbers will reach the service desks during long hours of the day for advice and assistance. Free time on different databases may also be available at regular intervals and this can be utilized to try a new database or to practice a search. Database producers also provide telephone numbers for discussing problems with experts who work with the database on a regular basis. Being alert to articles on search techniques and reading vendor newsletters carefully will also provide much practical assistance.

Learning to use a second or additional system must eventually be faced by most searchers as additional resources are acquired. Since the basic search techniques have already been mastered, a new system will usually just mean learning a different list of system commands to retrieve information and manipulate the search results. It is important to learn the unique characteristics of each system and the advantages each can offer. A comparison of the same database on different systems can provide a means of deciding which vendor to use if there are differences in the database search language or the way the database is mounted on the system that affect the results achieved. Often a searcher can learn the new system by using the manual and following a few searches as others are doing them. However, a careful step-by-step reading of the system manual is critical to alert the searcher to different components and access techniques.

A chart comparing the commands between systems is very helpful to have next to the terminal and, as more vendors are added to the library's resources, a quick source of the important commands of each system to consult when needed is imperative. Some vendors supply a brief guide to their command language and these should be kept near the searching terminal. In learning any new system, enough practice time is essential to reinforce the use of commands and specific techniques. To utilize a second system capably, it is necessary to have enough practice so that the searcher can change vendor systems when needed and use the new commands without confusion.

IMPROVING SEARCH SKILLS

Enough training, regular updates of techniques, and advanced workshops on a regular basis should provide the individual searcher with sufficient information to maintain knowledge of the systems being used and insure that the latest techniques are incorporated into the everyday searching responsibilities. Training does not guarantee that the searcher is efficient or really understands all the applications of advanced techniques. It is important, therefore, for the institution to have a plan for reinforcing information learned and evaluating searches to encourage the most optimum searching techniques.

Starting with novice searchers, there are a number of methods for providing additional support until searchers develop the necessary competence to approach searching with skill and confidence. Working with an experienced searcher in a mentor program, or being encouraged to consult other searchers when a search strategy is being planned, can be helpful. Standard practice searches can be used to review search techniques as results are compared among new and experienced searchers. Group discussions on the selection of terms, use of controlled vocabulary, developing search strategy, and review of online procedures will provide a broader base of information and make sure that searchers will not develop a narrow scope to their technique by only using the commands as they first learned them. If the service is new and no experienced help is immediately available, a network of support could be built with an online user group or among local libraries. Departmental librarians in a larger system could use the same approach to structure a review and assistance process. A comparison of the strategies for the same topic, a system of asking for help when a problem or particularly complicated search is undertaken, or reviewing completed searches through meetings, electronic mail, or telephone contacts will provide some support and evaluation.

Even experienced searchers can learn from each other and regular meetings to compare searches and problems will be beneficial. Discussions of the search interview, difficult strategies, unique solutions, and especially productive tactics can all be illustrated and reviewed. Suggestions of terminology, sources for consultation, and utilization of different databases may add an extra dimension that an individual alone may not think of. Reports from conferences, meetings, workshops, and the literature can also provide useful information. Searchers from a small library might meet regularly with an online users group to broaden their contacts and perspective. The process will be most effective if the meetings are regular and held at least monthly, while searches and problems are still fresh.

Sharing complicated searches can take advantage of individual searcher's expertise, although it is probable that the most profitable sharing is during the preparation stage or in reviewing the results, rather than at the terminal where discussion while online costs money. An experienced searcher could also have the responsibility of reviewing the search strategy preparation with all new searchers before they go online with a patron. The review of evaluations returned by patrons provides another source of information for improving search performance. Problem areas can be identified and a plan developed to improve skills, educate patrons for more realistic expectations, or in some cases to find the means of repeating searches that were unsatisfactory.

KEEPING UP WITH CHANGE

Despite excellent basic training and the development of skilled techniques by the searcher, nevertheless the opportunity and ability to keep up with new procedures, new technical developments, and new resources are critical. The rapidly changing online field from computer applications to information science and the deluge of literature from many sources require a systematic scheme for each individual to follow in order to take advantage of and to assimilate the most important developments.

Continuing Education

The attendance of additional training sessions by the regular searching staff should be expected. The library administration should understand the need for this planned updating of skills by providing the funds for travel and workshop fees. A workshop each semester for every searcher insures the opportunity to attend vendor update and advanced sessions as well as workshops by database producers. INSPEC, the Commonwealth Agricultural Bureaux, Predicasts, and BIOSIS are among these producers who put on programs to improve searching of their database(s). Sometimes there is no charge for attendance and they are often scheduled in different locations, which can be convenient.

While the vendor sessions will usually concentrate on overall system procedures, the producer seminars usually cover the structure and content of a specific database. Workshops at library schools or sponsored by online user groups can expose searchers to new resources, emphasize additional uses for databases, and enhance the understanding of strategy development. One searcher in a group can attend these sessions and report back to the others. Sharing the important hardware and software developments, new system techniques, and opportunities for new database resources is valuable for everyone and can help take advantage of each searcher's participation in these additional activities.

Practicing to Maintain Skills

Mechanical search skills and techniques can be kept up-to-date simply by going online often enough. If few searches are scheduled, practice time on the least costly files using questions asked at the reference desk can offer experience in developing vocabulary, search strategy, and system procedures. Even very brief searches on this basis will give practice in the development of answers to questions of patron interest. Preparing in-house bibliographies or verifying interlibrary loans are additional tasks for keeping search skills current. Any free time offered on new databases should be utilized. Free searches for faculty and students on these new files provide excellent experience.

Attending Conferences and Meetings

Attending national conferences such as the National Online Meeting and Online or those sponsored by the American Library Association (ALA), Special Libraries Association (SLA), or the American Society for Information Science (ASIS) is one of the best ways to find out about new developments and trends in the field. Special interest groups such as the Machine-Assisted Reference Section (MARS) of the Reference and Adult Services Division of ALA provide especially helpful information and bring together individuals actively participating in online searching. Papers and discussions often concern management of online searching, charging fees, new types of databases, and how other libraries handle problems or expansion of services. The exhibits at these major conferences provide a great deal of literature and an opportunity to talk with knowledgeable sales personnel. New equipment, new databases, and new system developments are often demonstrated here for the first time and there may be separate sessions for sales representatives to discuss their new products.

Local or regional online user groups often schedule valuable meetings on topics of current interest. These sessions may bring in prominent speakers or highlight local expertise. Important contacts can be developed for consultation when help is needed or for communicating new database information and search techniques. Reports by attendees and the sharing of information gained at meetings will make the most important news available to all the searchers and can help in planning for and adjusting to changes that may take place as new databases become available and new vendors are considered.

Reading the Literature

Reading newsletters—both printed and online, journal articles, reports, and proceedings of conferences—must be a continuous process. A large amount of information is being published and it is difficult to find the time to read and assimilate items of interest. Developing a core reading list for each searcher and the monitoring of supplemental material by the manager of the service is one solution. Reading responsibilities can be shared among the searching group. Circulating tables of contents and articles of interest, putting together files of information on specific databases, and organizing a collection of article reprints are all additional possibilities. Literature sources include:

Vendor Information · Reading the vendor newsletters is extremely important for each searcher. These sources include news of the system, announcements of database changes, additional resources, updates of the command language, future plans, and suggestions for improving searching technique. The online coordinator, manager, or a designated searcher should be responsible for scanning these newsletters and making changes in the manuals or adding notes to the appropriate database information sheets. In this way the newest information is readily available for all searchers. A file or notebook of these newsletters and the indexes that usually accompany them should be located in the searching office or near the terminal to allow for consultation when needed.

Database Information · In addition to the updates to vendor manuals, there are advertising, producer information, and articles about databases that appear in journals and newsletters. These items can all be kept in a file organized by database name. It is important to keep only current material and, therefore, the manager or one of the searchers should be responsible for reviewing and weeding.

Journals and Newsletters · Regular reading of the important journals directly related to online searching such as *Online, Database,* and *Online Review* is essential for keeping up with the field. Electronic journals such as the *Online Chronicle* on Dialog are even more current and include the full text of articles. New developments, new databases, news of the information industry, and articles on improving search technique, trying new systems, reviews of software, and comparisons of databases can be found in these publications and will prove to be extremely helpful.

The manager or individual searchers may wish to scan newsletters and other journals for articles of interest. *Information Intelligence Online Newsletter, Information Today, Database End-User*, and *Library Hi Tech* are particularly appropriate. Library journals such as the *ASIS Bulletin, Journal of Academic Librarianship*, and *College and Research Libraries* have frequent articles on online searching. Other journals with regular columns on online topics include: "Online Databases" in *Library Journal*, "Online Update" in *Wilson Library Bulletin*, "Databases" in *RQ*, "Reference Databases" in *Reference Services Review*, and "Sci-Tech Online" in *Science and Technology Libraries*.

A file of articles of interest or an in-house database of resource material would probably both be very helpful for an active group of searchers. To be useful it must be well organized and accessible by subject and database. However, the factors of having time to consult extra material, keeping the information up-to-date, being able to find what is needed, and having the time to organize it consistently are all considerations when planning this strategy.

Regular reading, attending meetings, and reviewing new information on systems and databases are of utmost importance. The best method of making this information available should be considered by the group of searchers in an institution. Once a plan is developed, the follow-through of circulating or distributing information and publications and keeping any files current become critical aspects. Consistent efforts to provide selective information for individual searchers may be the optimum approach for current awareness.

Bibliography

Bellardo, Trudi. "What Do We Really Know about Online Searchers?" *Online Review* 9:223–39 (1985).

Glunz, Diane L. "Quality Assurance in Computer Searching." *Reference Librarian* 11:277–92 (1984).

Jackson, William J. "Staff Selection and Training for Quality Online Searching." *RQ* 22:48–54 (1982).

Lamprecht, Sandra J. "Online Searching and the Patron: Some Communication Challenges." *Reference Librarian* 16:177–84 (1986).

Neway, Julie M. *Information Specialist as Team Player in the Research Process*. Westport, Conn.: Greenwood Press, 1985.

Pilachowski, David M., R. Patricia Riesenman, and Patricia Tegler. "Online Search Analyst and Search-Service Manager Tasks." *RQ* 24: 403–10 (1985).

Rettig, James. "Options in Training and Continuing Education." In *Online Searching Technique and Management,* pp. 149–59. Edited by James J. Maloney. Chicago: American Library Assn., 1983.

Tenopir, Carol. "An In-House Training Program for Online Searchers." *Online 6:20–26 (1982).*

_____. "Databases: Catching Up and Keeping Up." *Library Journal* 108:180–82 (1983).

9

BENEFITS OF ONLINE ACCESS AT THE REFERENCE DESK *220*

 Promoting the Search Service and Online Ready-
  reference *221*
 Providing Additional Assistance for Patrons *221*
 Focusing on Important Aspects *221*
 Finding Specific Information *222*
 Extending Reference Sources *223*
 Utilizing Instructional Potential *223*
 Searching Practice *224*

READY-REFERENCE SEARCHING *224*

 Online Resources for the Reference Desk *224*
 When to Choose an Online Source at the Reference
  Desk *227*
 Location of Equipment *229*
 Selection of Online System(s) for the Reference Desk *230*
 Personnel Preparation *231*
 Support Material *231*
 Procedure Manual *232*

CONTROLS FOR READY-REFERENCE SEARCHING *232*

COPING WITH POTENTIAL PROBLEMS *233*

GOVERNMENT PUBLICATIONS *236*

Online at the Reference Desk

Online database searching in the academic library is usually first provided to assist researchers who need to find specific, up-to-date information. The expertise, equipment, and organization required for a responsive and competent support for these clients is best concentrated in an online search service, usually established as a separate unit within the reference department. As reference librarians have become skilled and experienced at searching research topics, they have realized that this efficient method of finding information is useful for other information-seeking situations, particularly for answering certain questions at the reference desk. In addition, online assistance can be extended from the reference desk into other library operations with applications for bibliographic instruction, interlibrary loan, collection development, acquisitions, cataloging, and assisting librarians with their own research.

The scope of online searching within a reference unit of a research institution can include several service levels. The highest level of in-depth searching is provided by a search service where the skilled, personal assistance of a reference librarian is devoted to working with a patron on a research topic. The two individuals meet together to structure the search strategy and perform the online search, resulting in a bibliography—or data—that may be extensive, but that is carefully crafted to produce the needed information. There may be a fee charged for this information service.

Another level of information retrieval utilizing database resources is ready-reference. Searching can be made available with one or more computer terminals at the reference desk to aid in answering questions and assisting patrons with their library research. There are no patron fees for this component of information services that provides quick and efficient answers with a limited computer output. Online searching at the reference desk provides selective retrieval of information either from sources not available in the library or from databases that provide additional access points for the corresponding printed indexes.

Some factual information, brief bibliographies, or verification of incomplete citations are examples of responses suited for the computer-assisted retrieval of information. Reference librarians must be knowledgeable about both print and online sources, and must be able to select the most appropriate and the most efficient method of finding material pertinent to the patron's question. The library budget must include electronic resources in addition to printed materials as a necessary investment for adequate information services.

A third level of online reference services is the provision of equipment and passwords for patrons to do literature searching themselves. This extension to the use of printed indexes provides different challenges for reference librarians and a different type of assistance for students and faculty. Patrons may be charged a fee for connect time with an online source, or a CD-ROM unit may provide unlimited searching of a popular index. Each level of reference use is suitable for certain situations and information needs.

At the reference desk, not only do remote online databases provide resources to supplement the reference collection, but electronic access provides a different, and often more effective, method for identifying and retrieving needed data, references, directory, or encyclopedic information. Answering ready-reference questions from a larger aggregate of resources and being able to choose the most appropriate method of searching major reference works gives the librarian many alternatives for utilizing the best source and access method for the problem.

The database vendors have added to the usefulness of their systems for ready-reference situations by increasing the number of databases that are full-text encyclopedias, directories, and files of numerical data. Most of these provide answers to questions rather than bibliographies of source documents. However, even the bibliographic databases used most often for lengthy or extensive searching can be consulted at the reference desk to secure brief lists of articles or information from an abstract or other portions of a record.

BENEFITS OF ONLINE ACCESS AT THE REFERENCE DESK

A computer terminal at the reference desk provides an atmosphere of authority and expertise to this service point. Skillful reference librarians have another dimension of information access available to them. Students and faculty, many with their own microcomputers or proficient at searching the online catalog, increasingly expect computers to be a part of all modern services and will not be surprised to find that a computer terminal is being utilized at the reference desk to provide a quick online search. Positive aspects of online searching for ready-reference include:

Promoting the Search Service and Online Ready-reference

It may be important to make patrons aware of the distinction between scheduling an online search on a research topic that may have a fee for service, and receiving free information services at the reference desk, including a brief online search. Emphasis should be placed on providing the same basic information service for all library patrons with arrangements available for those who need more extensive and more personalized service. At the same time, the linkage between the reference desk and the search service is very important. Expertise gained by librarians in one level of service enhances skills at the other. Most important, patrons will receive appropriate assistance.

The visibility of the terminal at the reference desk helps bring attention to the online means of providing access to information and helps advertise the availability of an online search service. Whenever a quick search at the reference desk is not enough—more terms are needed, more manipulation of search strategy, and more citations printed—it is a logical step to refer patrons to the search service where they can have a more lengthy interview and the undivided attention of a search specialist. The provision of resources from older historical materials in print form to the newest information retrieval by electronic means furnishes a continuum of optimum resources.

Providing Additional Assistance for Patrons

Computerized retrieval of information allows the reference librarian to do more than just point out an index or give brief instructions on how to find information. A company address, the source of a biography, or the latest software for calculating income taxes can all be determined online to quickly provide the patron with information that may be difficult to find in a printed source. Students who have a problem finding articles on term paper topics in the printed indexes or who do not know where to start their research can be given a brief bibliography or a few citations that include indexing terms to encourage them and to lead the way to further use of the printed indexes. The patron needing a correct title or the source of a recent article can be given the information quickly and efficiently by scanning a number of years in a comprehensive database.

Focusing on Important Aspects

The reference interview determines the information needed by the patron. When a brief search appears to provide the best answer, the few subject terms or keywords that will be used must describe the particular approach to the topic. Selecting these words requires the patron to think through and articulate the important aspects of the subject. This experience is an important lesson for students, and the reference librarian can be a significant contributor to the process. Following up the interview with the immediate feedback of a quick search of an appropriate database secures an answer that may include factual data, illustrate the type of material that can be found, or indicate the amount of information available in the literature. The index or equivalent of the database can be suggested for finding more references. The process of searching terms and getting instant results, which may or may not provide the information the patron needs, can help in the selection of appropriate indexing words for using a printed source and can suggest that research topics must be carefully described in specific terminology.

Finding Specific Information

Patrons needing some very precise information from an online source may be impatient if they have to fill out a form for a search request, make an appointment at a time when a librarian is available, and return again to the library. Although a search service can often absorb on-demand searching, there may be many times when the question is so specific that a careful interview and search preparation is not needed; immediate access with a few search terms can very quickly produce the few citations or the desired information. If this request can be treated as a reference question and the search done at the reference desk, there is a minimum of paperwork and maximum efficiency. If there are any complications that show the need for more careful terminology, manipulation of the subject concepts, or the production of a substantial printout, the patron can be better served by the search service and the lengthier interview and search process.

A request for the results of a particular study can sometimes be satisfied by printing out the abstract that summarizes the important findings. The full text of articles and books is also available and these can provide a table of data, a paragraph of significance, or a whole article from a magazine missing from the shelf. Online directories, such as those that list large companies, can quickly furnish the names of executives, addresses, telephone numbers, and pertinent product and financial information. In addition, the newest terminology of students, writers, or scientists featuring very specific meanings can be searched online long before they are utilized as indexing terms in a printed source. Trying to find this information under general headings may be very frustrating for the student using the printed index and can be done very quickly online.

Extending Reference Sources

Additional online resources for ready-reference include the most recent issues of indexes usually available in the corresponding database before they are received in the printed form. A search of the most recent updates to a file will assist the patron who needs only the most current information to supplement what can be found in the library. In addition, databases are increasingly unique sources. While some may represent printed material the library does not own, others have no printed equivalents. These files provide valuable additional resources for information retrieval at the reference desk. Online encyclopedias, dictionaries, biographical information, and directories have greatly expanded the resources to be consulted.

Reference desks at different locations in the same building or spread out at branch libraries across campus can provide uniform access to information without building up duplicate and expensive holdings. This decentralization may be especially important support for scientists who find it inconvenient to go to a central library when they need information. Monitoring the ready-reference use of online databases can help justify the need to subscribe to a specific index that has shown heavy use online, or may provide data to show that some current holdings can be canceled when they are little used or expensive and the type of information usually needed can quickly be obtained from the equivalent database. Searching an index that is too costly to subscribe to, a directory rarely needed, or an abstracting service housed in another location may be very efficient access to these reference sources.

Utilizing Instructional Potential

Preparing for even a brief ready-reference search is a process that can be utilized to teach patrons about various aspects of library research. This can include a demonstration of how a thesaurus can assist in the selection of subject terms and the importance of using correct terminology. Choosing an appropriate source and discussing why the online or print version is a better choice can expand the scope of a patron's research efforts. Explaining the results of even a short search can include analyzing a citation, interpreting abbreviations, and determining the journals owned by the library. While discussing the search results, the librarian can point out additional resources or suggest a more comprehensive online search when that appears to be a more suitable approach. The personal interaction of the patron with the librarian finding some online information and explaining the process builds confidence and the patron will often ask more questions and come back for further advice.

Searching Practice

Quick searches at the reference desk are an opportunity for additional online practice. Logging on, selecting a database, searching a few appropriate terms, printing some citations, and logging off will help librarians maintain their familiarity and ease of online access as the basic procedures are practiced and reinforced. Even though this brief searching will not require the preparation and in-depth interview with the patron, nevertheless it is necessary for the librarian to be familiar with available databases and their contents as well as many of the techniques for searching. New searchers can concentrate on the most-used databases and the limited search language needed for brief queries. They will quickly learn to do limited, efficient searches. In addition, many databases, such as directories used at the reference desk, are different from the ones used most often for in-depth searching. The ready-reference use provides an opportunity for all searchers to try out many of these databases and to find out which sources provide the best answers to frequently asked questions.

READY-REFERENCE SEARCHING

It may take some time before librarians at the reference desk feel comfortable about, or even remember to think of, online access to information in the course of everyday information retrieval. The pressure of questions may make it difficult to take time to dial up a vendor and database when the first priority must be given to the person waiting for assistance at the reference desk. When the telephone is ringing and students are lined up with questions during the busy portion of the semester, it is usually impossible to try a new approach or to search a database unless the system is easily accessible. To overcome these problems, online database searching must be closely linked to reference activities and reference librarians must be encouraged to go online whenever appropriate. To accomplish this the equipment must be convenient, there must be sufficient funding for connect-time and printouts, reference librarians must be trained for online searching and must have a broad general knowledge of database resources, and the reference desk procedures must incorporate online access. At the same time, in most situations costs are an important concern; therefore, the procedures must include a means for monitoring and controlling them.

Online Resources for the Reference Desk

Increasing numbers of reference books, directories, and sources of factual information have become available online. These databases provide immediate access to information usually more current than their printed counterparts. It is often possible to secure the entire amount of information needed; otherwise, a source may be identified where the information can be found. Undoubtedly the availability of full-text databases and directories appropriate for ready-reference will increase substantially in the next few years. These resources, along with the many bibliographic files used extensively for more comprehensive online searching, add up to a sizable list of databases available to the library with a contract with one or more of the major online vendors.

Online Ready-reference Sources from Major Vendors · A sampling of databases (other than bibliographic files) that provide valuable online resources:

Full-text reference sources

> ACADEMIC AMERICAN ENCYCLOPEDIA
> EVERYMAN'S ENCYCLOPAEDIA
> IRS TAXINFO
> KIRK-OTHMER ENCYCLOPEDIA OF CHEMICAL TECHNOLOGY
> MENTAL MEASUREMENTS YEARBOOK

Indexes to reference sources

> ASI (*American Statistics Index*)
> BIOGRAPHY MASTER INDEX (index to 600 sources)
> INDUSTRY DATA SOURCES
> SUPERINDEX (indexes 2000 reference books)

Data sources

> CENDATA (Census)
> CHASE ECONOMETRICS
> D & B—DONNELLEY DEMOGRAPHICS
> HEILBRON (Organic Chemicals)
> PTS U.S. FORECASTS
> PTS U.S. TIME SERIES

News sources

> AP NEWS
> FACTS ON FILE
> NEWSEARCH
> STANDARD & POOR'S NEWS
> UP NEWS

Directory information

Biographical
AMERICAN MEN AND WOMEN OF SCIENCE
MARQUIS WHO'S WHO, INC.
STANDARD & POOR'S REGISTER–BIOGRAPHICAL

Organizations
ENCYCLOPEDIA OF ASSOCIATIONS
FOUNDATION DIRECTORY
FOUNDATION GRANTS INDEX

Computer products
BUSINESS SOFTWARE DATABASE
.MENU–INTERNATIONAL SOFTWARE DATABASE
MICROCOMPUTER SOFTWARE AND HARDWARE GUIDE

Business and industry
MOODY'S CORPORATE PROFILES
D & B–DUN'S ELECTRONIC YELLOW PAGES
D & B–DUN'S MARKET IDENTIFIERS (2,000,000 businesses)
STANDARD & POOR'S CORPORATE DESCRIPTIONS
THOMAS REGISTER ONLINE

Education
ACS (American Chemical Society) DIRECTORY OF GRADUATE
RESEARCH
EDUCATIONAL TESTING SERVICE TEST COLLECTION
NATIONAL COLLEGE DATABANK
PETERSON'S COLLEGE DATABASE

Medicine
COMPREHENSIVE CORE MEDICAL LIBRARY
CONSUMER DRUG INFORMATION FILE
DRUG INFORMATION FULLTEXT
HAZARDLINE (safety, regulations on hazardous substances)
HEALTH AUDIO-VISUAL ONLINE CATALOG

Other databases that provide specific information of value at the reference desk include those on patents, trademarks, standards and specifications, regulations, companies, books, and periodicals.

Accessing Local Databases · The library's online catalog is one local database that can be utilized at the reference desk. Other useful databases that may have been composed in-house can include holdings of a special local collection, indexes available in the reference collection by general subjects covered, a referral file, or a local history or newspaper index. Files stored on the academic computer can also be accessed through the terminal and modem at the reference desk.

When to Choose an Online Source
at the Reference Desk

Occasions when the brief search of an online database at the reference desk is especially appropriate are related to verifying citations, finding addresses, using sources not otherwise available, trying out new terminology, locating very recent information, or printing out brief bibliographies. Specific instances when searching an online database can be an efficient method of answering a question:

When Correct Citations Are Needed · Many patrons seeking help at the reference desk need to find information referred to in bibliographies. Other patrons may be trying to locate articles by using references received from a colleague or professor. When the citations are incomplete, the bibliography does not include the title, the journal abbreviation is obscure, the date is missing, or there are obvious errors, a search of an appropriate database can be made using the components that are available: title words, date, journal title, author(s), etc. Many years and several databases can be quickly scanned if necessary.

A brief author search may also identify the needed citation as well as find other works by that person. This information can complete a bibliography, identify a correct source or, if the patron plans to request the item on interlibrary loan, provide accurate information.

When Names and Addresses Are Needed · Some directories, such as STANDARD & POOR'S REGISTER or the ENCYCLOPEDIA OF ASSOCIATIONS, provide addresses of organizations and names of executives. Other information such as SIC codes, subsidiaries, financial information, and the date of the next annual meeting may also be available. Bibliographic databases, such as SOCIOLOGICAL ABSTRACTS, NTIS, or BIOSIS, include the address of the first author with the citation to the literature in the section of the record labeled the institution field. In other databases, sources of materials such as software or educational supplies will include the address of the producer or publisher.

When Reference Material Is Temporarily Unavailable · An index volume may be at the bindery, it may be mislaid within the library, or there may be an index issue that was not received. An online search can take the place of the missing resource, or when an index refers to an issue or source that is not available, more information can be found in the database. In many instances the citation and abstract can be printed out from the citation number in the index.

When Sources Are Not Available in the Library · A brief search may take the place of a costly index the library does not own. When the index is rarely needed, searching the equivalent database may be the most cost-effective way of providing the information. It is important, however, to make patrons aware of the availability of online databases when the library cancels or chooses not to subscribe to the printed equivalent. A record in the card catalog for the database, a sign next to the older section of the index, or a prominent list of databases with their corresponding indexes will draw attention to the online source.

Databases lacking a print form can provide a new and important reference source. Other databases that cover very narrow subjects can also provide unique information that may be used infrequently. COFFEE-LINE, POPULATION BIBLIOGRAPHY, WATERNET from the American Water Works Association, and WELDASEARCH are examples of these specialized sources that may match areas of subject interest on campus.

When Standard Reference Tools Require Another Method of Access · A quick online search of the database for an index or abstract the library owns may be used as a method of finding specific information difficult to identify under the structured headings of the printed index. Searching title words or terms in the abstract can produce a list of articles where a particular event, substance, or artwork was mentioned. Literature on a psychological test, for instance, can be retrieved online if the name of the test has been used in an article title, in the abstract, or as a subject heading. The computer can also combine two or more different concepts that cannot be found together in an index.

A scan of several databases in sequence for the number of items retrieved on a few subject terms can be used to indicate the most productive source for finding information. Search terms can represent popular subjects in the news or interdisciplinary topics. A citation retrieved by this simple free-text searching can be printed in a format that will list the subject descriptors to help a student find more references in the corresponding printed index. A source such as *Biological Abstracts*, that could provide a great deal of information for an undergraduate writing a term paper, may prove to be discouraging to use because of the large amount of foreign-language material. A quick search on the topic in BIOSIS, limited to English, will greatly increase the chances for the student to find articles he or she can use.

When Very Recent Information Is Required · Since databases are usually updated before the printed issues of indexes are received by the library, they can provide new information not presently available in print form. The first few references printed out on the topic will provide the most recent citations. Newspaper articles on terrorism, information on street drugs, the latest government regulations on toxic chemicals, or other time-important subjects are examples of search topics that represent frequent questions at the reference desk.

When the Time Span Is Unknown · A database search will cover several years of a printed index. When the patron does not know the appropriate date for the information needed, the search can save considerable time and be used to confirm when an event happened, such as tampering with Tylenol capsules. Even the number of hits for a topic over a sequence of years without printing out any citations will tell the patron which dates of the printed indexes would be the most appropriate. A search can cover several years of an index that might have to be searched a half year at a time in the printed form, or it can quickly retrieve information from ten or twenty individual issues before the cumulative index is received.

If it is difficult to determine the most appropriate index for a patron to use for a specific subject, the CROS or DIALINDEX databases on BRS and Dialog or another similar file of databases can be scanned to reveal the number of hits on a subject. When the files represent indexes that the library owns, the patron can be referred to the most effective sources.

When a Short Bibliography Is Needed · A limited number of references may be quickly printed out at the reference desk to assist students having difficulty finding any information on their topic. Almost any subject terms can be combined and will generally produce some results. Subjects that combine several major concepts can be very difficult to find in a printed source, but online these very different ideas can be easily brought together. A question on the effect of stress on concrete pilings used in bridge construction can suggest a quick search using one search statement, "stress" and "concrete" and "pilings" and "bridges," to produce a short list of appropriate references.

Repeated requests for information on popular term paper topics such as acid rain or spouse abuse can form the basis of brief subject bibliographies reproduced and distributed on request. These handouts can provide five, ten, or more citations and include suggestions of print sources where students can find more material.

Location of Equipment

The placement of the terminal will make a great difference in the amount of use for reference questions. Should it be located right at the reference desk? The answer may depend on the physical layout of the desk area, the number of librarians on duty at a time, whether a terminal can be restricted to reference desk use, the availability of a telephone line, and the security arrangements. It is probably most satisfactory if the equipment is set back from or faces away from the patron desk or access area. This location would make it easier to concentrate on the search procedure and there is less chance of interruption; there would also be more password security. If there is only one person at the desk at a time, it is especially important to have the terminal close by. If there is a terminal for utilities, such as for OCLC or RLIN, that can be used when needed for this purpose, the location may be limited by the local system connections. If possible, however, a machine dedicated to searching at the reference desk is the best arrangement, with a printer to record the results of the search for the patron.

If the search service area is nearby and there is more than one person at the reference desk, it is possible to step into that office for a quick search. While it is convenient to have use of the manuals and support material available there, this arrangement often makes it more difficult to separate the free brief information search from the more lengthy and often fee-for-service search. The number of passwords may also affect the reference use. The necessity of checking to see if a lengthy search is underway when there is a single password will make it impossible to conveniently respond to reference questions. It is certainly important to have a separate password for this purpose both for the ease of access and to help determine the costs for different activities.

Selection of Online System(s) for the Reference Desk

All vendor systems that the library has access to may be made available at the reference desk, or one may be selected that seems the most cost-effective, has the best subject coverage, or the material most likely to be needed.

Important characteristics for ready-reference systems are:

simple log-on procedure and commands that are easy to remember
databases that can be searched without codes or complicated strategies
databases that match subject interests of patrons
databases that are familiar and provide additional access points to heavily used indexes
databases that provide new reference resources.

If a single vendor is to be made available at the reference desk with a password for that purpose, the choice may be the vendor that most of the librarians search regularly; they will feel most comfortable with the search language and procedures. A better basis of selection would involve examining the types of questions most likely to call for an online source and determining the vendor of the most databases appropriate for these uses.

Personnel Preparation

All reference librarians should be trained to search the online databases for all the systems available at the reference desk. This training will include different techniques from those used for searching research topics. Special training is advisable to efficiently retrieve information from data and full-text sources. Dialog offers a Library Applications Seminar that concentrates on utilizing standard reference sources, searching full-text files, and techniques geared to finding specific information, all of which are important for reference desk applications. Each reference librarian should be familiar with the broad range of available sources, especially those useful for the library's clientele. This knowledge base is quite different from the subject or database concentrations valuable for the search service and in-depth reference questions. Practice time is important for trying out new databases and for comparing the answers to questions from online and printed sources.

It is imperative that all reference librarians have the same philosophy of service and make the same efforts to use online sources when appropriate. Otherwise the quality of service will be uneven and unfair to patrons. To provide the time and flexibility for searching, there should be enough staff at the reference desk during busy hours for each patron to receive an adequate interview to determine his or her needs. Searching at the reference desk could be initiated during those periods when there are two librarians available. With regular use, online resources will become more important and searching them a standard consideration. When librarians are subject specialists, the more difficult questions can be referred to the person with more online and subject experience in that field.

Support Material

A terminal at the reference desk must have some supporting documentation nearby to assist easy and quick access. The correct amount of material and good organization are particularly important here. Telephone numbers to reach the vendors, file numbers or codes for individual databases, and a list of the appropriate print formats may be enough. A manual of brief database descriptions such as Dialog's *Bluesheets* or BRS's *Aid Pages* will be more helpful. These can be limited to just those databases that are expected to be utilized. If there are bibliographic databases such as ERIC that will be relied on a great deal, a thesaurus for that index should also be kept near the terminal.

Search procedures for the reference desk include:

telephone numbers, including 800 assistance desk(s)
log-on procedures for each available vendor

limits and restrictions of ready-reference use (by database, cost, output)

major search protocols for each system

appropriate print formats

subject index to available databases

list of databases representing indexes held

list of databases representing sources not held by the library.

If a long list of available databases is to be utilized, it would be helpful to have a subject listing of files organized for quick consultation with subject emphasis, dates covered, and documents included.

Procedure Manual

A section of the online search service procedure manual can be devoted to use of online sources at the reference desk as outlined in chapter 6. The ready-reference manual should be brief and available when necessary to answer questions or to verify a procedure. It should be reviewed and revised frequently as technology, resources, attitudes, and the amount of funding change.

CONTROLS FOR READY-REFERENCE SEARCHING

In order to manage the costs and keep reference desk searching at a level of brief information retrieval, there should be some fairly precise guidelines established for using online sources. Regular review and change as experience is gained will help establish the most appropriate use of online databases for each library. A brief log and the monthly vendor bill can be used for monitoring the costs and types of searches conducted. It should be possible to recognize when there is a trend toward excessive or inappropriate online use. These records can also be used to calculate an average cost per search, which can be examined periodically and used to show the cost-effectiveness of using online sources. It may be found that the efficiency and funding are such that no constraints are needed other than the discretion of the librarian, and database access can be absorbed into the information retrieval process for use whenever needed. However, when costs and controls are a concern, procedures may be established to more closely regulate online use at the reference desk:

Limit use strictly to the discretion of the reference librarian. It is especially important for all the librarians to agree about when a search is appropriate. Have written guidelines,

Limit total usage to a certain amount of funding a month, or six months, or a year. This arrangement may be an especially appropriate plan when first using online resources at the reference desk until some indication of demand is established. The budgetary allotment may come from the total amount for all public services, or it could be included as part of the materials budget that encompasses other reference materials as well.

Limit use to specific databases. Depending on major patron interests, ready-reference use of databases could be limited to the MAGAZINE INDEX, ABI/INFORM or the Wilson indexes; several low cost databases; or to sources the library does not own. This procedure would reduce the overwhelming choice of databases available at the reference desk and extensive supporting search aids. Selected databases could also be chosen that primarily provide access to material the library owns. ERIC, newspaper indexes, and certain subject databases can be appropriate. These files will increase use of the library collection and will not require dependence on interlibrary loan services.

Review procedures regularly to be sure that online access is used when it provides an appropriate answer and that printed sources are used when indexing terms match the requested information, or browsing is important.

Review online search questions regularly to examine information requested and to decide if a reference book should be purchased instead of using the online source. The availability of online databases may also be considered when evaluating the reference collection.

Refer reference questions that require online access to subject specialists for the most efficient use of databases and better evaluation of online versus printed index. The specialist can also counsel patrons to try additional sources.

COPING WITH POTENTIAL PROBLEMS

Adding more procedures, a complicated piece of apparatus, and an overwhelming list of new sources to those already in place at the reference desk could cause confusion rather than increased efficiency. Reference librarians may feel that there is increased pressure to provide quick answers to information requests and that there are too many alternatives to cope with. Some causes of difficulties and methods of minimizing them can include:

Extended Searches · It is sometimes difficult to disconnect when the patron wants a little more information or another search term tried. The cost can increase quickly, as does the time involvement of the librarian. Specific guidelines for reference questions can set the maximum output of citations, search terms used, or cost of the search. It may be necessary to position the terminal away from the view of the patron, and if more interaction or more output is requested, patrons can be referred to the search service. Reference librarians should determine the specific information needed before logging on. Efforts should be concentrated on going online and offline quickly.

Terminal Security · If a portable terminal is kept at the reference desk, it can be locked in a desk drawer at night. Other searching equipment can be moved into a secure office when the reference desk is closed or fastened to a desk by adequate locks. A secure terminal at the reference desk is probably the best arrangement so the machine does not have to be moved in the morning and evenings, it is unnecessary to worry if the librarian is away from the desk, and it is available when needed.

Equipment · Problems with the machine, telephone, logging on, or other difficulties are always frustrating and will be even more so when patrons are waiting for a quick answer to a question. Front-end software for automatic logging on, a high quality outside telephone line, and the availability of backup equipment will lessen the potential for problems to develop. Equipment must be simple enough that changing ribbons or coping with paper jams in the printer can be easily handled. The search service manager can be a valuable resource for dealing with these matters, or one or two of the librarians can take the responsibility of reading the manuals and learning to deal with machine-related problems.

Increased Job Pressure · Students may want their term paper topics searched at the reference desk instead of reading printed indexes when they find their friends have received a good start on their papers with a brief online search. Unless clear guidelines are set for the use of online databases and the amount of information to be provided, there may be a few individuals who will want more than their share. Students can be asked to show that they have done some preliminary searching in the indexes before a database search is undertaken. A responsive search service, where more complex searches and more demanding patrons can be referred, will be helpful for maintaining the limited ready-reference search. It is also important that patrons have realistic expectations for the results of an online search. If students have received some explanations and comparisons of online and printed indexes during bibliographic instruction sessions, it will be a good basis for working with them at the reference desk. Reproducing short bibliographies on popular topics and making them available for students can sometimes take the place of answering repeated questions.

Additional Skills · Online database searching provides extensive information resources; however, the necessity of knowing what is available, remembering the procedures for accessing databases, and keeping this service efficient all increase demands on reference librarians. More training, more practice, and more alternatives for finding information require time, patience, flexibility, and intellectual vitality. Searching should not impact on one or two librarians, but should be shared by all reference desk personnel. It is also important that the procedures and support material at the reference desk be well organized so that searches can be performed easily to encourage the integration of this method of access into the overall ready-reference service. There should also be enough funding for this purpose so that the restrictions do not prevent true integration and so librarians receive enough practice on the job.

Time Requirement · A ready-reference search may seem to take quite a bit of time when the keywords must be discussed with patrons and the search carried out. However, the results must be the important aspect, and each patron should be given appropriate assistance. Any reference question may require additional explanations for using an index, finding correct subject headings, and reading the citations. Double staffing the reference desk will help so that either librarian can feel that he or she has time to do a brief search when that response is indicated. Reference librarians must have enough online practice so that they can quickly select the components of a topic, go online, retrieve the information, and log off. A major problem may be the time needed for training, practice, and study to keep up with the increasing number of online resources. The library administration must recognize the changing demands of reference desk work, provide adequate staffing, and adjust work loads so that librarians have the time to develop the necessary expertise.

Evenness of Service · It is important that all the reference desk staff are trained for online searching and that efforts are made for the service to be available for all patrons. Regular discussions of questions answered, limits on searches, procedures, and problems encountered are essential. The amount of assistance given to students for term papers, to faculty who insist on an online answer when a printed source is better, or the amount of searching for a business student researching a company should be reviewed and kept at a consistent level. New searchers can be paired with experienced librarians so that skills can be learned and reinforced.

Increased Interlibrary Loan Requests · Searching at the reference desk should be aimed at helping the patron find answers to questions or references to material that the library owns. Bibliographic databases can be chosen to provide search results that most closely match the library's collection so that patrons can find the material they need. Limiting the number of citations retrieved for a reference question, selecting only English-language articles, or particular types of documents will also help control the impact on interlibrary loan.

Increasing Costs · Increased funding may be required for providing optimum online ready-reference service. Most likely some adjustment of the reference budget will be necessary, along with a close look at service priorities. New sources of support should be investigated; these can include an examination of the reference book and journal budget and the possibility of canceling some expensive indexes or cumulations. If an index is canceled because the online version is available, it should be decided whether searches of these databases will be performed at the reference desk or referred to the search service for more extensive access.

Limits should be set. These could include time—for example, two or three minutes online—and number of citations, perhaps no more than ten. Particular databases may be emphasized for the type of information in them, the answers to questions most frequently asked, or the ones for which citations can be typed without charge. Particular vendors may be selected for reference desk activity: BRS because it is less expensive, or Wilsonline because the corresponding indexes are so often used by undergraduates.

GOVERNMENT PUBLICATIONS

Ready-reference use of databases will include finding information about publications of the United States government. The GPO MONTHLY CATALOG is the basic resource for the broad range of documents from federal agencies, Congress, and presidential offices. It is supplemented by many other files such as NTIS for technical reports, FEDERAL RESEARCH IN PROGRESS for ongoing federally funded research, the ASI (*American Statistics Index*) database for comprehensive coverage of the statistics collected by government agencies, and databases from individual government agencies representing subject areas such as agriculture, energy, medicine, water resources, and trade. The latest accomplishments of Congress and the most recent government regulations can be quickly determined online. This information is valuable both at the reference desk and within a government publications office that services a federal depository collection.

In addition, the GPO PUBLICATIONS REFERENCE FILE is an online source of information on documents that can be purchased by the public, selected by libraries for their collections, or used to find correct bibliographic information. The record includes stock numbers and prices and is updated biweekly to show the availability of documents.

The reference desk of the future may be identified by a bank of computer terminals. Already it is possible to have a terminal for searching a bibliographic utility such as OCLC or RLIN; one for the library's online catalog; a terminal with an acoustic coupler and a telephone for accessing remote databases; and a microcomputer for creating and utilizing in-house generated files. The developing gateway systems and new technology may well combine these functions into a single piece of equipment with the possibility of selecting the various resources as needed. At the present time the extent to which online searching has been made available to answer questions at the reference desk may well depend on the library budget, the availability of a terminal, backup assistance at the reference desk, the awareness of database sources by reference librarians and their training for accessing them, and the library's philosophy of providing optimum information services.

Bibliography

Belanger, Sandra E., and Nancy J. Emmick. "Use of Ready Reference Searching in Business Reference." *Journal of Academic Librarianship* 12:298–303 (1986).

Brownmiller, Sara, A. Craig Hawbaker, Douglas E. Jones, and Robert Mitchell. "Online–Ready-Reference Searching in an Academic Library." *RQ* 24:320–26 (1985).

Hitchingham, Eileen, Elizabeth Titus, and Richard Pettengill. "A Survey of Database Use at the Reference Desk." *Online* 8:44–50 (1984).

Holland, Maurita Peterson. " 'Real-Time' Searching at the Reference Desk." *Reference Librarian* 5/6:165–71 (1982).

Roose, Tina. "Integrating Online Searching with Reference Service." *Library Journal* 112:86–87 (1987).

10

BIBLIOGRAPHIC INSTRUCTION *240*
INTERLIBRARY LOAN AND DOCUMENT DELIVERY *242*
COLLECTION DEVELOPMENT *244*
LIBRARY TECHNICAL SERVICES *245*
    Acquisitions *245*
    Cataloging *245*
LIBRARY RESEARCH *246*

Implications for Other Library Operations

Online databases can provide information for internal library functions as well as for the library's clientele. Cataloging records, lists of publishers, journals and books, grant sources, and library literature offer a broad scope of online assistance for librarians. Just as database searching has been integrated into ready-reference, the convenience and efficiency of access to these resources can be an asset to the daily functioning of a library unit. However, as databases become significant library resources, some adjustments will be necessary to incorporate this online assistance into regular procedures.

Since database searching is a relatively new library service, different in organization from the traditional pattern and usually based on access to remote computer systems, there are necessarily additional costs and increased demands for equipment, supplies, and staff training. Funds for database use may generate an impact on budgetary allocations and increase competition for limited amounts of funding. The greater the commitment to free access, the more compromises that may be necessary in the budget. A high number of requests for scheduled searches requires increased searcher time as searchers work on an individual basis with faculty and students. This service commitment along with training, practice, and management tasks may impose a demand for more public service librarians, resulting in different staffing patterns. At the same time, other patron services may have to assume a lesser priority when online searches must be provided as promptly as possible. Establishing a search service or end-user facility may even cause a change in office space or the relocation of another library unit.

Other effects of online services include an impact on the use of journals and the need for more and different titles as the computer quickly and efficiently generates substantial lists of publications. Interlibrary loan services have to cope with more requests, the effects of higher expectations for quick access to information, and the problem of providing documents from obscure sources that are as easily identified online as those in local collections. As the information environment is changed by computer technologies, additional decisions will be required for collection development. Different patterns of usage must be recognized, consideration given to the full-text retrieval of articles on demand, and materials acquired in new formats. The management of library acquisitions will become increasingly complicated.

Other activities, such as bibliographic instruction, must also reflect the changing information field. Students' use of databases and the online catalog from remote locations will accentuate the need to help them understand the importance of learning search techniques and the appropriate use of online information systems. Bibliographic instruction must integrate electronic access to information into library research. With a more computer-literate student body, teaching methods may need to change and additional skills be included. It is a challenge to provide a balance between print and online sources. Different search techniques, the appropriate uses of an index and a database, and an understanding of the information to be found in an index or a database printout must be covered.

Computers have already changed many library operating procedures, and online database searching can be integrated into some of these internal processes. Ordering documents online, identifying new publications, and finding cataloging information are easily accomplished with an online search. Whether *Books in Print* is available on CD-ROM in acquisitions, or a database search is used in the planning for an online catalog, there are many opportunities for assisting library processes. Other library units may see changes in priorities, functions, and budgetary allocations as a result of the integration and expansion of online database searching.

BIBLIOGRAPHIC INSTRUCTION

As online searching becomes more of a regular component of information retrieval, it is increasingly important that bibliographic instruction programs include computer-access to indexes as part of the description of library resources and services available. Depending on the class level and research requirements of the students, this inclusion of database searching can be merely a mention that an online search service is available, the distribution of a brochure about the service, an explanation of a sample search, or a search performed with a small class grouped around the terminal.

Students finding that computers are part of their everyday lives, and who may be using them in classes or for entertainment, will find library research more interesting if taught from the approach of applying the decisions used for online searching to the strategy for finding information in printed sources. Focusing on the specific aspect of a subject; choosing keywords, descriptors, or search terms by using a thesaurus; developing the concepts of the topic and formulating a search strategy; these are procedures they can apply to searching both printed indexes and online databases. Selecting an index or database, considering the timeliness of the topic, the appropriate type of source material, and the amount of information needed are all part of this process. Presented in the right context and at an appropriate level and subject orientation for the class, it will help students think about their search procedures.

Wilsonline searches can supplement use of the Wilson indexes that freshmen will often recognize from use in high school and public libraries. Term paper clinics can also use this combination of databases and indexes as librarians work on a more individual basis with students needing extra assistance. Regardless of whether the bibliography was secured from the print index or the online database, students must still learn how to read citations and how to find books and serials in the library.

As CD-ROM becomes available for library patrons, the discussion of online searching will have to include a section on search techniques. If online searching is already a part of library research instruction, this will just be a short additional discussion on getting started at the keyboard and some basic search procedures. If it is important for students to also learn to use the printed index, they could outline their topic, find a few references in a printed index, and have their strategy for online searching checked by a librarian.

If the bibliographic instruction is for a research methods class, seminar, honors class, or group of graduate students from a department, they can participate in an online search on a topic appropriate for the class. Students can help select terms, suggest strategy development, assist in choosing a database, and watch the actual search, observing the resulting number of hits and some of the most recent citations. This type of session will often provide an opportunity to explain a complicated index and alert students to additional resources. The department may wish to supply funding for students to do a literature search as part of the preparation for their paper or seminar report. The student can prepare for the search by examining an appropriate printed index, selecting keywords, grouping them into concepts, and deciding how much literature is needed. Individual searches for class members extends the learning process and students have the advantage of reviewing their plan with a librarian, participating in the online search, and getting a good start on their research.

Materials in a handout for a large class can include a sample database search along with an example of the same topic as found in the printed index. The procedure used in the online search can be contrasted with the subject indexing of the printed version. Students who have learned to use the online catalog will find searching a database of periodical articles a logical next step. In any presentation or lecture, however, it is important to include a discussion of using an appropriate source and method for the topic and type of material needed. The online search is one choice, but printed indexes and other material may give better results.

Introducing online searching into bibliographic instruction will alert more faculty to the availability of online services. Some faculty will be more interested in bringing their classes to the library if an online search is part of the presentation. A database search can also provide a bibliography for a class that can be easily updated each semester. Students will be impressed with this modern approach to finding information; however, they must be able to find the documents they have identified. It can be very frustrating to have good references but not to be able to find the complete papers. The library procedures for finding journals and ordering through interlibrary loan must follow in a logical and successful sequence.

It is important, too, when discussing library research with a class to integrate the various electronic media available to patrons and to stress the similarities and differences of both procedures and materials found. The online catalog, online database searching, and CD-ROM are all electronic indexes to library materials and require use of a keyboard, some knowledge of search procedures, ability to read citations and translate this information into finding documents. A good learning experience will provide students with information-seeking skills that can be applied to later lifestyles and job situations.

Teaching research methods and search procedures can be part of every search undertaken. Not only can the search steps be explained, but also broader concepts such as the use of controlled vocabulary, the different types of literature retrieved, and the components of citations. Patrons can be alerted to print sources as well as other databases for more information.

INTERLIBRARY LOAN AND DOCUMENT DELIVERY

A search service utilized by research faculty and students will cause a noticeable impact on interlibrary loan services as requests for new and varied materials are processed. Patrons may expect even quicker interlibrary loan service since the online search was provided so swiftly. Requests from database printouts will include articles from the latest issues of journals, copies of patents, or papers from a conference that took place halfway around the world. Verification time will be saved if a copy of the citation, as printed out during a search, is attached to the interlibrary loan request and the database noted.

If the increase in requests is placing a burden on this office, patrons can be encouraged to include abstracts with their bibliographies so they can be more selective in determining the material needed. The patron's interest in foreign-language materials should be determined before printing out results, since these can usually be easily eliminated during the searching process. Enough of the record should be printed to make identification of the source materials as clear as possible for both patron and interlibrary loan personnel. It is also very important that the searcher makes sure patrons know how to read and understand their search results and that they know how to find journals and other materials available within the library. This educational process will save a good deal of time for both patron and interlibrary loan personnel.

Online searching can also aid the interlibrary loan process directly by assisting in securing correct citations and confirming the information in requests submitted by patrons. To correct or verify a citation, databases can be searched with even a few words from the title, linking them with "and" and limiting the search to the title field. Dialog has produced a bibliographic verification aid (its table 25), which lists the search commands for Dialog databases that restrict the search terms to the title field or to the year of publication, and the commands for keying the search to the corporate source, the journal title or CODEN. The various forms used for author's names in these files are included. With a request in hand, any necessary bibliographic information can be secured quickly by consulting this guide. Some online vendor systems have standardized the author and source listings for all bibliographic databases, making it easier to remember procedures. A search guide for this purpose could be prepared for all the library's available online resources and a clerk taught to efficiently search for this information.

The process of finding document sources can be assisted by ordering materials online. Many of the database vendors have contracted with information suppliers to furnish copies of articles and other items on request. These orders may be entered from the database where the item is listed, via a special order file, or by using electronic mail. Some suppliers will accept requests for materials found in other sources than databases. Since the patron usually needs to examine the printout first, and the library's holdings must be checked, the follow-up can be handled either by the interlibrary loan staff or by the searcher. Decisions about using an online document source and which staff member should do the actual ordering will depend on these factors:

patron's need for quick access to the document(s)
relative costs of online ordering vs. borrowing
interlibrary loan staffing
currency of the item
obscurity of the source and its availability elsewhere.

Online database searches for patrons require a commitment to help find the information referenced in the search results. Online ordering of documents should be a consideration.

COLLECTION DEVELOPMENT

Collection development in the academic library may be influenced by the growth in the amount of online searching. Databases provide greater access to journals that the library already owns and a demand is generated for additional titles. Articles in the newest issues of journals will be included in search retrieval, so patrons may look for these recent issues and any delay in checking them in will be noticed. New journals will also be in demand as citations from these sources are identified. Search results can be examined regularly and interlibrary loan requests documented to guide in the selection of new subscriptions. The frequency of citations for articles in journals in particular subject areas can be followed to note the need for these titles. An important consideration in selecting new journals for the library collection may be the indexing in one or more online databases. A search of several databases by the journal title or CODEN will indicate if a new journal is being included. This information is usually available online long before it is printed in the index list of sources.

Decisions about the format of new library materials will also be influenced by the availability of indexes online and the increasing number of full-text directories, some journals, and reference books that can provide an alternative to purchasing the printed form. A database can replace a cumulation of several years of an index while still having the printed information available even if it is less convenient. On the other hand, online access to an index that is rarely used or is expensive can make the information available in a cost-effective manner. Care must be taken that indexes or other items are not canceled and replaced by the online version when they are used for browsing by researchers, or when faculty want students to learn to use them. Relying on an online version puts pressure on reference librarians to provide a responsive search service. However, the resources of most libraries will be increasingly supported by the availability of full-text materials that are not available in any other form. NewsNet, for instance, can add more than 300 newsletters to the materials available for patrons. It will be an increasing challenge to make them easily accessible.

Online databases can supply bibliographies to assist in collection development. Searching BOOKS IN PRINT regularly will provide a list of the latest books for building a comprehensive collection in a specialized subject area. A bibliography of books and journals can assist in the development of the collection for new programs and research areas.

Book, journal, and software reviews aid in evaluating the quality and appropriateness of many types of new publications for the library collection. As electronic publications increase, it will become even more important to consider their acquisition online, on disk or on CD-ROM and to make the most effective use of them.

LIBRARY TECHNICAL SERVICES

Book acquisition, serials processing, cataloging, and other units within the library operation can utilize online databases for some of their information needs. Often selected databases may be used for specific purposes so individuals can be trained for a restricted amount of online searching.

Acquisitions

Identification of books from faculty requests, searching out new publications, and checking publisher's series can be accomplished online by utilizing a number of databases:

ASSOCIATIONS PUBLICATIONS IN PRINT
BOOKS IN PRINT
BOOKSINFO (English-language monographs from Brodart)
OCLC EASI REFERENCE
PUBLISHERS, DISTRIBUTORS & WHOLESALERS
WILEY CATALOG/ONLINE.

Serials can be identified, subscription costs determined, publishers addresses secured and pertinent information obtained from:

ULRICH'S INTERNATIONAL PERIODICALS DIRECTORY AND IRREGULAR SERIALS
     AND ANNUALS
CALIFORNIA UNION LIST OF PERIODICALS.

Materials currently available from the Universal Serials and Book Exchange can be determined from the database of that name on BRS and individual items ordered online.

Cataloging

As gateway systems are developed, OCLC, RLIN, and other bibliographic utilities will provide cataloging departments with easy access to BRS and Dialog. The OCLC database can be searched by subject on BRS. Cataloging information on books can be derived from the database, LC MARC, from the Library of Congress going back to 1968, and

REMARC, which covers from 1897 to 1980. These files provide many access points for finding records and verifying citations. Full cataloging information from the Library of Congress is furnished. Catalogers will be able to do their own literature searching and print out bibliographies on interpretation of cataloging rules, descriptive cataloging, or establishing authority files.

Catalogers should also be challenged to increase patron awareness of databases and to integrate them into the subject listing of material in public catalogs. Catalog entries for full-text online magazines and newspapers, CD-ROM databases, local databases, and the services of online vendors should reflect the availability of these resources.

LIBRARY RESEARCH

All librarians can also take advantage of the amount of information available in online databases to assist the work of library committees and managers who must make decisions about the organization and functioning of library systems. Reviews of new technologies, case studies of bibliographic instruction methods, or information on optical disks are examples of subjects that can be explored in ERIC, LIBRARY LITERATURE, LIBRARY AND INFORMATION SCIENCE ABSTRACTS or INFORMATION SCIENCE ABSTRACTS. Librarians with faculty status who are expected to participate in research and publication can prepare bibliographies and review the literature on their field of interest. The library administration can support these efforts by providing some funds for searching on topics that reflect the concerns of the library operation or the interests of the librarians. The library budget could include an allocation for these in-house uses and a specified amount for searching on research topics by each librarian.

As computers enter into the operation of more library functions, it will seem even more logical to the staff to utilize the information available by online database searching to support decision making and the development of new systems. The increasing number of pertinent online files has made this quick access to information very valuable. Every library staff member should be aware of these resources and know when they can provide appropriate assistance. At the same time, administrators must anticipate the changes made necessary by the incorporation of online systems. These adjustments will include both budgets and service priorities. Information services, the educational responsibilities of librarians, and library collection development are all changing processes that must adapt to new technology and its effect on scholarship.

Bibliography

Connolly, Bruce, and Cheryl M. LaGuardia. "The Impact of Database Searching on Interlibrary Loan—'Eliminating the Negative'." *Online Review* 10:185–89 (1986).

Dreifuss, Richard A. "Library Instruction in the Database Searching Context." *RQ* 21:233–38 (1982).

Rice, Barbara A. "Evaluation of Online Databases and Their Uses in Collection Evaluation." *Library Trends* 33:297–325 (1985).

Shill, Harold B. "Bibliographic Instruction: Planning for the Electronic Information Environment." *College and Research Libraries* 48:433–53 (1987).

11

ADVANTAGES OF USING A MICROCOMPUTER *250*
SELECTING A MICROCOMPUTER *252*
SOFTWARE TO ASSIST ONLINE SEARCHING *255*
    Software for Different Tasks *256*
    Level of Assistance *257*
    Accounting Features *259*
    Modifying Search Results *260*
    Features of Software Packages *260*
CRITERIA FOR SELECTING SOFTWARE PACKAGES *261*
    Basic General Features *261*
    Technical Specifications *262*
    Aids for Searchers *263*
SOURCES OF SOFTWARE *263*
    Database Vendors *264*
    Database Producers *265*
    Other Software Producers *265*
MANAGEMENT CONCERNS *267*
    Downloading Search Results *267*
    Procedures for Use of Microcomputers and Software *268*
    Training for Microcomputer/Software Search
      Assistance *269*

Microcomputers and Software

Microcomputers have been increasingly utilized for online searching during the 1980s. Most searching in the 1970s was performed on printing terminals at speeds that now seem slow. As the use of microcomputers proliferated, they became easily available for search terminals and sometimes were purchased for this purpose because of their potential usefulness for so many other library applications. The microcomputer has become the first choice for online searching over a printing terminal because of the assistance it can provide the searcher before going online, during the interactive search process, and for handling the search results after logging off. The automation of repetitious procedures, the ability to do as many operations as possible offline before or after making the connection with the database, and the capability to receive, store, and transfer the search results electronically provide many opportunities to enhance search efficiency. In addition, microcomputer systems can now provide assistance to those learning to be searchers, or can assume the role of an electronic intermediary to modify and simplify search procedures for individuals who wish to do their own searching.

Once microcomputers were being used in the library, individuals with programming experience began to take advantage of their potential by developing software designed to assist searchers using the machines as "dumb" terminals. Today, the availability of commercially marketed software for supporting search activities has so expanded that usually several software packages are available to meet the needs of the searcher in a variety of situations. However, choosing the best software and utilizing its capabilities to the fullest extent requires careful consideration and knowledge of developments in technology, search systems, and database organization. Using a microcomputer to provide readily available assistance during a database search has made the microcomputer with a selected software program an essential machine for efficient searching and the delivery of a quality information product.

Microcomputers arrived at a time concurrent with increased demands on online database searchers to remember and utilize efficiently more vendor systems, additional system commands, multiplying numbers of databases, and sophisticated techniques that frequently change and vary with the systems, the databases, and the type of information needed. It is increasingly difficult for the experienced searcher to keep up and for the novice searcher to catch up. At the same time, the amount of database searching continues to increase as more essential information becomes available and as the patron expects more services and faster answers to information queries. Searchers handling more requests on a wider variety of topics need assistance to concentrate on the intellectual components of the search while incorporating new techniques, remembering new system languages, and utilizing a multitude of new resources. In order to provide this help, and to keep the service for patrons at an expert level through staff changes and varying responsibilities, it is important to acquire microcomputers and software and utilize them to the greatest advantage.

Microcomputers are replacing all "dumb" printing terminals as costs continue to decrease, technology improves, and software performs more functions to aid the online searcher. The judicious selection of equipment and the training of searchers to make the most of electronic search aid features will improve searching efficiency and help deliver an improved information product to library patrons.

ADVANTAGES OF USING A MICROCOMPUTER

Justification for selecting a microcomputer for an online search service is concentrated primarily on improving the efficiency of searchers, automating the routine steps in a search process, making complex searches more cost-effective, and providing additional options for the delivery of search results. In addition, microcomputers can provide help for inexperienced searchers who are learning or who do not get enough practice. Microcomputers with appropriate software can assist even expert searchers by performing specific functions:

> *Automating the telephone connection and log-on procedure.* A single command and the telephone number is dialed for a local communications network. If the first telephone number is busy, another will be tried automatically. When the telephone connection is made with the communications network, the code is supplied for the online vendor and the password is sent to complete the log-on process. The searcher can then proceed with the search.

Providing a way to prepare a search strategy on the computer before going online. Queries can be typed, edited, and corrections made on the monitor before logon to the system and database. When the connection is made with the vendor and the database selected, the search terms are automatically sent line by line. Although this procedure can be interrupted by the searcher at any time, the interchange is carried out without operator prompting or hesitation.

Allowing typing ahead while a response is being received from a previous command. Database connect time is shortened by this ability to type in statements while the computer is working at another task.

Transferring the searcher to another database or another system easily without going offline, redialing, or starting over.

Storing software instructions, manual information, explanations of specific search procedures, and other search assistance in a help file to be utilized at the computer when needed during the search process.

Translating the search commands of one system into the correct commands for another. This capability allows an expert searcher on one system to search a database on another without needing to know the different command language used for that system.

Providing search assistance with menus and other aids to prompt the inexperienced or untrained searcher. This friendly approach is usually a slower method of searching but can be used as a means of learning to search, or a method for patrons to do their own searches. It allows the microcomputer to be used for different levels of search services.

Storing frequently used search strategies, SDI profiles, and standard search strings that can be recalled when needed. Searching of SDI profiles is more efficient when the stored strategies can be recalled, the statements sent quickly, and the results downloaded.

Storing search results electronically or downloading on a disk. The requested information can be given to the patron on a disk along with or instead of producing a typed printout. Search results can also be sent electronically to another computer.

Editing the completed search results to eliminate unnecessary citations or merging files to produce organized bibliographies and custom printouts.

Accumulating statistics automatically on search activity, use of various systems, and accounting information. Accurate and comprehensive reports can be quickly assembled.

The capabilities of microcomputers to assist searchers have increased dramatically in recent years. The equipment and software must be carefully selected to take advantage of these developments that will improve and help maintain an efficient search service.

SELECTING A MICROCOMPUTER

The campus computer center is a source for advice about choosing a microcomputer, and may even be able to provide equipment at a good price if there is a special arrangement for campus purchasers. For further assistance, searchers at other academic libraries can be surveyed for their comments on the use of different equipment and software. While most microcomputers can be used for online searching, to achieve optimum performance it is important that the microcomputer have the capability of performing as many of the supporting features as possible. Purchasing the software, microcomputer, and modem at the same time will insure compatibility and maximum proficiency.

When buying a piece of equipment such as a microcomputer, first decide exactly what tasks the computer is expected to perform. Will it only be used for searching by trained searchers? Will patrons use it to do their own searching? Will it be available for word processing? Does it need to be portable, or will it be attached to a permanent work station? Is security a consideration? The answers to these questions will help define the physical characteristics of the equipment. If the software is selected first, its description will list requirements for the microcomputer operating system, amount of memory, and type of modem.

A second element of the planning should include the search environment. As in purchasing any equipment for a search service, the location, space, lighting, and noise considerations must be kept in mind. Tables, work stations, chairs, and other pieces of equipment must be compatible with the search equipment and comfortable for the searchers and patrons. It may be important for the microcomputers to match equipment already owned by the library or on campus. Acquiring a standard type of microcomputer will make it easier to find backup equipment, share software, and transfer data from one machine to another.

A third consideration is cost. Available funding may limit options, but a high quality, standard microcomputer that will communicate at the faster rates and has as much storage as possible on a hard disk should be priority considerations for a versatile machine. When technology changes require new search equipment, this machine can be transferred to other uses in the library.

The installation of a microcomputer and associated software into a searching station will be easier if a systems librarian or a member of the searching staff is accustomed to the terminology and use of microcomputers, and experienced in using various types of software. Manuals are rarely clear and simple enough for the totally inexperienced user. Support from a computer center on campus, assistance from a software producer, and the advice of staff members with their own computers will help. With experience, the search service manager can learn to deal with the installation of software, the utilization of machine capabilities, and problems that searchers encounter as they try out new equipment.

The selection of a microcomputer will require examining the hardware or mechanical characteristics and related equipment that make up an online work station. Important features for a microcomputer are:

A standard operating system. The microcomputer should be compatible with other equipment in the library and on campus for potential networking. MS-DOS is the most common operating system. This specification usually indicates IBM or IBM-compatible microcomputers. Equipment must include a modem or have a serial port for attaching one, and be easily adjustable for speed, duplex (full or half), and parity (odd, even, or off).

Consideration of software. If specific programs are planned for the service, they should be tried out before purchase of the equipment, and a wide choice of programs should be available for the microcomputer selected.

The overall quality, noise generation, and speed of the package, which includes a monitor, modem, and printer.

The amount of built-in memory expressed as ROM, Read-Only Memory, or permanent instructions in the machine, and RAM, Random-Access Memory, temporary storage of information that is lost when the machine is turned off. A present standard suggests 256 K of memory, but a larger amount will increase software options and the versatility of operation.

Storage by floppy or hard disk. Maximum storage size is important to provide enough capability for storing and manipulating lengthy search results and to make the microcomputer adaptable. Two double-sided disk drives or a hard or fixed disk and one disk drive are usually required. Microcomputers for patrons to do their own searching may not need this large amount of storage space.

Construction of the microcomputer to allow further expansion of information storage or upgrades to the machine.

A *keyboard with clear labels,* easy and comfortable to use, and similar to an electric typewriter. A movable keyboard is the most convenient arrangement for a search service where the searcher is working with a patron. It should be a solid component of the microcomputer if it is to be used by patrons doing their own searching. There should be a large, clear return key, and a numeric keypad is desirable. Special purpose or function keys should be plainly marked and placed for ease of use. The cursor should be controlled by directional keys.

A *screen or monitor large enough for viewing by several people,* or a smaller screen if the equipment is for use by one person at a time. The image should be legible and sharp with good contrast. Amber or green colors on black are usually preferred. There should be no distortion or flicker of the image. Eighty characters wide by twenty-four text lines on the screen are usual standards. A color monitor should be considered, as some software and graphics packages will use color to enhance the messages on the screen. The equipment should be tried out in the search location to decide on the best type, size, and arrangement.

Synchronized speed of microcomputer, modem, software, printer, and other computer components. Search equipment should operate at at least 1200 baud with the option for faster communication speeds. Slower speeds may be satisfactory for menu-driven systems used by patrons.

Readable print quality from the printer, which should also be quiet, fast, and reliable. The operation and maintenance should be simple and putting in new ribbons, loading paper, and trouble-shooting paper jams should be logical, straightforward processes.

Support by the manufacturer. Good manuals, an 800 customer assistance telephone number, and a user group geared to the product can be important.

Servicing. Can equipment be taken care of on-campus, or should a service contract be arranged? Similar machines should be available for backup when necessary.

Configuration and capability. A modem may be built into the microcomputer or a separate external modem must be purchased to link the equipment to the telephone line. A direct connection will provide the best service. It must be capable of either full or half duplex modes with asynchronous communication. A baud rate of 1200 is preferable over 300; the capability of 2400 or higher is advisable. Some modems have a memory for storing telephone numbers and automating selected functions. Check on the versatility for pulse or touch-tone dialing, automatic dialing, and redial functions. Hayes is a standard; usually Hayes-compatible is specified. A modem with the capability of filtering out noise or static from the communications line is a valuable asset since interference becomes more pronounced as the speed of transmission increases. The modem must obviously be compatible with the microcomputer and the software.

Accessories for microcomputers can help solve environmental problems or make working at the machines more comfortable. These items can include surge protectors if the electrical system is subject to fluctuations; a disk file; antistatic floor mats; and glare-reducing screens. While available funds may limit the choice of microcomputer, there are many alternatives to consider among the standard operating machines. Emphasis should be placed on those features that assist in online searching, with a maximum amount of memory.

SOFTWARE TO ASSIST ONLINE SEARCHING

Communications software must be used with the microcomputer for it to function as a searching terminal. The major types of software are: communications, data management, spreadsheets, and word processing. Communication software aids the connection between the microcomputer and the host vendor system, provides an interface when needed for assisting search procedures, and can include some support features such as accounting or editing search results. Software can facilitate access to databases by experienced searchers or can simplify search commands so that undergraduates can do their own searching. Owning a number of software packages gives the microcomputer a wide range of capabilities. As vendor systems and clientele expectations change, the search service equipment can be adapted by changing the software. Searchers can decide what kind of assistance is the most helpful, and procedures can be developed to support the software features that make searching more efficient.

However, to increase the options of the experienced searcher, communication software must be carefully selected and the microcomputer must have the capacity to take advantage of the features desired. Most software is purchased as disks containing programs loaded onto a microcomputer to govern its actions until another program is entered or the machine is turned off. The machine must have enough memory to store the program and still receive and manipulate a sizable amount of information. If the software has been on the market for a while, published reviews will evaluate its features. A second or third edition will have improved the product. Nevertheless, the software must be easy to install, use, and must be helpful and unobtrusive during the search process.

Most communications software provides the capability of downloading search results onto a disk. The patrons need only know that search results are in an ASCII compatible format; they should then be able to read and manipulate this file of search results on their own computers.

Software for Different Tasks

To assist online searching, communications software is marketed with an increasing number of names and options. Software packages often contain programs for a number of operations that can be used separately or can be linked for various functions. Features provided by these systems usually fall in one or more of the following general categories:

Presearch Connection, or "Gateway" Software · These programs perform the tasks required to gain access to the vendor system or database: dialing and redialing a series of telephone numbers until contact is made, making the connection, and sending the password. The primary function is automating the link between the search microcomputer and the host system.

Intermediary, Interface, or "Front-end" Software · This software performs the gateway function and accomplishes additional tasks before, during, and after the search. The searcher may choose assistance during the interactive search process with procedures simplified to the point that he or she is asked for responses to questions that define the search topic, help choose a database, convert common terms to the more sophisticated terms of the database, and perform the Boolean logic. The software may be constructed to interact with a specified database, a group of databases from a single vendor, or a wide range of sources. It may also be geared to different levels to assist the trained searcher or the novice with no searching experience. Some packages allow the searcher to choose the amount of assistance given by selecting either menu-driven or command-driven interfaces.

Developing the search strategy on the computer while offline and then uploading or sending the commands in sequence will assist the experienced searcher, but must be arranged so that the searcher maintains control and an interactive capability. It must be possible to override pretyped commands. Sending the search results to a printer or downloading to a patron's disk are further options that help the searcher provide a more versatile product for the patron. Some software can also act as an emulator—an interface that allows the searcher to use the commands from one database system to search that of another unfamiliar vendor. Expertise on one system can then be utilized in the second system.

Record keeping may be a feature of intermediary software that automatically records the search activity: the database used and the length and cost of each search. These data are cumulated to provide weekly or monthly reports.

Postsearch Processing · The same software or a different package may be required to manipulate results after signing off the database system. Potential operations include converting records to a form suitable for handling in a different program; mathematical calculations or statistical analysis of data; reformatting citations and sorting them; editing bibliographies, organizing, and indexing them; and other changes in the output to improve or alter the final results. The patron can be provided with a selected bibliography, a classified mailing list, or an analysis of the data secured online.

Level of Assistance

Software is designed to provide various amounts of assistance for searchers. It can have a minimal effect on experienced searchers, who will barely notice that their software dials the telephone for them and permits downloading of the search results on a disk, but is "transparent" or nonintrusive during the online database search session. In contrast, other software guides the patron or researcher by asking for a response at each step of the search, from selecting the appropriate database to printing the citations or data received.

Software may be command-driven or menu-driven. Command-driven software requires training and experience, since search statements ask directly for an action to take place. This characteristic is important for more complex, lengthier searches. The results are delivered much quicker and more efficiently than menu-driven software, which provides a list of options and proceeds when the choices are made. A menu system directs the untrained searcher at each step and is best for brief and simple searches. Potential assistance provided by software packages for online searchers with varying amounts of experience:

Assisting experienced searchers:

dial and redial to link with the telecommunications network
automatic log on and off the search system
search term preparation and editing on the computer before con-
    necting with the database system
automatically sending prepared search statements or uploading
storing profiles and search strategies to recall as needed
downloading of search results to a disk
merging files from various vendors
sending results to patron electronically
automatic search accounting, collection of statistics.

Assisting inexperienced searchers:

menu assistance when needed with unfamiliar procedures and
    sources
option of bypassing commands and steps as proficiency develops
availability of help screens with instructions and search aids
emulator for searching new system with familiar search language.

Assisting patron search:

helping choose search terms
database descriptions provided to aid in selection
menus or graphics to simplify search techniques
system tutorials, prompts and instructions.

Software for experienced searchers can assist the routine procedures of a search, but must not limit or restrict the flexibility of the
search system. Such system features as sort, limit, search operators,
and all format options provided by the database vendor must be fully
usable. Minimum assistance provided should include the storage of a
list of telephone numbers representing TELENET and TYMNET and
other communications systems. Other numbers representing different
networks or databases can be included and should be activated by hitting a single key. The desired telephone number should then be selected and automatically dialed, with a sequence of other numbers
tried in turn when there is no response or the line is busy. This capability may be supplied by a "smart" modem or be part of the communications software. An automatic logon to the desired system should take
place once the connection is secured.

Search preparation on the microcomputer before connecting to the database assists an inexperienced or slow typist and allows errors to be corrected. The searcher preparing a search with a patron present can confirm the basic strategy, add or change synonyms and various spellings, and review them on the computer monitor or screen before the search begins. A signal to the microcomputer will activate the telephone connection, sending the password and connecting to the database. The prepared search will then be sent automatically as a block or line by line to the host system and the results transmitted back to the microcomputer. The searcher should be able to interrupt this automatic sequence at any point and to assume an interactive exchange.

The results of the search should be printed, downloaded to a disk, or captured in the buffer or internal memory of the microcomputer. A signal should activate an automatic logoff. The searcher should be able to turn on the printer or the storage disk as needed. Usually the fastest transmission from the database is accomplished by storing or downloading on a disk with printing taking place when offline. The faster equipment makes the results available immediately and only for special printouts will there be a need for ordering offline prints from the database vendor.

Software geared for patron use takes the place of the searcher as intermediary. The guided systems are usually easy to use, utilize plain language terms, take more time to carry out a search, and generally restrict the resources that can be accessed, flexibility, or the ability to use all the functions of the database vendor. Communication with the patron will usually be in the form of questions with responses selected from menus or graphics that utilize boxes or forms, and may include explanations or help screens. These systems make it easy to do brief, uncomplicated searches.

Accounting Features

Software packages that include accounting features may provide a billing statement or invoice for patrons at the end of a search session. Usually some of the information is entered by the searcher before the start, such as date, name of patron, department, subject, charge code, and searcher's name. When the search is completed and the accounting key is struck, the files used, elapsed time, and search costs are automatically recorded.

This data is accumulated and daily, weekly, or monthly reports can be prepared. Summaries will include a list of searches by the names of searchers, databases, patron names, and vendors. Reports can be printed out regularly and are especially useful when it is important to keep track of costs or budget preparation is underway.

Modifying Search Results

Patrons can be advised that search results downloaded on a disk are in the ASCII format, and that any compatible word processing program can be used to access the information. Vendors are increasingly providing formats that will tag components of the records for easier use in word processing, or data can be printed out in a manner to facilitate transferring the figures to a spreadsheet program or statistical package. Both of these options are designed to minimize the amount of manipulation or reentry of data for further processing.

The software package being used to assist online searching may include a component for manipulating records after they are downloaded, or the library may own a word processing, bibliographic, or other program for this purpose. The computer can enhance the search results in a variety of ways to provide a better product for the patron or to make an edited bibliography for library uses. Some capabilities are useful for the searcher, while other applications can be better handled by the patron.

Features of Software Packages

For the searcher:

> Improving the appearance of the search results. A cover sheet can be automatically prepared with the patron's name, date, and search subject. Other information can be added to identify the library and searcher.
>
> Eliminating inappropriate citations.
>
> Merging two or more files and eliminating duplicates.
>
> Editing records to retain only necessary information.
>
> Standardizing records to one format for bibliographies.
>
> Converting field codes and similar tags to full name for easier identification.
>
> Sorting by various fields to organize library guides, bibliographies for classes, and reference lists for researchers.
>
> Adding information to the records such as those items held in the library system.
>
> Creating current awareness publications for faculty.
>
> Sending an entire file to a patron via electronic mail.
>
> Saving a search and using it to demonstrate the search process for students.

For the patron:

> Eliminating unnecessary material including records not relevant to the topic; system banners and search statements; or fields such as identifiers, indexing terms, and subject codes.

Reformatting records to a standard citation for consistency with patron's bibliographic file or publication need.

Adding notes to the records about content or adding other references from a personal file.

Transferring data to a spreadsheet and statistically analyzing data to produce tables and graphs.

Ranking records by the occurrence of important words.

Sorting by author, title, or other significant category. Creating an index to the file.

Using as a minidatabase and searching with Boolean operators.

CRITERIA FOR SELECTING SOFTWARE PACKAGES

Essential features of any software selected to assist online searching are: automatic dial and redial from a list of stored telephone numbers, log on, log off, and other repeated sequences of commands activated from specific keys; static control; and downloading search results to a disk. Some of these features may be performed by software that is a component of the modem. The need for other functions and the various levels of assistance will depend on the individual situation, the searchers' experience, the type of searches performed, and the databases used most often. As more helpful features and conveniences become available, software should be examined carefully for the versatility of the operations and whether additional features are limited to particular vendor systems, selected databases, or specific situations.

Basic General Features

Software producer is reliable and experienced.

Good reviews and recommendations by other searchers are available. Be sure that the package has been tested and used by others.

Good documentation has been prepared: a user manual with clear examples, a newsletter.

Clear and complete directions allow for installation with ease.

There are different versions for different types of microcomputers.

Options furnish various levels of assistance for searchers. They should provide for skipping steps or moving to a different level as experience is gained. Both command-driven and menu-driven systems are provided.

Access to several vendor systems is possible. All searching functions are available regardless of database vendor system accessed.

Related software components for word processing or data manipulation are available.

Revisions and updates are produced at regular intervals. Supplied free, by subscription, or sold as new editions.

A demonstration disk covers all functions.

Customer service includes an 800 telephone number for extended hours.

A limited amount of training is required to use the software competently. (Is a tutorial disk available?)

Cost is related to convenience and to the number of features provided.

Technical Specifications

standard ASCII (American Standard Code for Information Interchange) format that enables computers to recognize and exchange information

asynchronous communication

compatibility with microcomputer and modem

amount of memory required of microcomputer

filter capability to detect and suppress line noise

passwords masked or erased as received

text scrolls to review content of buffer

easy-to-find break key with a signal long enough to interrupt the communication

logical, simplified language for controls and actions

telephone numbers and passwords stored and easily changed

printer operation control

status reports on the screen, which relate buffer contents, room on disk, printer on/off, online/offline, accounting in operation, and insert mode

function keys (preferably ten to twenty) that can be programmed for specific tasks

marking and editing buffer contents before downloading to disk

downloading in ASCII format

accounting and search statistics gathered for as many activities as possible and covering all search services utilized.

Aids for Searchers

easy-to-remember commands

logical, step-by-step search procedure

simple, clear use of keys on keyboard

search strategy preparation and editing before online connection

automatic dialing, redial, and log on to system
help files that can be called up during search
storage and recall of search strategy
ability to modify or recall last command
type ahead as responses to search statements are received
ability to standardize command languages among vendor systems
tutorial disks for learning software procedures
uploading of blocks of prepared statements to search system
downloading capability to receive information and transfer it to a
     disk
frequently used strategies or other text stored to recall when set-
     ting up or when needed during an online search
ability to manipulate downloaded search results
creation of files, such as list of patrons and search topics.

Reviews of software by librarians who have tried a variety of packages for online searching will provide the best guidance. It is especially important that the software producer has made provisions for changing conditions through providing regular updates and/or creating new editions as necessary.

SOURCES OF SOFTWARE

Communications software can be developed in-house, or public domain software can be copied from another disk or downloaded from an electronic mail system. Commercially produced software can be purchased from a software distributor, an online vendor, or a database producer. For consistency, reliable assistance, and continued development of new options for searchers, a package from a commercial source is first choice. As competition increases among the software producers, costs should decrease and products improve, so choices should be reviewed regularly. While there are inexpensive basic programs available for less than $50, software from the major producers can be expected to cost between $125 and $500, with packages for related services an additional fee. Some software packages are created to access one or two primary database system(s) and, although they can be used as a gateway to search other vendor systems, when this occurs the major software features are not available. It is easier to devise a software product that provides extensive assistance or does more tasks if it is limited to a specific vendor database system.

Examples of some popular software packages currently being used to assist online searching include those in the following lists. All generally provide the essential features, including preparing search strategy offline and uploading, and downloading the results.

Database Vendors

Dialoglink, Dialog Information Services, Inc.

for experienced searchers
microcomputer: IBM, DOS, 128 K memory
access to Dialog, Knowledge Index
menu system, which can be bypassed for native mode
can be used to access other services
features include type ahead, recall/modify last command, help
    screens
collects data on search activity, costs
prints individual search or summary reports
two modules: *Dialog Communications Manager* and *Dialog
    Accounts Manager*
evaluation disk available.

Searchmaster, SDC Information Services

for end-users
microcomputer: IBM, DOS, 128 K memory
access to BRS, Dialog, NLM, ORBIT
can be used to access other systems
gateway service provides automatic dial up and log on. Scripts
    can be written to perform specified search functions. Can be
    used to restrict searchers to particular databases or types of
    searches.

Wilsearch, H. W. Wilson Co.

for end-users
microcomputer: IBM, DOS, 128 K memory
access only to Wilsonline
menu system or native mode
help screens, menus for subject areas, databases, search terms
licensing fee, charged by number of searches
demonstration disk available.

Database Producers

microCAMBRIDGE, Cambridge Scientific Abstracts

for end-users
microcomputer: IBM, DOS, 128 K memory
primarily for access to Cambridge Scientific Abstracts' data-
    bases on Dialog: AQUATIC SCIENCES AND FISHERIES ABSTRACTS, CON-

FERENCE PAPERS INDEX, ISMEC, LIFE SCIENCES COLLECTION, OCEANIC
ABSTRACTS, POLLUTION ABSTRACTS
menu system, which can be bypassed
other Dialog databases can also be accessed
demonstration disk available.

microDISCLOSURE, Disclosure Information Group

for end-users
microcomputer: IBM, DOS, 256 K memory
assisted searching of DISCLOSURE database on Dialog
menu system, which cannot be bypassed
no uploading; does not utilize all Dialog features.

Search Helper, Information Access Co.

for end-users
microcomputer: IBM, DOS, 128 K memory; Apple II, 64 K
  memory
access to Information Access Company's databases: MAGAZINE
  INDEX, NATIONAL NEWSPAPER INDEX, TRADE AND INDUSTRY INDEX, LE-
  GAL RESOURCE INDEX, NEWSEARCH and MANAGEMENT CONTENTS
menu system, limited searching flexibility
does not download
subscription, fixed rate per search.

Other Software Producers

Crosstalk, Microstuf Inc.

for intermediate-level searchers
microcomputer: IBM, DOS, 96 K memory
command-driven
script files can be created to automate particular functions.

Pro-Search, Personal Bibliographic Software

for experienced or end-users
microcomputer: IBM, DOS, 256 K memory
access to Dialog, BRS
native mode or menu system
can access other systems
high-level mode provides choices from database descriptions,
  lists of subject terms, other help screens

can use selected Dialog commands to search BRS and reverse procedure

can activate saved search strategy at any time before or during search

accounting of Dialog and BRS activities; prints cover sheet, reports

related software: *Pro-Cite* and *Biblio-Link* for converting downloaded records to standard format and preparing bibliographies

demonstration disk.

Sci-Mate Searcher, Institute for Scientific Information

for end-user

microcomputer: IBM, DOS, 128 K memory

access to BRS, Dialog, NLM, ORBIT, Questel

menu or command systems

provides passive mode for other systems

related software: *Sci-Mate Manager* and *Sci-Mate Editor* for managing bibliographic files and preparing records for publications.

Search Works, Online Research Systems, Inc.

for experienced searchers

microcomputer: IBM, DOS, 256 K memory

access to BRS, Dialog, NLM, ORBIT

provides type-ahead, search statement recall and editing, scrolling

includes online search guide that can be called up on or offline for brief explanations of commands, procedures, and formats for the four systems

accounting functions, cover sheets, reports

provides postsearch processing including ranking, sorting, and indexing.

Features that the software provides should be carefully considered and matched to the needs of the library and comfort of searchers. Software reviews can be found in current journals such as: *Online, Database, Library Software Review, Microcomputers in Libraries, Small Computers in Libraries, Library Journal, Wilson Library Bulletin* and *Database End User*. Databases that include software reviews are: .MENU—THE INTERNATIONAL SOFTWARE DATABASE, the MICROCOMPUTER INDEX, the MICROCOMPUTER SOFTWARE AND HARDWARE GUIDE and the ONLINE MICROCOMPUTER SOFTWARE GUIDE AND DIRECTORY.

MANAGEMENT CONCERNS

Downloading Search Results

Downloading is the term usually used for transferring information from a database or host computer system to a smaller computer and retaining it on an electronic storage device, such as part of the machine's internal memory or buffer, or on a separate disk. Patrons may request delivery of search results in this form instead of printing. Usually downloading is a matter of convenience for the patron, who may have access to a microcomputer for editing the results, or who wishes to add the citations to a file of references maintained on his or her own microcomputer. The speed of information transmission by new microcomputers and software has made downloading a convenient method of capturing the results of a search. In addition, data storage capacity for microcomputers has increased while costs have decreased dramatically. Many different commercial software packages are available for manipulating these standard text files. BRS has always tagged the components of records and Dialog now provides a specific format with tagged fields for assisting in the use of downloaded bibliographic records. Dialog also provides a report output for numerical databases that tabulates figures to assist in the conversion to a spreadsheet program or statistical package.

Considerable controversy about copyright regulations has accompanied the technological developments of microcomputers with commercial software, which has made it a relatively simple process to receive transmitted data at increasingly faster speeds and to store greater amounts of information at a relatively small cost. The one-time use by an individual and retention of downloaded records for a short time is generally considered "fair use" of the material. Since search costs usually include citation fees, the patron or the library has paid for retrieving the information. Although increasingly fast microcomputers can download these records very quickly, the costs per citation can be more significant than the online connect-time charge. Any effort to keep a personal file of references current must result in other searches of the producer's database. Downloaded searches delivered to patrons should include a notice that identifies the owner of the database source and the copyright regulations in effect.

However, any other use of downloaded records for purposes such as a minidatabase, a published bibliography, or plan for distributing multiple copies of the material should only be done with the approval of the appropriate database producer. This procedure is necessary if any of these applications are for a commercial product. Many producers have policies for such situations and will give permission for reuse of the records for certain purposes or provide a contract with set charges per citation.

Procedures for Use of Microcomputers and Software

The procedure manual should have a section for the selection and use of the microcomputer and software, including:

Equipment should meet standard specifications. Both microcomputer and software packages should be purchased with the approval of a systems librarian or someone responsible for computers in the library or on the campus.

Only the search service manager, systems librarian, or other designated person should change any of the machine configurations. The responsible person should be contacted for assistance if any problem arises. A backup person familiar with the equipment will assure the availability of adequate expertise.

Software commercially produced is preferred so that staff turnover will not result in the library owning a program no one understands.

One copy of the software should be purchased for each microcomputer used for searching. Most packages are not copy-protected and should be kept in a master file for backup with a copy on the microcomputer it is used with. The software can either be loaded on the hard disk or copied onto a floppy disk for use with the machine.

A procedure should be established for evaluating new software and updates to packages in use. New software should be purchased when additional features are significant.

The search service manager will review all the functions offered by the software and select those best suited for the library situation.

As additional software packages are purchased, an inventory should be maintained for control over this material. All disks should be clearly labeled and maintained in a suitable environment.

Manuals for microcomputers and the software packages should be kept in a convenient location near the equipment.

Staff shall have adequate training before operating the microcomputer(s) and utilizing new software.

Regular searcher meetings should include discussions of search options provided by software packages and maximum use of equipment features.

Use of the microcomputer should be limited to specific personnel. The search service manager or head of public services or reference may approve use by other individuals. Tasks for the equipment may be limited to online searching for patrons on commercial vendor systems (as opposed to access to the campus computer), short searches by reference librarians, and library-related projects. Priorities may be established with searchers working with patrons first; searching for reference questions or interlibrary loan verification, second; and library research, word processing, and personal use a last priority, which can be bumped by a request for a patron search.

Searches that result in lengthy printouts of more than a few citations should usually be downloaded to the buffer or a disk to take advantage of the maximum speed of communication. When the search is concluded, the results may be transmitted from either the buffer or the disk to the printer for a hard copy. Offline printouts should only be ordered when appearance is important or the searcher does not wish to print off an extensive bibliography.

Each searcher is responsible for any search results or strategies stored in the microcomputer memory or buffer. Information that needs to be retained should generally be transferred to a separate disk kept by the searcher.

A policy should be established for the length of time downloaded search results will be retained in the library on a floppy or hard disk. Stored search strategies should be reviewed regularly.

Downloading will be performed with consideration for the copyright laws, which generally means one copy of search results may be downloaded for patrons for their personal use.

Training for Microcomputer/Software Search Assistance

Good software does not replace the need for the searcher to be skilled in negotiating with the patron, developing search strategy, or competency in other facets of searching online databases. Searchers should understand that software provides assistance for very specialized tasks, or more general help for inexperienced searchers.

Introducing the use of a microcomputer and software to a search service will require searchers to learn new procedures. A formal session can be held with all searchers, or individual tutoring can take place to review the new protocols, the method of handling disks, the options for search procedures, and accounting features. Microcomputers offer the opportunity to provide additional services for patrons such as cover sheets for search results or downloading. These procedures may be entirely new capabilities for the experienced searcher and the increased options bring more and different steps to remember. Manuals should be available to all searchers.

Regular review of the procedures should reinforce the time and cost saving features. Preparing strategy on the microcomputer before logging on and then typing ahead as the search is underway are both techniques that can be used to produce a cost-effective search and help compensate for poor typing skills; however, this takes careful planning. Downloading allows receipt of lengthy search results at maximum speed, but the searcher must have an extra disk available, know how to delete old searches, what to do when the disk is full, and how to transfer the information. The printer can produce a copy during the search and after the search is completed from either the buffer or the disk. Additional functions can be learned as they become available on new editions of the software. It is difficult to find the time to learn and practice new techniques, especially when adequate searching can be done with established methods, but once the next step is made to faster systems and assistance with routine procedures, it would be difficult to go back to straight searching. It is also a waste of equipment if the microcomputer is used only in a terminal mode without taking advantage of the many options available to give the searcher more time for the search itself, rather than managing the hardware.

The availability of a menu-assisted search system may be valuable when an appropriate database is available from a vendor the searcher is not familiar with. This end-user software can also be used to start the training of new searchers; to initiate staff who have never used a microcomputer and who will be operating one in another library position; and to teach support staff who may be doing some limited online searching, such as for interlibrary loan verification or for completing book purchase requests.

Assistance provided by a good microcomputer system has become very important for searchers at all levels of experience. Choosing from hundreds of databases, remembering several complex system procedures with different command languages, learning about content and structure of the databases, and recalling techniques to improve efficiency or to incorporate the newest upgrades to the systems are incredibly demanding of librarians who perform searching as only a part of their responsibilities. Machine control of the routine portions of the search process is increasingly necessary, but this help must not limit the options and interactive searching capabilities. Even the most experienced, expert searchers who find that they can press a button to be automatically logged on to a system, send an already prepared search strategy, type ahead to continue the search, and quickly download the results and log off, will be converts to microcomputer assisted searching and will be eagerly awaiting the next edition of the software.

Bibliography

Casbon, Susan. "Online Searching with a Microcomputer—Getting Started." *Online* 7:42–46 (1983).

Clancy, Stephen. "Do It for Less! A Comparison of Low-Cost Communications Software for the IBM PC." *Database* 9:52–61 (1986).

Garman, Nancy. "Downloading . . . Still a Live Issue? A Survey of Database Producer Policies for Both Online Services and Laserdisks." *Online* 10:15–25 (1986).

Hawkins, Donald T., and Louise R. Levy. "Front End Software for Online Database Searching. Part 1: Definitions, System Features, and Evaluation." *Online* 9:30–37 (1985); "Part 3. Product Selection Chart and Bibliography." *Online* 10:49–58 (1986).

Public Access Microcomputers in Academic Libraries: The Mann Library Model at Cornell University. Edited by Howard Curtis. Chicago: American Library Assn., 1987.

Tenopir, Carol. "Online Searching with a Microcomputer." *Library Journal* 110:42–43 (1985).

12

PROVIDING END-USER SEARCHING *276*
    Reasons for Offering End-user Searching *276*
    Problems of Providing End-user Searching *276*
    Academic End-users *278*
USER-FRIENDLY SYSTEMS *280*
    Major Vendor Search Systems Designed
      for End-users *281*
    Front-end Software *282*
    Intermediary Host System *284*
    Local Databases on Floppy, CD-ROM,
      and Laser Disks *285*
SETTING UP AND ORGANIZING FACILITIES
  FOR END-USER SEARCHING *289*
    Space and Equipment *289*
    Management *291*
    Costs and Charging Fees *292*
SELECTING AN END-USER SERVICE *293*
    Factors to Consider *294*
    Important End-user System Features *296*
TRAINING THE PATRON SEARCHER *298*
    Training Goals *299*
    Methods of Training End-users *299*
FINANCIAL CONSIDERATIONS *302*
ROLE OF THE INTERMEDIARY *303*

Online Database Searching
by Patrons

Using a computer instead of a printed index to find information is an increasingly popular choice for patrons of an academic library. This option may be the only practical method of providing online searching for a substantial number of undergraduates and other patrons who would like to use library resources independently. In many instances patrons are already using terminals to search the public catalog, so it is a logical step to use a similar technique to find references in journals. As more faculty and students have microcomputers available in the laboratory, office, dormitory, and in their homes, they will be accustomed to using them for a variety of tasks and will feel comfortable sitting at a computer work station to find the information they need. Patron or end-user searching in this context refers to the access of commercial online databases, usually in the library, by individuals who expect to utilize the information themselves.

As online databases have developed, searching them to retrieve desired information has meant learning complicated and exacting techniques. Some of the procedures for searching may have changed over the years, but this has usually meant that there are even more access points to search larger files, and making the correct decisions quickly at each step demands concentration and experience, with backup by good system manuals. Obtaining passwords; logging on and off; learning about the databases' subject and document content, indexing procedures, and vocabulary; using new versions of equipment and different types of software have added to the complexity for the occasional user. In addition, the various database systems require knowledge of different search languages, separate contracts, and varied options that may be available on one system and not another. The proliferation of databases and directory, full-text, and numerical files, each requiring a different approach for the searcher, has added to the knowledge base needed to effectively search for information on research topics.

Now many of these complicating factors have been bypassed or solved by one or more of the simplified systems for the inexperienced searcher. Different intervention points between the searcher and the database have provided a number of choices for simple database search systems. These options include a user-friendly search language offered by the database vendor, software for this purpose mounted by the searcher on a local microcomputer, or an intermediary system that can be accessed online to communicate with the unskilled searcher, converting common language into necessary search protocols, carrying out the search, and delivering the results. The database may be located on a remote computer or locally on a CD-ROM disk. However, as these simplified search systems are developed, they usually result in a less versatile system, often limited to particular databases or specific search procedures. They produce, then, a different level of searching neither precise nor comprehensive. The results of a database search by an easy-to-use search language will not have the probing and selectivity of the expert search system, but will usually retrieve some information on a subject that has been defined by a few key words and that may be entirely adequate for the patron.

Although there are many choices among the end-user systems to solve the interface problems between patron and database, other factors may limit their use in libraries. Costs are always an important item, and finding space in the building, the demand on a limited staff, and the need for new equipment, furniture, additional telephone lines, the training of both staff and patron, and possibly charging a fee are necessary considerations. One of the difficult problems is that only one person can use a computer terminal or work station at a time. If a lengthy search is needed, there must also be time allotted to printing the results. Even two, three, or more machines limit access to a selected few of the many students needing to find some articles when papers are due and reports must be prepared. Methods of scheduling machine time, limiting usage to prepared search topics, or to a specific amount of time online can be management intensive and may not be worth the investment. Applying access barriers also limits the value of the systems for browsing and learning to search effectively. At other times, during vacations or between semesters, the equipment may sit unused. The choice between an economical system that only has charges when used and one that is very expensive, but has no limit to time "online," is a difficult one.

Some scientists may have already learned to search databases, but found they did not use them enough to remember the procedures. On the other hand, students may be eager to try online literature searching, since some may be already using the home-oriented services such as CompuServe and are using computers regularly for their class assignments and laboratory projects. While these patrons will appreciate finding microcomputers in the library, there are others who may have never used a computer. Among this latter group are some very knowledgeable about the literature, and others who have rarely consulted library resources. Online vendors, database producers, and software publishers are increasingly attempting to assist these patrons at all levels of computer and bibliographic expertise by providing systems that are easier to use, or interfaces that translate common language into the specific search commands of the major online database systems. As more full-text and numerical databases become available, there may be increasing interest and usability for the patron who will be able to find entire articles and specific data online. Finding the information rather than references to the literature will appeal to patrons who do not want to make the effort to track down references or who need only a few facts. However, the library is an especially important place to use computer-assisted information retrieval because it supplements the access provided by printed indexes and brings online retrieval close to the supporting documents. Not only can the library provide this literature, but librarians can assist the novice searcher when problems arise. These patrons may need assistance when learning to use the equipment and some of the database systems. Librarians are a logical choice to take on this training of end-users. They can make sure that patrons know about the various methods of finding information and when each method is most appropriate.

One major function of end-user systems is to take some of the pressure off the library search service by having patrons run their own simple and routine searches. The quality of the search service for providing in-depth and precise searches on research topics can be jeopardized by an overload of requests. The system of appointments and working with patrons on an individual basis requires a time commitment to provide an effective product. By developing a do-it-yourself searching system as another alternative to the scheduled online search or the use of a printed index, the patron can be encouraged to use the most satisfactory information retrieval system. Brief searches that secure a small list of references or less precise information on well-defined subjects can easily be done by the patron. Even if librarians feel concerned that the library user may not be finding sufficient information, the individual may be very pleased with the results, since he or she needs only a few citations to get started on a research project. Many individuals, and especially busy faculty members, will not wish to learn to search even a friendly system when they need information that is comprehensive, up-to-date, with complex terminology and requiring careful planning. They will continue to rely on a trained and skilled searcher.

Branch or departmental libraries may be especially appropriate locations to implement an end-user service. There may be more flexibility in organizing services, and databases and training can be focused on a specific subject area. The clientele is also likely to be more uniform as far as experience with computers and requirements for library research are concerned.

PROVIDING END-USER SEARCHING

Many library patrons are in a hurry to find information and will use computers to search for literature online if the computers are available and easy to use. Not only is this a faster method than searching a printed index, but the individual can usually receive a printed copy of the reference list. The many information sources available to patrons can include citations to journal articles, full-text magazine articles, and data such as cost of living or census figures. Not all of these may be of interest to the library's clientele, but more resources are constantly becoming available.

Reasons for Offering End-user Searching

To relieve the search service of performing brief, simple searches
To help develop the independence of library patrons
To make it easy for patrons to do an online search on their topic
without having to find a librarian and make an appointment
To allow patrons to do a search and get some immediate results instead of having to explain the topic to someone else who will do the searching and who may not understand the problem
To provide a method for offering online searching for large numbers of undergraduates
To attract students to the library and to increase their interest in information retrieval
To use as a means of teaching information seeking skills for current work and future career applications
To encourage patrons to learn greater appreciation for the search process and what an online search can produce
To use as a tool to encourage patrons to learn more about indexes and other library resources
To create more use of library materials, especially journals
To enable the library to offer low-cost or free online searching
To generate excellent publicity for the library.

Problems of Providing End-user Searching

Only one person can use a microcomputer or terminal at a time.
Patrons may expect to find the full text of articles, and they may not realize what they are searching.
Patrons may not understand when other sources will provide better or more information.
Online systems are not usually suitable for general or historical questions.

Librarians must be responsible for one more service and may have to provide more training, supervision, and maintenance of additional equipment.

May mean more scheduling, records, additional charging system.

Patrons may need help with search technique, interpreting results.

Librarians will be expected to know more about microcomputers, additional online systems, and how to cope with a wider variety of searching problems.

Additional costs for access to databases, equipment, supplies, space, furniture, staffing.

The critical elements in developing the capability for patrons to do their own searching are simplicity and results. Presuming that patrons are interested in becoming more independent in their library research, they will wish to access databases as easily as they have used printed indexes. As work progresses toward making the online catalog accessible to the public, the same must be done for online databases. Whether the library's choice is to provide online access to one of the major vendors, to an intermediary online system, or to information stored locally on a CD-ROM disk will not matter to the patron primarily interested in finding needed information. However, librarians cannot just provide passwords that will allow access to databases, but must supply equipment and space for patrons to use them. The equipment must be secured, and placed next to a telephone if online access is made available. If the service is successful, there will be much demand for more equipment, passwords, and telephone lines.

An online service for patrons to use can be considered another index—available for patrons to use without intervention or assistance unless they ask. In this case the most simple, self-explanatory process is needed. CD-ROM can fit in this category, since it is always available without having to make a connection to a telephone line. In addition, the searcher does not have to be efficient, but can browse the file until something appropriate is found. If, however, the system provided for patrons is based on a connection with a remote computer, there is need for efficiency and a responsibility for librarians to teach both faculty and students how to use online services effectively. This can be as casual as help on an individual basis at the terminal, or as formal as classes on search techniques. The academic librarian must also consider how to integrate database searching into the procedures for library research and how to teach searching skills that will be appropriate for both printed and online sources. An important aspect is making sure that the patron knows what method of information retrieval is most likely to result in the desired material.

An easy-to-use online system does much of the work. It asks questions or provides a menu of choices to help make the decisions that mark the progress of a search. Some programs can interpret an individual's ordinary language and convert it into the correct form of search statements. But the most successful interpretation of common vocabulary cannot make up for fuzzy thinking or a search on a general subject that could be better approached in a printed index. Simplifying computer-assisted systems usually means that the number of tasks that can be accomplished is also reduced; consequently it is often not possible to search by fields, by concept codes, and other components of the database record. These features are usually not important factors, as most patrons will limit their searching to a few subject terms. When the topic becomes more complex and more comprehensive coverage of the literature is desired, it is then essential to examine the terminology, work out a search strategy, and utilize the more sophisticated procedures of the direct database access.

Costs play a role here, as they do in all online searching. The uncertain charges for a single search and the very high cost of a CD-ROM unit that allows unlimited searching at one price make choices difficult. Major questions to answer when it is decided to turn some searching over to patrons include what is the best type of systems for the library's clientele, how to make enough equipment available, what are the costs and how to finance them, and how to integrate the various information services.

Patron searching increases independence for finding information in the library, relieves the search service of performing simple searches, and provides an additional avenue to teach about library resources. Problems include funding for this additional service, more responsibilities for librarians, and the need to be sure students understand the place of online searching among other library access tools.

Academic End-users

The academic library patrons who are potential users of a self-service online search facility include:

Undergraduate Students · Students are not surprised to find microcomputers in the library; many of them will have used computers in elementary school and throughout their school careers. With some colleges requiring microcomputers for incoming freshmen and using computers in classes, students may have more experience with computers than the searchers, who have limited their involvement to searching online databases. Students are often impatient with printed sources and may be easily discouraged when they do not quickly find useful articles. Many students need only a few citations for a term paper or a class project. The computer offers a fast method of finding some references and is a more interesting challenge than the printed index; a printer to copy off the results is popular.

Most students are usually not as concerned about the source they are searching as they are in getting results. If they have to sign up for a time on the computer or sit through a training session first, there are many who will choose the more familiar printed index. For their purpose, the simpler the procedure the better, and information from a small selection of databases covering a good range of popular, business, social science, and general science periodicals, even if they do not include the latest issues, will be satisfactory.

Researchers: Faculty, Staff, and Graduate Students · The wide use of microcomputers in laboratories and offices has made them a familiar sight on campus, and they are used by staff and students for many purposes such as collecting data, analyzing results of experiments, writing reports with word processor programs, maintaining a reprint file, or participating in a conference on an electronic mail system. Expertise and practice on various projects has given individuals confidence that they can do their own literature searching with equal ease when they need a bibliography for a publication, a reference for a particular procedure, or an investigation into a new area of research.

While it is important that researchers realize the value of working with a trained searcher for extensive and precise information retrieval, literature searching by this group should certainly be satisfactory for scanning the literature, finding a few references on a topic, or searching for publications of other scientists. For more comprehensive retrieval of information they must be made aware of the online search service and the availability of expert searchers to achieve optimum results. Many researchers want to find information when they need it and are frustrated if they have to make an appointment and wait for a convenient time to do a search with a librarian.

It is important that researchers receive prompt attention when they need extensive or more complex searches; otherwise, they will settle for less effective but speedier results. There are faculty who follow the literature closely and others who have been working with a searcher for literature retrieval for many years and now feel that they understand the process well. They may choose to learn the standard search systems and maintain expertise in a few databases. Other faculty are too busy to be interested in doing their own searching and do not often come to the library. These individuals will continue to ask for help and will still send graduate students to do much of their literature retrieval. Librarians will be utilized as consultants to advise on search techniques and database contents.

Graduate students are often the most confident of their computer expertise and their ability to find needed information. Technicians, "postdocs," and visiting researchers are all patrons with critical literature needs who may wish to do their own searching on a system with clear directions and current information, a selection of databases in their field, and search procedures that allow flexibility and in-depth search capability. The newest developments are usually very important; therefore, online access to the latest database updates may be a critical aspect of searching by this group. A branch or specialized library serving a clientele with relatively uniform interests such as biosciences, health, or physics departments can concentrate on offering the appropriate sources.

Teaching Faculty · Computers in the classroom for special projects and laboratory assignments are becoming common. Some faculty will be eager for their students to extend their library research techniques by finding information online and may be more encouraged to seek the assistance of librarians for bibliographic instruction when online sources are included. Other faculty may wish to restrict students to traditional printed sources so that they will learn basic information retrieval skills. Teaching faculty, themselves, may want to learn how to do online searching to keep up with the expertise of their students and to acquaint their classes with systems available to most of them after graduation. They can use library microcomputers to prepare reading lists or supporting material for assignments. Teaching faculty generally need access to the major subject databases, but the concentration for classes should be on databases where the library owns a significant part of the resources being indexed. Currency of material is important, as is the ability to follow changing political, social, and scientific developments.

USER-FRIENDLY SYSTEMS

Libraries providing access to online databases for individuals must select the system carefully to supply appropriate resources and procedures that can be easily understood by a clientele with widely variable skills. It is important that the operating mechanics do not interfere with literature retrieval, since the major objective is to help patrons find the information they need, not how to operate a microcomputer.
    Libraries wishing to offer this type of service can choose from a number of different approaches. A popular choice has been the modified versions of the major vendor database systems. A second approach is to use a front-end software package for the microcomputer that can simplify the command searching of the various standard database systems with menus and help screens. A third type of end-user system is providing access to an intermediary computer that receives simple commands from the searcher and translates them into a system lan-

guage, searches one of a number of databases at any one of several major vendors, and transmits the answer to the patron, who may not be aware of the source of the information. Simple procedures may also be available to search databases available in-house or on the campus mainframe computer.

Examples of these different types of systems for inexperienced searchers, along with their advantages and disadvantages follow.

Major Vendor Search Systems Designed for End-users

The number of databases available from the simplified system of a major database vendor may be less than those used for command searching, and availability may be limited to off-peak or evening hours. Searching is by simple commands or a menu system. It is necessary to dial up the vendor, log on, do a search, and log off. The library service must be organized to keep track of elapsed time as patrons use the system, keep control of passwords, provide basic search training, and have a staff member available for assistance. All new versions or improvements are handled by the vendor; updates to the files are regular, and vending systems can be acquired that can log on and off the systems, keep the passwords secure, and collect funds for elapsed time. Printing citations must be managed separately.

BRS After Dark and Kowledge Index from Dialog are examples of systems designed by large database vendors for untrained searchers. They are available during off-peak (evening) hours, include extensive selections of databases, are inexpensive, and usage can be charged to an individual's credit card. At higher cost BRS also offers BRS BRKTHRU during regular working hours, a menu-assisted search system for their entire list of databases. Regular searchers of the BRS databases can also choose to use a menu system instead of the command language for an additional fee.

Database vendors and producers are both sources for specific subject services. The Dialog Business Connection provides menu-driven access to a selected group of business databases. Emphasis is on factual information rather than bibliographic. The searcher concentrates on the data needed; the source database for that information is not identified. While targeted to novice users, some experience and training in using codes and working with subject terms may be needed. BIOSIS has announced the BIOSIS Connection, planned to make available a variety of databases for both menu and expert access.

BRS After Dark has a one-time subscription fee of $75 and a monthly minimum of $12. BRS BRKTHRU has an initial fee of $75 and the searcher pays only for use at about half the rate of the standard BRS service. Dialog charges $35 for a password for the Knowledge Index and database use is at a flat rate of $24 per hour. Dialog's Business Connection requires a sign-up fee of $145 ($120 for Dialog subscribers) and online usage is charged at $85 per hour.

Advantages of Vendor Online and User Services

Broad selection of databases is available.
Databases are familiar, since they are the same as those offered through the library's search service.
Either a terminal or a microcomputer can be used for searching.
Search costs are generated only when system is used.
Searching at nonprime times may cost less.
Updates and improvements to the files are automatically provided by the host.
Information is current with latest update to database.

Disadvantages

Not all databases offered by the vendor may be included.
Resources are limited to those on the system accessed.
Patrons may need assistance in preparing search strategy and using Boolean logic.
Help with commands and procedures may be needed.
A monthly minimum fee may be charged.
Supporting manual with clear procedures is needed.
Modem and telephone connection are required.
It may be necessary for a librarian to log on and off.
Line noise and system down are potential problems.
Hours of availability may be restricted.
Staff must be available for assistance and security of equipment, passwords.
Time must be scheduled and monitored, and number of citations printed must be verified.

Front-end Software

Software selected for a microcomputer can be utilized to help the novice searcher select an appropriate database, choose search terms, and carry out the search. Usually menus are displayed to guide the patron's choices and establish the correct procedures. The program may supply descriptions of the databases and detailed directions at any point when the "help" key is struck. Automatic telephone dialing, logon and uploading of the search strategy are additional features. The patron can choose to type the results or download to a disk and some programs include further capabilities for editing the results or creating reports.

Some of the more popular software packages include: *Pro-Search*, *Dialoglink,* and *Sci-Mate Searcher*. These assist searching of the regular online vendor systems. *SearchHelper, microDISCLOSURE,* and *Wilsearch* limit access to certain databases. *SearchHelper* is designed for the Information Access Company's databases, such as the MAGAZINE INDEX and TRADE AND INDUSTRY INDEX, microDISCLOSURE accesses only DISCLOSURE on Dialog, and *Wilsearch* is specifically for searching the familiar H. W. Wilson databases such as READERS' GUIDE or the EDUCATION INDEX. *Grateful Med* from the National Library of Medicine provides menu-assisted access to the MEDLARS database. In some cases menus can be bypassed for command searching of the database. Some software is constructed to assist searching only certain systems or databases, while others provide help with many systems.

Software searching packages will usually vary in cost between $30 and $900. Software that restricts searches to a selected group of databases may be available for an annual fee that pays for a prescribed number of searches, each producing not more than ten to twenty citations. For instance, *Wilsearch* retrieves up to ten references per search and, depending on the subscription rate, each search can cost from $1 to $5.

Advantages of Front-end Software

Short, simple searches are easily conducted.
Online assistance before connection to database can make search time more efficient and cost-effective.
Available all hours the vendor is available.
Assisted access to all databases on major systems may be provided.
Menu systems are usually easy to use and require minimal instruction.
Assistance provided to instruct new searchers.
As searchers become more experienced, search steps can be bypassed.
Telephone connection and logon are performed automatically.
Patrons can be offered a group of databases that are especially appropriate for their needs.
A prepaid subscription may include inexpensive searches.

Disadvantages

Microcomputer with modem is required.
Telephone line must be available.
Searching capabilities may be limited.
Searchers may require assistance to understand procedures and to use Boolean logic.
Use by patrons will generally require monitoring, and if there is not

a prescribed number of references per search, time used and citations printed must be controlled.

Library must contract with each system accessed.

Databases are charged at regular rates unless prepaid arrangement.

Databases accessed may be restricted to a specific group of sources.

New software may be needed each time the vendor system makes any changes.

Intermediary Host System

These gateway services provide a link to a variety of databases. The searcher is connected to a remote host computer that provides menu systems to assist the searcher to develop a strategy. The system selects an appropriate vendor system and database, converts the searcher's terms to conform to the vendor's search language, searches the database, and transmits the results back to the searcher. EasyNet is one that offers access to over 800 databases. InfoMaster, IQuest and Searchlink are similar. Charges are a standard amount per search statement on one database with a prescribed number of references obtained, but there is no charge when there are no results. The searcher can choose to bypass some of the menu procedures and can select a database directly if desired. Help is offered online from EasyNet. When a question is sent, a response is returned from a librarian on the staff.

Charges on these systems usually include a low connect-time fee and a cost per search that delivers a specific number of citations. Easynet charges about $8 per search (ten references) with a surcharge for some databases and an extra fee for more information, such as abstracts, plus a low connect-time charge. An annual subscription of $550 provides ten passwords and searches beginning at $5. Other contract options may be arranged. This type of database access will do most of the work for the patron and provides very broad resources. It will be satisfactory for simple searches where only limited output is needed.

Advantages of Intermediary Host System

Access to extensive resources is provided.

Separate contracts with different systems are not necessary.

Either a microcomputer or a terminal can be used.

No cost is charged if no citations are received.

Charges for connect time are low.

No adjustment is needed when online vendors change procedures.

Patrons with a wide variety of interests can be served.

Passwords can be supplied for individual sessions to determine charges.

System can supplement a search service to provide databases that are rarely used.

Simple commands can be translated to those necessary for searching specific databases.

Credit card charge can be accepted.

Disadvantages

Source for searching cannot be controlled.

Flexibility of search process is limited.

System may be costly for the amount of results obtained.

System cannot take advantage of specific features of particular systems.

Searching procedures cannot be controlled.

Telephone line and modem are required.

Local Databases on Floppy, CD-ROM, and Laser Disks

Databases can be purchased or leased from the producers. Online database searching during the 1960s and early 1970s was often made available by purchasing magnetic tapes and mounting them on the main campus computer; this can still be done today. To make them available for untrained searchers, software must be devised or purchased that will make them easy to use. This type of system may be suitable for the campus with a computer network that can make both the library's online catalog and a selection of databases available in all the campus buildings. The resources must be appropriate for this broad scope of patrons and must be used enough to justify the subscription costs. In addition, as the searcher gets farther away from the reference desk or the library, it becomes increasingly important for the search procedures to be simple and clear, with directions to seek assistance at the reference desk when there are questions or more extensive searching is required.

Portions of some standard databases are available for purchase or subscription on floppy disks, while large databases may be obtained on compact optical disks (CD-ROM) or laser disks that can store much more information than the floppy. The cost of the database in these cases is a set amount and can provide as much searching as desired without connect-time or print charges. Since the holdings are local, there is no telephone connection needed. Although both historical and current information are available, sometimes on separate disks, usually the library must have a subscription for updates provided on new disks, which are supplied monthly, quarterly, or annually. The associated software to search these databases is usually designed for the end-user and access is simple with menus or assisting screens. To read CD-ROM and laser disks there must be an additional piece of equipment attached to the microcomputer. Databases on CD-ROM or laser disks may be costly; they must be purchased singly and only selected ones are available at this time.

While database producers are making available an increasing number of the online bibliographic files in disk format, there are also many numeric databases, such as census reports and government statistical data, stock prices, and company financial information. Directories such as *Books in Print*, encyclopedias such as the *Academic American Encyclopedia*, and information on drugs and chemicals are other examples of available resources. Locally developed files of data may also be provided by faculty for their students.

Databases on Floppy Disks · Portions of databases can be purchased on floppy disks. These contain several hundred citations and are usually accompanied by a search program disk. Searching is geared to the end-user and there are no connect-time charges. BIOSIS B-I-T-S, ERIC MICRO*search*, and MICROACCESS from the MICROCOMPUTER INDEX are examples. Numerous disks are necessary to increase the quantity of information available. Disks may contain numeric information as well as bibliographic. MICRO/SCAN DISCLOSURE II comes in two versions with financial information on 5,000 and 9,000 U.S. public companies, respectively. TRINET has data on three diskettes to provide economic census data for marketing and industrial analysis.

Subscriptions are relatively inexpensive. ERIC MICRO*search* disks cost $7.50 each. Usually two are delivered quarterly, each containing 250 to 350 citations.

Databases on CD-ROM · CD-ROM stands for Compact Disk-Read Only Memory. It also refers to a small, sturdy, less than five-inch disk that holds more than 200,000 pages of typed information and is read by a laser beam. This medium has only recently become the basis for the storage of databases and their distribution to search locations. While searching is on an interactive basis with the contents of the disk, there is no method for adding the latest information. A subscription brings a regularly updated disk. Most CD-ROM operates with a CD-ROM reader connected to an IBM microcomputer.

CD-ROM is being used in many cases to supply several years of a database. Usually a set of disks will furnish back files plus a current disk that is replaced periodically. Silver Platter, Inc. for instance, provides PsycLIT on two disks covering 1974 to the present with quarterly updates. ERIC, back to 1966, on as many as four disks is available from many sources including Dialog's "Ondisk" program and OCLC. While an increasing number of individual databases are available in this format, DATEXT, Inc., has combined recent segments of six online business databases on U.S. public companies to produce monthly CD-ROM disks in four subject areas: consumer, industrial, technology, or service. They can be subscribed to singly, or as a package. Digital has created subsets of other databases such as COMPENDEX or NTIS that are on selected subjects such as electrical and computer engineering or environmental health and safety. They are updated quarterly.

Access to the information on CD-ROM depends on software usually developed for the particular product. It may be available separately on a floppy disk or be incorporated as part of the information on the CD-ROM. The sophistication of procedures varies but several levels of expertise may be available. While some are very similar to those for searching online databases with Boolean logic and free-text searching, others provide only a menu system. Sometimes the menu system can be bypassed for more efficient command-driven retrieval. The greatest advantage of a database on CD-ROM is the unlimited searching provided at a prescribed cost. This characteristic makes the availability of the database very close to that of the printed index. With an attached printer the patron can receive a copy of the search results and downloading will permit editing the citations or manipulating the data.

Since the information on the CD-ROM cannot be changed, various arrangements are made to provide current material. New disks quarterly, semiannually or annually are common, and in some cases interim material is provided on a floppy disk. Access to the equivalent database through the same microcomputer can furnish the very latest information. *Wilsondisc*, for instance, has the Wilson indexes available on CD-ROM covering varying years back to 1981. There are four different access modes from browse to expert and the equipment can be used to access both information on CD-ROM or to provide dial-up access to Wilsonline. It will be, therefore, suitable for use by both trained searchers and end-users.

InfoTrac is a system based on twelve-inch laserdisks that provides access to 900 general periodicals with monthly updates. A work station is composed of one to four microcomputers with laserdisk players and printers. The menu search system has proven to be very popular with undergraduates.

Costs for CD-ROM include about $1,000 for a CD-ROM reader to attach to a resident IBM microcomputer with hard disk. An H. W. Wilson work station that includes an IBM microcomputer, monitor, printer, compact disk player, and modem is $4,700. Some CD-ROM disks are sold, some are leased, and some are acquired by subscription. Silver Platter is now offering ERIC with annual updates for $330. PsyCLIT back to 1974 and a current subscription with quarterly updates is $5,000. Dialog's ERIC on CD-ROM is $1,450 a year for the database back to 1966 and with quarterly updates. The twelve Wilson indexes can be purchased on separate disks with various years of coverage, updated and cumulated quarterly and no additional charge to search the database for $1,095 to $1,495. Most databases are in the range of $1,000 to $8,000 depending on the specific database, time coverage, and frequency of updates. Charges can be more if the equipment is included. Complete work stations from InfoTrac with monthly updated laser disks begin at $8,500 per year. ERIC from Dialog for 1981 to the present will be leased for $1,950 to $3,450 depending on the coverage. Academic discounts are sometimes available.

Advantages of Local Database Systems

Subscription cost is set to simplify planning and budgeting.

No additional costs for heavy use makes it ideal for offering free searching.

Complete package of equipment and disks can be purchased or leased.

System is an excellent medium for training searchers.

No connect-time or citation charges are assessed, thus allowing unlimited browsing.

Equipment is not tied to a telephone line.

There are no telecommunications costs or problems with line noise or system down.

System is always available, no need to dial-up or log on.

Search language is usually easy to use. Different skill levels may exist.

Full use of Boolean operators and other search features can be provided.

Response time can be immediate.

System is very useful for access to older online files.

Single CD-ROM disks provide large storage capacity.

Files can be selected to meet needs of clientele.

Potential exists for many enhancements to search capabilities.

Linkage of several user stations may be allowed.

Multiple copies may be available for nominal cost.

Disadvantages

The field is rapidly changing, and standards are developing.

A CD-ROM reader to attach to microcomputer must be purchased.

The system is expensive, especially if not heavily used.

A budget allocation will be needed to offer free usage.

A separate contract may be needed for each database acquired.

Each database may have a different search language and procedures.

Response time may be slow.

Some search procedures may require extensive training to use.
Microcomputers must have sufficient storage capacity, around
640 K.

The result is more equipment to service.

Disks will need to be acquired, cataloged, and claimed. May need
multiple disks for extensive coverage of years, selection of databases.

Disks must be handled and stored.

Up-to-date information may not be included.

SETTING UP AND ORGANIZING FACILITIES
FOR END-USER SEARCHING

Providing facilities for patrons to do their own searching requires the
selection of the type of system to be used, management of computers
or terminals, space for individuals to use work stations, planning for
limits or controls, managing the flow of patrons, waiting lists when
necessary, and sometimes the additional collection of fees and money
management. Patrons may need training or guidance and staff must be
available for questions.

Space and Equipment

The library may have a single microcomputer or terminal next to the
reference desk or a microcomputer laboratory with many machines
and a staff member to supervise. The larger facility, when available, can
be used for students and faculty to do word processing, use their own
programs and disks, work on class homework, and search databases
online or on CD-ROM. If printers are available, they will be very popular and may require some controls to keep the paper consumption at a
modest level.

This equipment should be set up with consideration for its availability, security, and visual impact. The equipment should be located
near the reference desk in order to foster the image of the computer as
one of several methods of finding information. Reference librarians can
not only answer questions about the database content and search process but can also suggest alternate approaches such as printed indexes,
reference books, or the card catalog. It is important that patrons are
aware of the facility, and seeing others using it is one of the best advertisements. Access to online databases will require a telephone connection. Some possibilities for setting up equipment:

Microcomputers Near Reference Desk · One or more microcomputers located in an area within sight of the reference desk will provide

some security and assistance will be available when needed. If online access is offered during evening hours, equipment used during the day for searching may be available. The simplest arrangement is to have a dedicated microcomputer that is wheeled out into a public area and returned to a locked room when a staff member is not around. There must be a telephone line available if an online system is used.

CD-ROM or Laserdisk Work Stations · These units should be set up with a consideration for comfort and the local environment, since there will be less inclination to restrict users to short time periods. Ideally, the stations should be placed near the printed indexes to emphasize the availability of other sources. The distance from the reference desk may depend on the need for security of the equipment. If there are a number of disks to use there must be a method and place for checking them in and out.

Microcomputer Laboratory · A room of microcomputers may be housed in the library, but managed by the computer center on campus. Nevertheless, this offers a group of machines that could be utilized for providing access to online databases for library patrons wishing to do their own searching. The usefulness will depend on the location in the building and its relationship to other reference resources. Staff or students responsible for the room should be given an orientation to library resources and encouraged to direct students to the reference desk for assistance with their topics or to find more material. If the room is not close to the reference desk, it is even more important that there be some way to indicate that more help and other sources are available.

Search Room · A room of microcomputers and work stations devoted to online resources for patron use can concentrate the search activity into one area; access can be controlled and telephone lines can be installed, and manuals, thesauri, and search aids can be housed there. Supervision would be managed by library staff and students who could provide help for patrons. Preferably this room would be separate from the search service where librarians and patrons carry out more complex searches together. It is important to separate the two levels of service activity and to limit distractions for both efforts.

Management

Reference librarians need to know how to use all the search systems offered for patron use in order to answer questions and advise on procedures. New developments must be monitored and changing patterns of library use should be noted so adjustments in library staffing and services can reflect patron needs.

One reference librarian with some microcomputer experience should be in charge of end-user searching to manage the service, monitor procedures, and conduct training sessions. If possible, the search service manager should be in charge of the end-user facility in order to integrate the two services and assure the most appropriate use of these systems. As the facilities expand, the search service manager could be responsible for the equipment and vendor relations and another reference librarian or searcher could manage the everyday activities of the end-user facility, including training patrons when necessary. Communication must be fostered between the two areas, with management a cooperative and yet separate function.

Vendor Systems, Equipment, and Supplies · The selection of an end-user service will be the responsibility of the head of public services or the reference department, a systems librarian, and/or the search service manager. Equipment should be coordinated with the library's present equipment. The database systems may be offered by an online vendor already under contract to the library; software may already be owned by the library and used for command-level searching in the search service, and a CD-ROM player may be added to microcomputers already in the library. Selection of new equipment and vendors should follow guidelines already established for the search service, taking into consideration the different clientele and aim of the service. Supplies should be managed by a clerk.

Training End-users · Patrons may learn how to search by experimentation, counseling, tutoring, workshops, or a course in bibliographic instruction. The method of teaching may be determined by the complexity of the system chosen. Vendor training may be considered for the more complex sources, although brief introductions by a reference librarian may be enough. Training should focus on integrating this method of searching into the other information retrieval methods available in the library.

Help or counseling at the patron facility or a nearby computer should not impact on service at the reference desk. Students can help supervise, answer questions, and provide monitoring of the equipment, or librarians can share the hours of responsibility.

Hours of Operation · Ideally, all hours the library is open should feature searching. Limitations may be set by the type of system or the availability of personnel; however, patron access should be as easy and convenient as possible.

Controlling Usage · Some method may be needed to manage patron access to the databases. Use of the system can be limited to fifteen minutes, but this must be monitored in some manner. The sequence of patrons, whether by signing up on a list, making an appointment, or on an availability basis, must be considered. Students may be limited to one search per day, two or three a week, or by some other system. The number of terminals or microcomputers will have an effect on the need for a sign-up or an appointment system.

Students may be required to have some instruction first. Reading a manual, attending a training session, following an online tutorial, or using a computer-assisted instruction program are some possibilities. Students can be asked to fill out a search form outlining their strategy and have it checked by a librarian before using the computer.

Costs and Charging Fees

Costs of providing another library service must be considered carefully. The equipment, vendor contracts, and database charges are only a small part of the impact on the library budget. Any demand on staff time is very expensive. Building changes and telephone lines may be necessary to accommodate a viable facility for more computers. However, the benefits for library patrons and the wish to keep up with a changing academic and information environment may make adjustments in other services and the impact on staff worthwhile. Charging for this type of service can be an alternative, but would still only provide a portion of the costs. Since this service can be aimed at undergraduates, there should be extra effort made to find enough funding to heavily subsidize, if not to provide it free of charge.

The price of CD-ROM is substantial, but it may provide a better alternative to printed indexes than an online database source because it is available without intervention of the librarian. It is also online all the time. Costs are known and, therefore, can be budgeted. These factors make it an ideal system for offering free searches for undergraduates.

If fees must be charged, this is one more system to collect money for, keep records, and process paperwork. Fees can be levied by the amount of connect-time used, the number of citations printed, or a standard amount per question. If access is controlled by passwords, a single fee can be charged for each password that entitles the patron to a scheduled amount of time. An example of a fee could be $5 for half an hour with maximum use one hour or a standard $3.50 per search. It is best to collect the money before the search and then refund it if there are problems getting online or a system is down.

Online systems that will charge to credit cards provide one method of collecting fees. A vending system that automatically logs on and off and allows a defined period of search time is another. Otherwise, monitoring time, printing, and collecting cash can require a great deal of staff time.

SELECTING AN END-USER SERVICE

The decision to acquire an online database system for patron use is made; now considerations to select a system must include the information needs of patrons, the amount of assistance that can be devoted to service users, and the value or amount of use for the costs generated. The end-user service should aim for a level of service between the sophisticated search service and the use of the printed indexes. The patron should be able to perform simple searches to produce a limited output appropriate for the class project or survey of the field of investigation. The amount of help provided the patron should depend on expertise and experience.

One of the first considerations is the clientele to be served, type of resources they need, and the demand for this service. If the primary purpose is for undergraduates, the system must be simple with clear directions and provide a good general database that includes a broad range of periodicals. If the clientele are researchers in a particular subject area, the databases must be appropriate and utilize more flexible search systems with Boolean logic.

The next aspect should involve the amount of independence desired for the patron's use of the equipment. Should the student or faculty member be able to come into the library and carry out a search without the intervention or assistance of a library staff member? If some assistance is needed, should it be right at the terminal as part of the search procedure, provided by a person who is available near the equipment, or should training sessions be offered before searching? The decision may depend on whether the goal is to provide a searching facility for the patron wishing to find information, use this computerized service as a tool to support bibliographic instruction and increase the involvement of students learning library research methods, or increase patron skills and knowledge of electronic information retrieval, which will be part of their preparation for careers and future information seeking experience.

Factors to Consider

When choosing an end-user service, it is first necessary to decide between accessing an online vendor system or establishing a local database, such as a CD-ROM or laserdisk system. Some considerations include:

Scope of Resources · A CD-ROM system allows the selection of a single database that may be satisfactory if it meets the major needs of the library patrons. Additional databases may be purchased as needed. A limited range of databases are available through a friendly system such as BRS After Dark or Wilsonline. A very broad scope of resources can be obtained with a single comprehensive system such as EasyNet.

Investment for Start-up · Will totally new equipment be needed, or will equipment on hand be utilized? Are additional components necessary? If complete work stations are purchased, the initial costs will be substantial. In addition, initiation or password fees for an online database system, software, or CD-ROM equipment and subscription fees add to the required investment.

Reputation of Vendor, Producer · Any system must be assured of continued support and maintenance from the vendor. Read reviews, talk to other librarians using the system or software, discuss vendors at meetings of online user groups. Some determining factors may be how long they have been in business, how long their product has been on the market, the services they offer, and their reputation for reliability.

Location in the Building · Placing the system next to the reference desk will provide maximum assistance with resulting demands on the reference librarian. Locating the system near indexes will help to integrate this method of finding information, as long as the system is easy to use and self-explanatory. Equipment placed in a microcomputer room usually means that there are students or staff on hand to help with technical problems, but arrangements must be made in all cases to have adequate assistance available when needed.

Impact on Staff · Staff time will be required to assist patrons with the database systems. Even simple procedures will often generate some questions. Setting up for the day, putting away at night, assisting with online or offline procedures, hiring and training students to oversee the operation will be added responsibilities. Are other staff available who can be taken from some other operation to assist with this service?

Patron Independence Desired · A simple menu system on a local database can usually be operated by patrons with the least amount of assistance. Since the amount of connect time is not a consideration, browsing and experimentation will help provide results. An online database that requires Boolean operators will require some training for effective searching. Assistance to log on and off a system will require contact with the library staff. The choice may depend on computer skills of clientele, complexity of topics searched, and staff time available.

Amount of Use Expected · Heavy interest among students and faculty may dictate a CD-ROM unit for unlimited searching. If most needs are supplied by printed indexes, an online connection for occasional use of a database may suffice.

Best Medium for Patron Needs · A single database for a clientele with relatively uniform interests; a system with levels of access for different amounts of user expertise and experience; a broad general database for undergraduates; and a selection of the major subject databases for researchers may fit the needs adequately. A menu or Boolean logic system or choice of expertise can be found to meet the requirements and experience of patrons.

Changing Technologies · As equipment is improved and systems change it is often difficult to know when to adopt a new service or when to buy the equipment. It is important to purchase standard systems that can be modified easily or come in units linked to provide additional patron access. Equipment such as that for CD-ROM may come as a package with a subscription to the database. If the producer maintains an investment in the equipment, changes and upgrades will be their responsibility rather than the library's. Usually costs will decrease after new systems are on the market for a while. Waiting until a new technology has been tested in the field is always a good idea.

Up-to-date Information · A system online to a major vendor will provide access to the latest updated files. CD-ROM units may be replaced monthly, quarterly, or annually. Researchers will usually need the most up-to-date information. Undergraduates do not usually require files that contain the most recent publications, although current topics in the news are popular subjects for term papers.

Cost-effectiveness · Start-up costs may be significant and contract and billing options will vary with different systems. There is also a potential cost for upgrades to equipment, software, and systems. Contracts should be examined to see if there is a reduction in charges for group participation, or for a larger subscription payment. Online databases where payment is based on connect time are the best option for limited or sporadic access. CD-ROM is very expensive, but if demand is great, the ability for unlimited searching may make it cost-effective. Any intermediary vendor such as EasyNet is also costly, but charges are only for searches that are successful. The budget process is enhanced if the charges are stabilized and predictable; the same is true for patron searches if a fee is levied. A standard cost per search makes it easier to plan for both patron and library. If patron fees are collected, there is additional management responsibility for handling the money, figuring charges, and keeping records.

Important End-user System Features

Equipment

Hardware needed. Amount of computer memory required for software, downloading, storing search programs. Does it come with the contract or database? Is it leased or purchased? Disk drives required: Single, double, or hard disk?

Telephone line requirements

Speed of transmission, response

Print quality and speed

Versatility of equipment. Is it keyed to a specific use or is it general purpose equipment adaptable for other work?

Ability to link additional work stations or easily expand facilities. Security necessary for equipment, software, passwords

Inability of patron to alter message on screen

Software simple to use, easy to learn and capable of performing as many features as possible, such as using Boolean logic, saving searches, downloading, and keeping accounts.

Producer Support

Availability and quality of the manuals, training, and support by the manufacturer

Responsiveness from producer such as service desk, help online

Hours of availability—evenings vs. daytime vs. 24 hours

Stability and vitality of system producer/manufacturer for continuing the product and incorporating new technologies

Quality of online help screens. Availability at any time during search

Response time. Costly if using online system, waste time if local database

Planning of vendor for system/software/hardware upgrades

Availability of a demonstration disk or free trial period.

Searching Procedures, Flexibility

Simplicity of protocols and directions with clearly defined choices

Ease of use by patrons who have never used computers

Choice of menu system or ability to use Boolean logic. May depend on needs, training of patrons

Amount of training needed by patrons for adequate search quality

Amount of help needed by novice searchers. Try out on students

Complexity of log-on and log-off procedures

Assistance in selecting a database, the amount of information provided on each source

Ability of search language to recognize common and new terminology

Ease of viewing or printing search results; if not successful to know what to do next

Availability of limits to time period, language, type of document

Capabilities such as Boolean searching, truncation, word proximity, range of dates, uploading

Ability to repeat a step in a menu without going back to the beginning of the search or to skip steps or move to a more expert search level

Number of steps in menu selection process. If too long it will be frustrating for patrons after they have used it several times as it is too time consuming. It is desirable to be able to do several steps at one time (stacking them)

Ability to limit searches to certain databases

Browse ability without extra costs. Available with a floppy or CD-ROM disk of a database, or searching on EasyNet when there are no hits

Printing versatility—specific fields printed, several choices available.

Resources

Variety of sources available; full-text, bibliographic, directory, numeric. Specific databases may be important

Availability of backfiles and time periods covered

Frequency of database updates, new software, new CD-ROM disks

Supplement to already available resources. Different method of access to heavily used indexes such as ERIC. More coverage of time, more current

New resource for departments or units on campus for which library resources are lacking

Availability of full-text support—online or in the library.

Costs

Start-up costs for specialized equipment, telephone lines

Cost for amount of use. An expensive CD-ROM product may be very cost-effective if based on the number of times it is used

Ability to set cost per search

Options for charging patrons such as credit cards, vending, machine-readable cards

Selection of contracts. (Can a better price be obtained by paying ahead?)

Additional Features

Special functions such as term weighting, highlighting search words, sorting results

Accounting features to monitor activities, produce reports

Capability for post-processing: Downloading as ASCII file, making charts, analyzing data, editing and indexing bibliographies, merging files.

TRAINING THE PATRON SEARCHER

Reference librarians should try out and learn to operate the end-user system selected. They should be able to answer questions about resources, search techniques, or machine problems. Other questions that will be generated by an end-user service will include those about how to use microcomputers and software and the availability of systems for the online user at home. If the end-user service is close to the reference desk, it may be used to answer reference questions. This will familiarize librarians with the procedures and content, but must be used this way with caution to keep the system accessible for patrons. Nevertheless, this type of usage will give librarians a good background to assist patrons.

Patrons may need more education and assistance with a system that uses Boolean logic than one using a menu system. Menu systems usually provide screens for each step of the search process and guide the user to making choices for subjects and databases and can often be used by someone with no experience. To use Boolean logic a user must understand the procedures for combining terms and how the different operators enlarge or restrict groups. It is probable that all users will benefit from training on organization and execution of the search. Any discussions of search technique should be sufficiently broad and inclusive to encourage use of other sources and to assist in finding materials. The patron needs to know when to search online, when to use a printed index, and when to have the assistance of a librarian for a more complex and exhaustive search.

Training Goals

Two types of basic training are brief sessions to describe the purpose of the system, the primary search techniques for simple searches, and the supporting documentation that is available; and more extensive instruction that can either be a component of established lectures to classes on library research, or sessions concentrating on the use of computer systems to assist literature retrieval but including other sources as well. Training goals should include:

Providing an understanding of online searching and when it is an appropriate choice for information retrieval. Relate to online catalog and printed indexes.

Assuring familiarity with operation of the microcomputer, how to turn it on, how to log on, how to connect to the database, and how to log off. Should include knowledge of the keyboard and where the various function keys are located.

Familiarizing patrons with the scope of resources available online and their print counterparts. Knowledge of how to find out more about databases and how to identify those in particular fields.

The importance of terminology and how to determine keywords necessary for a productive search on a topic.

Basic search strategy development specifically related to computer searching, but with the same principles used for any library research.

How to carry out a simple search.

Providing confidence that equipment is easy to use, online searching is a logical process, and good results can be obtained.

Ideally there should be some method for patrons to practice before running up online costs. This may not be necessary for a local system where the amount of connect time is unlimited, although if a practice database is available, it will free the end-user facility for experienced patrons. A practice microcomputer could have a small downloaded database available with some exercises to illustrate the searching procedures and features.

Methods of Training End-users

There are different methods of training end-users. The training must fit the type of searching available and the expertise of the patrons both for using microcomputers and for bibliographic research. The amount of staff time is also a factor. Are librarians at the reference desk able to assist patrons using search equipment? Can some hands-on training be part of regular bibliographic instruction classes, or is assistance provided near the equipment? Some possibilities include:

No Training · Just provide the facility for online searching, enough signs and manuals, and many patrons will find enough information on a trial and error basis. Printed material can advise on the basic steps.

Search Counseling · May be needed by students before a search to plan their topic, select terms, and review procedure. After the search, students may need assistance to evaluate their results and sometimes to try another approach. This service may be more important when using an online system where each search or connect time generates additional costs.

Manuals and Handouts · Manuals for the operation of the microcomputers, the software, and the end-user system should be available and provide clear directions for the patron. Handouts may be prepared listing the principal commands, the resources available, and any directions for scheduling, costs, and time or citation limits. Good examples and sample searches to illustrate procedures and commands are very helpful in assisting patrons to understand how to do their own searching. A form with spaces for search concepts can be used to illustrate Boolean logic and for organizing search steps.

Tutorials or Computer-Assisted-Instruction (CAI) Packages · When online tutorials from the software producer or online vendor are available, these can assist individuals willing to take the time to learn more complex techniques and strategies. This program could be set up on a second microcomputer or made available in a microcomputer laboratory. Reference librarians can also guide students by making appointments for helping them individually at the terminal.

Lectures and Workshops · Lectures for specific classes or groups such as graduate students should generally include the larger context of library research in order to give an overall view of resources, both online and print, that are available and how to find them. An outline for a class presentation can include the following material about online searching that patrons can do themselves:

Explanation of the system and end product. Definitions of terminology such as that for citation, record, field, database, and thesaurus.
Databases or resources available. Subjects covered, dates, and materials included in the database.
Comparison between searching databases and corresponding index(es). Advantages and limits of each. Describe appropriate use of each, and need for analysis of subject and approach desired. Include relationship to online catalog.
Subject selection. Topic must be clearly definable and narrow

scope. Use of controlled vocabulary versus free-text. How to utilize a thesaurus. Examples of good search topics and poor ones. Organizing the topic and breaking it into concepts described by keywords. Developing a search strategy.

Boolean logic if appropriate; otherwise the choices presented by the menu system.

Displaying and/or printing results.

Logging on and off.

Search aids available. Using the system manual.

Sample search. Use topic of current interest or appropriate for group.

Practice time. May include assignment to complete.

Teaching Faculty to Search · Special workshops may be sponsored for faculty to introduce them to the service so they can perform their own searching, or so they can send students to the library for this purpose. Emphasis can be placed both on the assistance it provides for students who need to write a paper, and the easy access to materials for research, writing grant proposals, and writing for publication.

Researchers may use the menu searching systems, or may wish to learn the command language for direct searching of databases that interest them. This will require more intensive training sessions and practice time. If they have their own passwords and plan to search from the laboratory or office, some introductory workshops with emphasis on the printed form of the databases may be all that is necessary. Library searchers can be of special help to tutor faculty and to answer questions. Researchers may wish to do either their own searching and downloading or take search results to edit and then integrate with an online reference file of their own. They may only be interested in one or two databases most appropriate for their area of specialty.

Faculty may not wish to invest the necessary time to learn to be good searchers. However, a preliminary introduction will acquaint them with the resources available. Researchers should be reminded of the availability of the library's search service, which will combine their understanding and expertise with that of the trained searchers.

Access Outside the Library · Patrons may be searching the online catalog in their office, laboratory, or dorm. If databases have been mounted on the campus computer or faculty and students have their own passwords to online systems, it may be necessary to go to the field—the departments—to do instruction, answer questions, and remind them of other resources available at the library. It is important for librarians to be knowledgeable about the many different uses of the microcomputer, software, and the various friendly systems that provide capable support for information retrieval.

Other Microcomputer Training · Teaching faculty and graduate students how to evaluate and use the software that can in turn be used to manage reprint collections may be considered an appropriate function of librarians. Particularly if there is a microcomputer laboratory in the library, these programs can be demonstrated and various packages made available for faculty members to try out. The library can also make the software available for faculty to check out and try on their own machines.

FINANCIAL CONSIDERATIONS

End user searching is often instituted to provide free searching for students. This type of service is difficult to handle if librarians must meet with individuals and do the search. CD-ROM has provided a method of stabilizing costs so they can be budgeted. Special funding may be secured from a grant, class donation, or alumni gift to establish this type of service to take care of initial costs of equipment and implementation. In order to provide a free service, however, the library must find a way to budget for the continuing costs which can include:

> service or password fees of online database vendors
> upgrades to software
> individual search charges for connect time and citation fees
> subscription to service on the basis of a per-search fee
> subscription to CD-ROM for unlimited searching
> paper, ribbons, and computer servicing, which can be substantial
>   when available for public use
> funds for expansion as service demands increase.

It is assumed that staffing is by adjusting the present work responsibilities. Possibly an undergraduate program or research group could underwrite this service, but once established it will be difficult to discontinue if the funding does not continue. If a fee is to be instituted in order to begin this service, patrons can be charged:

> a standard amount for a search
> an amount for time online, such as five dollars for ten minutes
> for prints only.

Or to help control costs, limits can be established such as:

> limiting access to two or three searches/semester/student or to a
>   specified cost/search
> creating a schedule for signing up for particular time segments
> requiring a training course before using system
> assigning presearch work in the printed indexes.

Rather than using restrictions or charges, the aim should be enough education and guidance so patrons use the most appropriate method for their research. One goal of patron searching should be to make it as available as the printed indexes. Budgeting for the costs will require a careful examination of service priorities.

ROLE OF THE INTERMEDIARY

The librarian has an important role in the establishment of online searching by patrons. This role, as an advisor, educator, and sponsor, is an important aspect of integrating these resources into the information seeking process. Patrons will, more than ever, need guidance, knowledge of library resources, and services to aid their efforts. The balance between establishing the independent library researcher and making the librarian an indispensable part of the process must be determined, with emphasis placed on providing the most appropriate service for the patron. Educating patrons about available resources, how to access them, and how to find the information they need are a vital responsibility.

Determining when and how to make online systems available for patrons, how to pay for them, and how to use them to best advantage are considerable challenges. The many options for end-user searching require a careful look at the requirements of library patrons, the funding available, amount of staff management needed, and resources to be gained. Gateways to some of the online services through systems already available in the library may offer a cost-effective approach. Searching BRS online through OCLC, or using EasyNet through the American Library Association's electronic mail service, ALANET, may be appropriate.

Many library patrons are eager to do their own searching. The opportunity to browse through a database, find some records of interest, and print them out to take away is very attractive. Many are probably willing to pay for the convenience of a system that is easy to use, responsive, and contains material of interest; however, this opportunity to find information with the assistance of a computer should be made available to as many patrons as possible. They will especially appreciate this facility if it is usually available to use when needed. Planning must consider the impact on staff, as librarians will need to assist this process while still maintaining information services at the reference desk, and a responsive expert database search service for more complex subjects. Integrating the search service, searching at the reference desk, and searching by patrons into an overall information retrieval service that takes advantage of the capabilities of librarians, patrons, and computers and provides the most effective approach that is easy to use, accurate, fast, and within budget limitations will be a continuing challenge.

Bibliography

"End-User Searching Services." SPEC Kit No. 122. Washington, D.C.: Office of Management Studies, Assn. of Research Libraries, 1986. 112 pp.

Helgerson, Linda W. "CD-ROM: A Revolution in the Making." *Library Hi Tech* 4:23–27 (1986).

Janke, Richard V. "Online after Six: End User Searching Comes of Age." *Online* 8:15–29 (1984).

LaBorie, Tim, and Leslie Donnelly. "Vending Database Searching with Public Access Terminals." *Library Hi Tech* 4:7–10 (1986).

Miller, David C. "Evaluating CDROMS: To Buy or What to Buy?" *Database* 10:36–42 (1987).

"Planning for End-User Searching: A Checklist of Questions." RASD Occasional Papers No. 1. *RASD Update* 8:14–16 (1987).

Tenopir, Carol. "Four Options for End User Searching." *Library Journal* 111:56–57 (1986).

13

CHALLENGES OF DIVERSITY *307*
      Computer Expertise *308*
      Impact on the Reference Librarian *308*
      Dependence on Equipment *309*
      More Choices *309*
      More Service Demands *310*
      Lack of Standardized Protocols *310*
      Providing the Information *310*
      Electronic Reference *311*
SUCCESS FACTORS *311*
      Knowing the Patrons' Requirements *312*
      Effective Promotion *312*
      Timeliness *313*
      Searcher Expertise *313*
      Adequate Finances *314*
      Competent Management *315*
      Support of Library Administration *315*
      Excellence *315*
A READING LIST *316*
      Current Awareness *316*
      Directories *317*
      Associations/Conferences *320*
      Indexes to the Literature *321*
      Major Journals *322*
      Other Journals *322*
      Books *324*
      Columns *325*
      Software/Hardware/CD-ROM Reviews *325*
      Bibliographies *326*
      Annual Reviews *326*

Diversity, Success, and Change

Librarians are in the midst of the changing information environment. The development of electronic technologies is affecting the library workplace, attitudes, and expectations of patrons, the retrieval and delivery of information, and the challenges facing librarians as professionals. Academic and special libraries, where research and business interests require accurate and current information to compete in scientific fields and the marketplace, have often been in the forefront of developments that provide better services for their patrons. The librarian's outlook is increasingly worldwide as text and numerical data is retrieved from an ever-growing body of publications produced around the globe.

The information explosion in recent decades has required the applications of new technologies to increase control and access to this growing body of knowledge. Automating information retrieval is much more than using electronic access instead of printed indexes. It is the ability to quickly sort through thousands of references to find one, or a few, that can offer an answer to a question or a report on work done on a specific problem. It is also the means of providing individualized service for researchers with comprehensive bibliographies or selected references on current topics. New methods of finding information require librarians to learn different procedures, know more about machines and technical processes, and continually keep up with new opportunities, new applications, and new resources. To take advantage of computers, optical disks, and electronic systems, it is extremely important to assess and thoughtfully select and implement the most appropriate new developments.

CHALLENGES OF DIVERSITY

The changing composition and competence of the student body, emphasis on research and publication for professors, and the demand for better teaching and more basics for undergraduates, are part of the constantly changing impacts on the academic information environment. Online searching of remote databases must be managed with flexibility in order to change with different demands. To provide effective information services, librarians must cope with a number of challenging situations that require imagination, initiative, and flexibility to insure that online information services achieve their potential in the academic library.

Computer Expertise

The rapid development of computer technology has emphasized the diversity of library patrons, just as it has had an effect on different elements of society. Most entering students have now been exposed to some computer experience. Children at very young ages are learning about computers and may even have an opportunity to try Dialog's program, Classmate, geared to elementary and secondary school classes. It is important to recognize this changing background of college students and to know that their approach to learning may be different.

In the future, as now, however, there are students who have no interest and feel no need to deal with computers. These students may include many older individuals encouraged to pursue college degrees at later stages in life. This group may not have an understanding of computer-assisted techniques, but may be very anxious to take advantage of newer methods and aids to learning. The range of expertise, experience, and enthusiasm challenges the efforts to make the electronic delivery of information accessible to all. Assisting patrons at the reference desk, through bibliographic instruction, end-user training, and tutorials, as well as on an individual basis, provide a range of approaches to deal with patrons on many levels.

Impact on the Reference Librarian

Automating information services should increase productivity, expertise, and efficiency. However, the requirements for more education, online practice, taking care of machine problems, keeping more records, handling money when fees are charged, making appointments, and working with individual researchers adds new demands on reference librarians and rarely replaces other responsibilities. These new skills may enhance collection development activities, improve status in the academic community, and make the career of an academic librarian very exciting, yet it can also mean a great deal of pressure to perform more duties at a higher competence level with a continual need to learn more and to keep up with the changing online environment. New responsibilities have added a great deal of diversity to the work loads of reference librarians. However, managing priorities and balancing time demands are necessities for public service librarians who must provide effective information services.

Dependence on Equipment

More dependence on effective computer-assisted retrieval of information also means becoming more vulnerable to electrical problems, machine failures, and poor telephone connections. Every public services librarian must learn how to put paper in printers and fix paper jams, what to do when the computer returns with an inscrutable message or a line of garbled letters, and when to abort a search. Backup machines and substitute systems can be crucial.

Developments in computers have made information available from any location. Despite this convenient access, only one person can use a terminal or computer at a time, and providing better service for patrons by installing an online capability for independent use may mean waiting lines and impatience with machine problems. As computers become faster and responses more immediate, the expectation is for them to work still faster. Any lags in communications become increasingly frustrating. As more equipment is acquired, still more is needed with more versatility, more memory, and the ability to accomplish more tasks.

An institution can never quite keep up with the latest developments. Even the newest piece of equipment may be out of date by the time it is installed. Yet waiting for the next breakthroughs for more power and more memory at lower costs can stifle implementation. Decision makers must be as informed as possible, dealing with the equipment available at the moment, and choosing standard systems that can be upgraded when needed.

More Choices

As computer systems become more friendly with assistance from front-end software, interfaces, menus, and more built-in flexibility, there are increasing numbers of databases to choose from, more choices for online access, and more references to sort through to find information in standard databases. It is more difficult to provide comprehensive information on a subject or to maintain precision when searching for specific subject material. The amount of information easily retrieved may overwhelm the patron. The growing number of easy-to-use systems for searching do not usually deal with the complexity of the databases or the need for precision of information retrieval.

Concentrating on a few systems that will provide most of the information needed by an institution's patrons and educating them sufficiently so they know the best approach for their topics of interest may be one answer to information overload and having too many choices to make.

More Service Demands

Librarians are in a position to be increasingly helpful for researchers, and yet can only carry out an online search with one individual at a time. This time restraint may make it impossible to reach more than a small percentage of those who could benefit from this service. Librarians must utilize a diversity of methods for providing user services so patrons can access CD-ROM databases, do their own searching online, take advantage of online resources for brief queries at the reference desk, and receive extensive personal services for complex problems and precision retrieval. Providing a large enough range of access tools with guidance for using the most appropriate method should help both patron and searcher.

Lack of Standardized Protocols

Although computers can store amazing amounts of information, can find small bits of data, and can provide great diversity of resources, many available systems are not standardized, are often difficult to use, and cannot be integrated. When an intermediary computer or software is utilized to interpret the different procedures or languages and convert them to a standard set of commands, the common language that results limits taking advantage of particular file access points and the precision available via specific commands. Each database, CD-ROM, and each vendor system must be accessed one at a time, each often by its own unique language and procedures and utilizing approaches geared to the individual files. Gateways broaden the diversity of resources available to a user of a few systems but do not assist the searcher who must learn new procedures, access codes, and terminology regardless of the method used to achieve access to a database.

Providing the Information

Patrons and librarians must realize the difference between accessing secondary information sources and securing primary literature. Patrons need more than places to look—they must be provided with the information they need with the assurance that it is accurate and timely. Computers offer the means of access, but it is up to the searcher and the library to make sure that references can be followed up with full-text online, full-text on optical disks, copies of printed journals, and/or efficient interlibrary loan services.

As different types of databases increase, it is also important to know how to access files of data collections. These may be local databases on the academic computer, the electronic equivalent of a reference handbook, or collections of figures on companies, census, or physical properties of chemicals. Extensive subject knowledge is needed in some cases to find relevant information. The continually increasing numbers of these different numerical files will emphasize the need for close collaboration between researchers and information providers.

Electronic Reference

Ready-reference services at the information desk or on the telephone will increasingly rely on electronic resources. An entire collection of reference works may be available on a single CD-ROM disk. The online catalog, information sources only available electronically, and the ability to find a specific bit of information from a large database are increasingly important.

Accompanying the expertise necessary to access these resources are the responsibilities for educating and assisting patrons using microcomputers, improving search techniques, and selecting online resources. In addition, the reference librarian must still communicate with the patron to determine the question to be answered by using good interpersonal skills during the reference interview. This critical aspect of information delivery is not affected by the availability of online resources.

The many contrasts that must be met by the librarian providing information sources and the patron who needs assistance in finding pertinent information will continue to challenge this generation of online information specialists.

SUCCESS FACTORS

The academic libraries with busy reference departments accessing online resources as needed for their campus constituents have put together, perhaps by trial and error or else by careful planning, the many elements that result in a successful information service. Some of the important factors include:

Knowing the Patrons' Requirements

Librarians must be acquainted with the activities of their patrons in the laboratory and classroom; the information needed and approaches they use to write grant proposals, classroom assignments, scholarly articles, or reviews of the literature in their field; and the language of the disciplines from psychology to organometallic chemistry. This familiarity will make the joint efforts of librarian and scientist or scholar beneficial for both participants. The knowledge of the librarian with online resources, search techniques, and the terms used in the pertinent literature can work synergistically with the practical and theoretical background of the scientist or scholar to enhance the information retrieval process and to produce results that meet the expectation of the patron for the latest developments in the field or an extensive coverage of work already accomplished on a particular topic.

Another important aspect of meeting the needs of patrons is the careful examination of online database vendor systems in order to acquire resources that meet the subject interests of the academic and research programs, those that augment heavily used library materials, and others that extend the library's resources and enlarge information opportunities. Knowledge of departmental programs, research institutes, clinical interests, and changing research fields of faculty members is essential.

As librarians gain experience and work closely with researchers, teaching faculty, and students, they will understand better the use of information in the various fields, recognize when responses to requests must be prompt, and be able to interpret a subject discipline in terms of access to information geared to an individual's requirements. Not only must librarians be able to produce accurate and timely information when it is needed for the researcher, but different levels of service must be provided for the student, the patron who wants to do library research independently, and the answers that must be immediate at the reference desk. Understanding these requirements and responding in an appropriate manner will help achieve responsive and useful services.

Effective Promotion

Patrons must know about database resources in order to request their use or consider this option for finding information. Marketing; education in the classroom and the library lobby; personal interaction on scholarly matters; and the availability of adequate signs, indexing in the card or online catalog, and notices near the indexes will help alert the academic patron to online services.

The enthusiasm of the public service librarians and the patrons themselves for this service will help to advertise online resources. However, part of the education process is making sure that patrons have realistic expectations. An online database search may not be the best procedure for finding a mathematical formula, and even promising subjects may not produce the results that a researcher expects. Searchers must know when an online source is appropriate and when an index or handbook will provide better answers, and they must be able to communicate the reasons to patrons in a logical and convincing manner. Patrons must understand that while using a computer to aid literature searching provides great assistance, preparation and planning are needed to achieve optimum online retrieval, and other methods or sources may be more appropriate.

Timeliness

Searches performed as soon as requested may be the best service that can be offered for faculty working in medical fields, genetic manipulation, or in competitive business-related research. Quick searches are important for the time-impacted professor or graduate student and a brief search on a simple topic or a few facts or procedures on very specific subjects can be adequately accomplished by an experienced searcher with little or no preparation. Subjects needing more comprehension or broader coverage are usually handled more effectively if an appointment is set up for a later date to allow for adequate planning.

It is extremely important to recognize the priorities and demands that patrons have on their time and to be sensitive to these pressures. If a search service becomes overwhelmed with requests, so that flexibility is very limited, plans must be made to get more equipment, passwords, searchers, or an end-user facility to allow patrons to do some of their own searching, reserving the more complex problems for the search service. Ideally, it should be easy for patrons to schedule a search, to have a question answered online at the reference desk, and to find equipment for doing their own searching.

Searcher Expertise

Searchers must be familiar with the online databases, the content, the years included, and the regularity of updates, the various emphases of similar files, and must know the printed indexes and their corresponding major databases. This knowledge of available resources must include access points, relevant thesauri, and major unique characteristics of databases.

Searchers must have good training, attend advanced training sessions, have enough practice if they are not regular database searchers, and feel comfortable at the keyboard. In addition, searching techniques must be up-to-date, flexible enough to allow for different databases, and competent to provide efficient information retrieval. Different databases and systems must be used interchangeably whenever necessary. Time is required for searchers to develop this expertise so they are confident and unpressured as they work with patrons.

A quality search service depends on capable individuals who have encouragement and financial support from their institution to develop and maintain the status of an expert searcher. They must have not only technical skill, but a knowledge of resources and the various choices for accessing them in order to make the best response to a question or to find information on a particular subject.

Adequate Finances

The use of online resources for all appropriate occasions at no cost to the patron is a very desirable, but difficult, goal to reach. Adequate support of an institution's online searching requires that service priorities be examined, methods of funding explored, budgets carefully adjusted, and costs controlled. It is often necessary for a search service to acquire new equipment, new peripherals, new software, equipment servicing, and to pay subscription fees plus search costs. These expenditures must be determined and then balanced among the other budgetary demands for more journal subscriptions, more books, and other services.

Purchasing the newest technology can be expensive, especially if a microcomputer quickly becomes too small, too slow, or inadequate for the next piece of software or a request for downloading. Selecting standard systems, waiting for reviews to know that others have worked out most of the problems, leasing equipment, or selecting modular systems so new units can be purchased when needed will reasonably insure the investment in costly equipment. Starting an online service with a minimal outlay and increasing the capability and services gradually will allow for planned expansion.

There should, however, be as few obstacles or impediments as possible to the delivery of information. If a fee is charged or restrictions are made on search topics, the number of searchers, or the amount, length, or cost of a search, there will be some patrons who will not have adequate access to this form of information retrieval. To find sufficient funding will require an objective look at the goals of the library and making choices for resources and services. The most important objective of information delivery is to supply the answers via printed or electronic means, depending on which method is more suitable for the question. Budgetary decisions are often difficult, but must be geared to the library goals for services.

Competent Management

Online services require organization, procedures, extensive training, special equipment and other arrangements unique when compared to the operation of other library units. The demands on staff time, fiscal resources, and building space can affect all the other library services and functions. Besides concern for the impact on staff and budget, there is a special need for management that can organize responsive online services for the exceptional, specialized, research-oriented clientele even while electronic access to information is integrated into general reference activities that serve every student, staff member, and professor on campus.

Procedures must be efficient and yet flexible enough to meet patron needs that are usually irregular and unexpected. To best utilize staff and finances, schedules, training, search records, money handling, data collection, reports, and evaluations must be prepared, monitored, and conclusions utilized for improving and expanding services. The rapidly changing information delivery field makes it necessary for continual awareness of new developments and applications of interest to libraries. Assessing these developments and making decisions about when to implement them requires a knowledge of patron interests, the fiscal status of the library, the planning of library operations, and the implementation of new technologies.

Support of Library Administration

Administrative and staff support for online services is crucial to providing strong online services. Each step, from a single terminal for online access to databases, to an expanded facility encompassing CD-ROM equipment, requires changing the environment for staff and patrons. Smooth adjustments to these changes will require good public relations, effective education of patrons, and the cooperation of the library administration. Confidence in competent management of these services will encourage expansion when needed and good communication within the library will alert the administration to new opportunities and needs for improved information services. The adjustment of priorities for budgetary items, personnel time, and library services must be a continuing effort as effective information retrieval services are developed.

Excellence

Librarians must work for more services, better and freer access to information, dependable equipment, systems designed for the convenience of patrons, ease of use, choices of access routes to materials, and appropriate results. Above all, the retrieval of information must be accurate and timely. There must always be flexibility to change ideas, priorities, and to try out new methods of applying technology.

The ultimate challenge is to shape the library of the future into an effective manager of information: Not a warehouse of documents, but a cohesive unit integrating physical objects with electronic access to worldwide data. Making these resources available for every patron, student, scholar, or researcher at the level and depth needed will require dedication, a broad view of information access and retrieval, and good management.

A READING LIST

Keeping up with new database opportunities, new equipment, and different methods of applying electronics to the information field is a constant challenge. It is essential to read relevant journals, talk to colleagues, attend meetings, know where to look up information about online databases, learn what to read on new systems and technologies, and how to find out about the availability and quality of CD-ROM and other optical materials. Some of the most important current resources are included in this bibliography:

Current Awareness

For news of developments in the online field, industry changes, new databases, equipment and software.

DataBase Alert. Vol. 1– . (Monthly; monthly, annual indexes). White Plains, N.Y.: Knowledge Industry Publications, 1983– .
   Newsletter reporting new databases, changes in online files, online vendor status and price changes. Companion publication to *DataBase Directory.*
Information Hotline. Vol. 8– . (11 issues/year). New York: Science Associates/International, 1976– .
   Brief paragraphs cover international news about new databases, new publications, and the online industry.
Information Intelligence Online Newsletter. Vol. 1– . (10 issues/year). Phoenix, Ariz.: Information Intelligence, 1980– .
   New developments in the online industry, online services and products. Selected articles printed from the database, ONLINE HOTLINE. Available on a diskette.
Information Retrieval & Library Automation. Vol. 9– . (Monthly). Mt. Airy, Md.: Lomond Publications, 1973– .
   News articles on new techniques, equipment, software, publications.

Information Today. (Monthly except July/August and November/December). Medford, N.J.: Learned Information, 1984– .
"The newspaper for users and producers of electronic information services." Newspaper format; latest news of the information industry.

Library Hi Tech News. Vol. 1– . (Monthly except July/August). Ann Arbor, Mich.: Pierian Press, 1984– .
News of automation developments in libraries and new developments in the industry. Each issue includes LHTN bibliography on the application of new technologies for libraries and information centers.

THE ONLINE CHRONICLE. (Updated biweekly). Weston, Conn.: Online, Inc., 1984– . Online database, File 170 on Dialog.
Full-text international news of the online industry. Expanded version of the "News" section in *Online* and *Database.* Includes section for job openings and register of available online professionals.

ONLINE HOTLINE NEWS SERVICE. (Daily updates). Phoenix, Ariz.: Information Intelligence. Composed of two databases, ONLINE HOTLINE, 1982– , and ONLINE LIBRARIES AND MICROCOMPUTERS, 1983– .
Full-text records of articles on current online topics. Selected articles from ONLINE HOTLINE published in *Information Intelligence Online Newsletter.* A printout of the entire ONLINE HOTLINE database is the *R1++ Online Hotline Printout. Information Intelligence Online Libraries and Microcomputers* is the hardcopy edition of the database ONLINE LIBRARIES AND MICROCOMPUTERS. Both databases are available on diskettes (monthly updates).

Optical Information Systems Update. Vol. 5– . (Biweekly). Westport, Conn.: Meckler Publishing, 1986– .
Newsletter of optical storage and publishing. Companion to *Optical Information Systems.*

Directories

Resource publications for information on databases, online vendors, database producers, and availability of CD-ROMs. Provide address, telephone numbers and often key personnel.

Cane, Mike. *The Computer Phone Book: Directory of Online Systems.* New York: New American Library, 1986. 685 pp.
Directory and user's guide to the end-user databases such as BRS After Dark, Knowledge Index, Dow Jones, EasyLink, and NewsNet.

CD-ROMS in Print. (Annual). Westport, Conn.: Meckler Publishing, 1987– .
Currently available CD-ROMS with version number, purpose,

price, publisher, system requirements. Includes directory of producers.

Computer-Readable Databases: A Directory and Data Sourcebook. 2 vols.: *Science, Technology and Medicine* and *Business, Law, Humanities and Social Sciences.* Edited by Martha E. Williams. Chicago: American Library Assn., 1985.

Available online from Dialog as DATABASE OF DATABASES (Quarterly Reloads). Provides extensive information on publicly accessible databases.

DataBase Directory. (Semiannual). White Plains, N.Y.: Knowledge Industry Publications, 1985– .

Supplemented by monthly newsletter, *DataBase Alert.* Available online through BRS as KNOWLEDGE INDUSTRY PUBLICATIONS. Provides contents of worldwide numeric and bibliographic databases available in North America, producers, pricing. Subject, database name, producer, and vendor indexes.

Directory of Online Databases. Vol. 1– . (Quarterly). New York: Cuadra/Elsevier, 1979– .

Two directory issues per year, each with one update. Indexes include: name, subject, database producer, online service, telecommunications network, and master index.

Directory of Periodicals Online: Indexed, Abstracted & Full-Text. 2nd ed. Vol. 1., *News, Law and Business;* vol. 2, *Medicine and Social Science;* vol. 3, *Science and Technology.* Washington, D.C.: Federal Document Retrieval, 1986.

Online locations of approximately 25,000 periodicals indexed in over 375 databases. Gives addresses of vendors and producers.

Encyclopedia of Information Systems and Services. 7th ed. Vol. 1, *United States;* vol. 2, *International;* vol. 3, *Indexes.* Edited by Amy Lucas and Kathleen Young Maraccio. Detroit: Gale Research, 1987. 1900 pp.

Detailed descriptions of international electronic information systems, products, databases, and services. Indexed by organization name, personal name, function, software, database, geographic location and subject.

Guide to CD-ROMs in Print. (Annual). Westport, Conn.: Meckler Publishing, 1987– .

Lists products, availability, system requirements, prices, services, company names, contract information.

"International Comparative Price Guide to Databases Online." *Online Review.* (Semiannual). February and August issues.

Directory of databases offered by more than one online vendor service with the producer, subject, and online vendors. Prices are given in U.S. dollars for the minimum and maximum charge per online hour, the online hit charge, and the price for an offline print.

Laserdisk Directory. 4 Parts. *Database,* June and August; *Online,* July and September, 1986.

Gives description of the product, type of laserdisk, compatibility, producer, availability in 1986, price, contract provisions for return of disks, and other restrictions.

Microcomputer Market Place. Vol. 1– . (Semiannual). New York: R. R. Bowker, 1985– .

Microcomputer and CD-ROM manufacturers and distributors, software publishers, periodicals, manufacturers of peripherals and supplies, associations, services, conferences.

MICROCOMPUTER SOFTWARE & HARDWARE GUIDE. File 278 on Dialog (Monthly reloads). New York: R. R. Bowker, current.

Extensive listing of software programs and hardware systems. Gives title, producer or manufacturer, compatibility, operating systems, price, ordering information.

North American Online Directory. (Biennial). New York: R. R. Bowker, 1985– .

"A directory of online information products and services with names and numbers." Alphabetical and classified lists of databases, database producers with addresses, phone numbers, key personnel. Broad coverage includes networks, associations, user groups, consultants, trade shows, periodicals, and newsletters.

Online Bibliographic Databases: A Directory and Sourcebook. 4th ed. London: Aslib, distributed in the United States and Canada by Gale Research, 1986.

Includes 250 bibliographic databases, directory of online vendors and general index.

Online Database Search Services Directory. A Reference and Referral Guide to Libraries, Information Firms, and Other Sources Providing Computerized Databases. 2nd ed. Edited by Doris Morris Maxfield. Detroit: Gale Research, 1987.

"Provides detailed descriptions of the online information retrieval services offered by public, academic, and special libraries, private information firms and other organizations in the U.S. and Canada." Indexed by organization name, acronyms, subject, databases, online systems, search personnel.

Optical Publishing Directory. (Annual, two or more updates/year). Medford, N.J.: Learned Information Inc., 1987– . (Supersedes *Optical/Electronic Publishing Directory*).

Comprehensive directory of optical products. Listings of CD-ROMS presently for sale, producers, hardware, service vendors, new products.

Reston Directory of Online Databases: Your Computer's Phone Book.
Reston, Va.: Reston Publishing, 1984.
"A travel guide to the world of information that can be called up on
any computer."
*Small Computers in Libraries Buyer's Guide and Consultant Direc-
tory.* (Annual). Westport, Conn.: Meckler Publishing, 1987– .
Product/Service listing and vendor section.
SOFT. Database on BRS (Updated monthly). Weston, Conn.: Online,
Inc., current.
Currently available software packages. Gives specifications, de-
scriptions, applications, costs, and hardware requirements. Over
5,000 packages.
The Software Catalog: Microcomputers. (Semiannual with semiannual updates). New York: Elsevier, 1983– .
Produced from .MENU—THE INTERNATIONAL SOFTWARE DATABASE
(Monthly updates) on Dialog (File 232). Includes descriptions of
software packages for microcomputers, producers and distributors, compatibility, minimum memory required, prices, and date
of release.

Associations/Conferences

Presentations include online searching topics; opportunities are provided to meet colleagues; exhibits display newest products.

American Society for Information Science. (Annual Meeting).
Proceedings published by Knowledge Industry Publications,
1937– .
International Online Conference. (Annual Conference). December,
London.
Proceedings published by Learned Information, Oxford, 1977– .
Machine-Assisted Reference Section (MARS). Reference and Adult Ser-
vices Division, American Library Association, 1977– .
Meets and organizes programs annually for the ALA Conference.
"Messages from MARS" published quarterly in *RASD Update,* the
newsletter of the division. Committees work on various projects to
assist online database searching in libraries.
National Online Circuit. 1980– .
Meets at the *Online* and *National Online* Conferences. "Circuit
News" column in *Online* and ONLINE CHRONICLE. Maintains contact
with online user groups across the country and publishes a list of
them annually.
National Online Meeting. (Annual Conference). Spring, New York.

Proceedings published by Learned Information, Medford, N.J.,
1980– .
Online 8?. (Annual Conference). Fall.
Proceedings published by Online, Inc., Weston, Conn., 1979– .
Optical Information Systems Conference and Exhibition. (Annual).
Sponsored by Meckler Corp. 7th Annual, New York City, December, 1987.
Software/Computer/Database Conference and Exposition for Librarians and Information Managers. (Annual).
Proceedings published by Meckler Publishing, Westport, Conn.,
1986– . Sponsored by the *Journal of Small Computers in Libraries.*

Indexes to the Literature

Abstracts and indexes provide access to the current and older literature, both in printed form and as an online database.

Computer and Control Abstracts. Vol. 4– . (Monthly; semiannual index). London, Institution of Electrical Engineers, 1969– .
Includes section on information science and documentation that covers information services, dissemination of information, information storage and retrieval, and bibliographic systems. Classified arrangement, author, subject indexes. Part of the INSPEC database (Monthly updates).
Current Index to Journals in Education. Vol. 1– . (Monthly; semiannual indexes). Phoenix, Ariz.; ORYX Press, 1969– .
Covers 780 major journals in education and includes online searching in libraries and educational institutions. Author, subject, journal contents indexes. Included in the ERIC database.
Information Science Abstracts. Vol. 4– . (Monthly; annual index). New York: Plenum, 1969– .
Covers books, journals, conference proceedings, reports, and patents. Includes every relevant item discussed in the *Annual Review of Information Science and Technology.* Subject and author indexes. Equivalent database INFORMATION SCIENCE ABSTRACTS (Bimonthly updates).
"LHTN Bibliography." (Monthly except July/August). *Library Hi Tech News.*
Current index to articles, book reviews, and conference proceedings. Subjects include databases, laser and optical disks, and online database searching. Index also recorded on machine-readable data strips in the newsletter.

Library and Information Science Abstracts. Vol. 1– . (Monthly; annual index). London, The Library Assn., 1969– .
International coverage of journals, books, reports, conference proceedings, theses, dissertations. Classified arrangement, subject, author indexes. Equivalent database LISA (Monthly updates).

Library Literature. (Bimonthly; annual cumulation). New York: H. W. Wilson, 1936– .
Author and subject index to 200 worldwide periodicals, books, pamphlets, films, filmstrips, microfilms, and theses. Equivalent database LIBRARY LITERATURE (Semiweekly updates).

Resources in Education (RIE). Vol. 10– . (Monthly; semiannual indexes). Washington, D.C.: National Institute of Education, 1975– .
Abstracts educational documents. Indexes by subject, author, institution, publication type, clearinghouse number/ED number. Included in the ERIC database.

Major Journals

Required reading for all online database searchers. Articles on searching technique, management topics related to online searching in libraries, applications of new developments, and news of the field.

Database: The Magazine of Database Reference and Review. Vol. 1– . (Bimonthly). Weston, Conn.: Online, Inc., 1978– .
Articles emphasize database content, search techniques, comparisons between databases, and discussions of new database developments.

Online. Vol. 1– . (Bimonthly). Weston, Conn.: Online, Inc., 1977– .
"The magazine of online information systems." Articles emphasize impact of electronic and optical systems, searching technique and procedures, and current issues in the field.

Online Review. Vol. 1– . (Bimonthly). Medford, N.J.: Learned Information, 1977– .
"The international journal of online information systems." Articles on topics of interest to searchers worldwide. News of international developments.

Other Journals

New titles are continually appearing to increase this list of journals that cover various segments of the online information field providing a broad exposure to developments in and applications of computers, CD-ROMS, and database systems.

CD-ROM Review: The Magazine of Compact-Disc Data Storage. Vol. 2– . (Bimonthly). Peterborough, N.H.: CW Communications, 1987– .
Articles on new developments in CD-ROM and CD-I, applications, buying guides, and related subjects.

Database Searcher: The Magazine for Online Database Users. Vol. 3– . (Monthly except July/August). Westport, Conn.: Meckler Publishing, 1987– . (Supersedes *Database End-User*).
Covers industry developments, online and database news, new products, search techniques, and end-user searching.

Electronic and Optical Publishing Review. Vol. 6– . (Quarterly). Medford, N.J.: Learned Information, 1986– . (Supersedes *Electronic Publishing Review*). Articles, reviews, news with emphasis on information in electronic form.

The Electronic Library. Vol. 1– . (Bimonthly). Medford, N.J.: Learned Information, 1983– .
"The international journal for minicomputer, microcomputer and software applications in libraries." Subjects include information technology and its impact on libraries, hardware and software developments and reviews, and library systems and networks.

Information Intelligence Online Libraries and Microcomputers. Vol. 1– . (Monthly except July/August). Phoenix, Ariz.: Information Intelligence, 1983– . Looseleaf format.
Subjects include microcomputers, databases, software, telecommunications, networks, meetings, and publications related to libraries. Available on a diskette.

JASIS: Journal of the American Society for Information Science. Vol. 1– . (Bimonthly). New York: Wiley, 1950– .
Scholarly articles on basic information science and theory with applications for online searching.

Library Hi Tech. (Quarterly). Ann Arbor, Mich.: Pierian Press, 1983– .
Lengthy articles with broad coverage of new technologies of interest to libraries.

Microcomputers for Information Management: An International Journal for Library and Information Services. Vol. 1– . (Quarterly). Norwood, N.J.: Ablex, 1984– .
New applications of microcomputers, latest news on hardware and software, and industry trends.

Optical Information Systems. Vol. 6– . (Bimonthly). Westport, Conn.: Meckler Publishing, 1986– . (Supersedes *Videodisk and Optical Disk*).
Subjects include CD-ROMs, laserdisks, and videodisks.

Small Computers in Libraries. Vol. 1– . (11 issues/year). Westport, Conn.: Meckler Publishing, 1981– .

Short practical articles on library uses of microcomputers including online searching.

Books

Selected list of recent books on online searching, microcomputers, CD-ROMs, and related topics.

Alberico, Ralph. *Microcomputers for the Online Searcher.* Westport, Conn.: Meckler Publishing, 1987. 299 pp. Supplement to *Small Computers in Libraries,* vol. 3.

Downloading/Uploading Online Databases & Catalogs. Proceedings of the Congress for Librarians, February 18, 1985, St. John's University, Jamaica, N.Y. Library Hi Tech Special Studies Series, No. 1. Ann Arbor, Mich.: Pierian Press, 1985. 136 pp. Includes annotated bibliography, 1974–1985.

Essential Guide to CD-ROM. Westport, Conn.: Meckler Publishing, 1986. 189 pp.

Falk, Howard. *Personal Computers for Librarians.* Medford, N.J.: Learned Information, 1985. 174 pp.

Ferrarini, Elizabeth M. *Infomania: The Guide to Essential Electronic Services.* Boston: Houghton Mifflin, 1985. 314 pp.

Gilreath, Charles L. *Computerized Literature Searching: Research Strategies and Databases.* Boulder, Colo.: Westview Press, 1984. 177 pp.

Glossbrenner, Alfred. *The Complete Handbook of Personal Computer Communications.* 2nd ed. New York: St. Martin's Press, 1985. 546 pp.

Hoover, Ryan E. *The Executive's Guide to Online Information Services.* White Plains, N.Y.: Knowledge Industry, 1984. 296 pp.

Humphrey, Susanne M., and Biagio John Melloni. *Databases: A Primer for Retrieving Information by Computer.* Englewood Cliffs, N.J.: Prentice-Hall, 1986. 384 pp.

Klingensmith, Patricia J., and Elizabeth E. Duncan. *Easy Access to DIALOG, ORBIT, and BRS.* New York: Marcel Dekker, 1984. 220 pp.

Managing Online Reference Services. Edited by Ethel Auster. New York: Neal-Schuman, 1986. 408 pp.

Numeric Databases. Edited by Ching-Chih Chen and Peter Hernon. Norwood, N.J.: Ablex, 1984. 332 pp.

Online Catalogs, Online Reference: Converging Trends. (Proceedings of a Library and Information Technology Assn. Preconference Institute, June 23–24, 1983, Los Angeles.) Edited by Brian Aveney and Brett Butler. Chicago: American Library Assn., 1984. Library and Information Technology Series, No. 2. 211 pp.

Online Searching Technique and Management. Edited by James J. Maloney. Chicago: American Library Assn., 1983. 195 pp.

Online Searching: The Basics, Settings & Management. Edited by Joann H. Lee. Littleton, Colo.: Libraries Unlimited, 1984. 164 pp.

Public Access Microcomputers in Academic Libraries: The Mann Library Model at Cornell University. Edited by Howard Curtis. Chicago: American Library Assn., 1987. 211 pp.

Reference and Online Services Handbook: Guidelines, Policies and Procedures for Librarians. 2 vol. Edited by Bill Katz. New York: Neal-Schuman, 1982, 1986.

Columns

News and discussion of current issues in the online field are provided by these regular columns in major library journals.

Library Journal. "Online Databases."
RQ. "Databases."
RSR: Reference Services Review. "Databases."
Science and Technology Libraries. "Sci-Tech Online."
Wilson Library Bulletin. "Online Update" and "Connect Time."

Software/Hardware/CD-ROM Reviews

Reviews of specific products to aid in selection and purchase.

Booklist. (Bimonthly September–June; monthly July and August).
   Section on "Microcomputer Software" providing brief reviews.
CD-ROM Librarian: The Optical Media Review for Information Professionals. Vol. 2– . (Bimonthly). Westport, Conn.: Meckler Publishing, 1987– . (Supersedes *Optical Information Systems Update/Library & Information Center Applications.*)
   Product reviews of optical media, news, and articles about hardware, software, updates and backfiles, and applications in libraries.
Computer Equipment Review. Vol. 3– . (Semiannual). Westport, Conn.: Meckler Publishing, 1981– .
   Reviews of computer equipment and peripherals.
Computer Review Index. Vol. 1– . Schenectady, N.Y.: Schenectady Public Library, 1986– .
   Index to critical reviews that cover computer hardware, software, peripherals, and online services.
Library Software Review. Vol. 1– . (Bimonthly). Westport, Conn.: Meckler Publishing, 1982– .

Articles and reviews on commercial software for libraries. Includes new applications such as optical products.

Software Reviews on File. Vol. 1– . (Monthly). New York: Facts on File, 1984– .
Looseleaf service that reprints reviews from microcomputer journals. Indexed by producer, title, hardware, and subject.

Bibliographies

Comprehensive coverage of the literature on online database searching.

Byerly, Greg. *Online Searching: A Dictionary and Bibliographic Guide.* Littleton, Colo.: Libraries Unlimited, 1983. 288 pp.
Hawkins, Donald T. *Online Information Retrieval Bibliography, 1964–1982.* Medford, N.J.: Learned Information, 1983. 311 pp. Updated annually in *Online Review.*

Annual Reviews

Annual Review of Information Science and Technology. Vol. 1– . (Annual). White Plains, N.J.: Knowledge Industry Publications, for the American Society for Information Science, 1966– . Edited by Martha E. Williams.
Lengthy documented articles written by international specialists. Major topics vary each year.

Index

accounting
  procedures, 136–137
  records, 135–136
  software, 259
acoustic coupler, 69–70
acquisitions, assisting, 245
advisory committee, 108, 149
associations, online related, 320–321

bibliographic instruction, 31, 223,
  240–242
bibliographies, reading list, 326
books, reading list, 324–325
brochure, 113
budget proposal, search service, 48–49
budgeting, 101, 117–122. See also fees;
  finances
building location, 35–36, 289–290

cataloging, assisting, 245–246
CD-ROM, 285–289. See also local database systems
  directories, 317–320
  impact on instruction, 241
  reviews, 325–326
  selection, 293–298
clientele
  academic, 9–11, 33–35, 278–280
  off-campus, 32–33
collection development, impact on,
  244–245
command-driven software, 257–258
communication costs, 43
communications software, 255–266
conferences, online related, 213–214,
  320–321
continuing costs, search service, 45–46
controls

costs, 101–103
end-user services, 292
ready-reference searching, 232–233
coordinator of search services. See search
  service, management
copyright, downloading and, 267–268
cost estimating, search service, 40–46
costs
  continuing, 45–46
  controls, 101–103
  end-user services, 292
  equipment, 41–42
  initial investment, 40–42
  operating, 45–46, 118–119
  overhead, 121–122
  personnel, 44
  searching, 15–16, 19–20, 61–63
  site preparation, 41
  support materials, 42
  variable, 43–45, 120–121
courses on online searching, 207
current awareness sources, 214–215,
  316–317

database costs, 43–44
database producers, directories, 317–320
database producer software, 264–265
database producers, 8
database resources, 57–61, 64–65,
  151–152
database vendors. See vendors
databases
  bibliographic, 58–59
  on CD-ROM, 286–289
  directories, 317–320
  on floppy disks, 286
  growth in number, 7–9
  nonbibliographic, 59

demonstrations, 82, 113
directories, 317–320
document ordering online, 243–244
downloading, 260, 267–268
  copyright concerns, 267–268

end-user searching, 20–21, 273–304
  advantages, 276
  CD-ROM, 285–289
  controls, 292
  data collection, 171–172
  equipment, 162, 289–290
  evaluation, 163, 185–187
  fees, 292–293
  on floppy disks, 286
  intermediary host system, 284–285
  on local databases, 285–289
  problems, 276–277
  search evaluation, sample form, 187
  software, 258–259, 260–261, 282–284
  summary of searches, sample form,
    191
  vendor search systems, 281–282
end-user services
  clientele, 278–280
  costs, 292
  facilities, 289–290
  finances, 302–303
  management, 161–162, 290–292
  procedure manual, 161-163
  selection, 293–298
end-user systems, 280–289, 296–298
end-users, 278–280
  training, 163, 298–302
equipment, 249–255, 309
  management, 89–90, 151, 158–159,
    162, 234
  ready-reference searching, 229–230
  search service, 11–13, 41–42
  selection, 67–70, 252–255
evaluation
  end-user searching, 163
  patron satisfaction, 109–111
  procedures, 157–158
  sample forms, 185–187
  search services, 108–111
  searchers, 110–111, 203–204
expenses. See costs

facilities for end-user searching, 289–290
facilities management, 87–93
faculty, 9–11, 33–35, 77, 242, 279–280,
  301–302
fee structure, 127–132

fees, 16, 122–132, 155
  advantages and disadvantages, 125–127
  cost recovery, 128
  end-users, 292–293
  none charged, 124
  standard charge, 130–131
  subsidized, 128–130
  surcharge, 131–132
finances, 117–138, 314. See also costs;
  budgeting; fees
  end-user services, 302–303
  management, 100–103
  procedures, 155–156
  ready-reference searching, 236
financing the search service, 15–16,
  19–20, 52–53, 132–134
forms, 79, 172–191
forms, examples
  appointment calendar, 178
  evaluation, patron searching, 187
  evaluation, search service, 185–186
  financial summary, 189
  interdepartmental authorization, 177
  online literature search request,
    173–174
  online search authorization, 177
  patron searching summary, 191
  ready-reference searches, summary,
    190
  search form, print and online sources,
    184
  search log, public terminal, 182
  search log, reference desk, 182
  search planning, 183
  search service billing, 179
  search service log, 181
  statistics sheet, 188
  undergraduate search request, 176
free searches, 124, 137
front-end software, 256–257
  for end-users, 282–284
funding for online services, 52–53,
  132–134

gateway software, 256
goals and objectives for online services,
  26–33, 144–145, 158, 161
government publications, ready-reference
  searching, 236–237
graduate students, 9–11, 33–35, 279–280

indexes to online literature, 321–322
information delivery, 220–223, 310–311,
  313

information services, 18–19, 29–31, 38, 224–229
integrating online searching, 18–19, 29–31, 38, 277–278
interdepartmental authorization, sample form, 175, 177
interlibrary loan
  assisting, 242–243
  impact on, 236, 242–244
intermediary host system, 284–285
intermediary role of librarian, 303

journals, reading list, 322–324

keeping up-to-date, 111–112, 212–215, 316–317

librarians, changing environment for, 21–22, 303, 307–311
librarians, expertise, 31–32
library administration, support of online services, 315
library, electronic information delivery, 3–5, 307, 310–311
library operations, impact on, 48–50, 239–246
library research, assisting, 246
library schools, training searchers, 207
library staff, orientation, 81, 205
local database systems
  advantages and disadvantages, 288–289
  producers, 286–288
  selection, 293–298
local databases for end-users, 285–289

management, 85–115, 315
  of changing environment, 111–112
  of costs, 101–103
  of development, 114–115
  end-user services, 161–162, 290–292
  of equipment, 89–90
  of facilities, 87–91
  of fees, 127–132
  fiscal, 100–103
  of public relations, 112–114
  for quality services, 103–112
  of records, 92–93
  of searchers, 93–100, 105–106
  of security, 90–91
  of vendor relations, 88–89
manager of ready-reference searching, 158

manager of search services
  characteristics, 86–87
  responsibilities, 85–86, 145–150
manuals, vendor, 14–15
menu-driven software, 257–258, 277–278
microcomputers
  advantages for searching, 250–252
  hardware features, 253–255
  installation, 37, 253
  procedures for selection and use, 268–269
  reviews, 325
  search service, 68–69
  for searching, 12–13, 249–255
  selection, 252–255
  training for use, 269–270
modems, 12, 69–70

online industry, history, 7–9
online literature, reading list, 214–215, 316–326
online resources for ready-reference searching, 224–226
online resources, growth, 7
online search authorization, sample form, 176–177
online search request, sample forms, 173–174, 176
online services
  funding, 132–134
  history, 5–6
  initiating, 25–53
  success factors, 311–316
online vendors. See vendors
operating costs, search service, 45–46, 118–119

password security, 91
patron fees. See fees
patron needs, 77, 106–107, 202–203, 221, 312
patron searching. See end-user searching
patrons from off-campus, 32–33
personnel. See searchers
policy and procedure manual. See procedure manual
precision of search results, 108–109
presearch interview, 198–199
printers, search service, 70
procedure manual, 141–164
  database resources, 151–152
  end-user searching, 161–163
  equipment selection, 151, 158–159, 162

330   Index

procedure manual (cont.)
  evaluation, 157–158, 161, 163
  finances, 148–149, 155–156
  manager, ready-reference searching,
    158
  manager, search service, 145–150
  microcomputers and software,
    268–269
  outline, 143–144
  ready-reference searching, 158–161
  records, 156–157, 160–161
  search procedures, 153–155
  search service, 144–158
  search service guidelines, 152–153
  searchers, 150–151
  staffing search service, 145–151
procedures
  accounting, 136–137
  efficiency of, 103–105
  microcomputers and software,
    268–269
  promotion. See public relations
proposal to initiate online services,
  25–53
public relations, 80–83, 112–114,
  312–313

reading list, 214–215, 316–326
ready-reference searches, summary, sample form, 190
ready-reference searching, 158–161,
  219–237
  advantages, 220–224
  choosing a vendor system, 230–231
  controls, 232–233
  data collection, 171
  equipment, 229–230
  evaluation, 161
  online resources, 224–226
  problems, 233–236
  procedures, 158–161
  records, 160–161
  search aids, 231–232
  training searchers, 231
  when to go online, 159–160, 227–229
recall value of search results, 108–109
records, 135–137, 168–172
  automation, 170
  data tabulation, 170–172
  management, 92–93
  procedure manual, 156–157
  search log, 168–169
reference collection, impact on, 30, 223

reference librarians, impact on, 17,
  234–235, 308–311
reference services, 17–18, 29–31,
  158–161, 219–220, 235–236, 311
researchers, assisting, 9–10, 28–29, 33,
  279–280
reviews, computers, software, CD-ROM,
  266, 325–326

scheduling searchers, 93–95
scheduling searches, 98–100
SDI, 29, 154
search aids, 14–15, 42, 79–80, 231–232
search authorization, sample forms, 177
search definition, 169
search log, 168–169
  sample forms, 179–182
search planning, sample forms, 180,
  183–184
search procedures, 76–79, 153–155,
  198–201
search service
  accessibility, 106–107
  advisory committee, 108, 149
  billing, sample form, 178–179
  budgeting, 48–49, 101
  cost estimating, 40–48
  data collection, 92–93, 170–172
  environment, 87–88
  equipment, 11–13, 67–70
  evaluation, 108–111, 157–158, 184–187
  facilities, 87–91
  finances, 15–16, 19–20, 52–53,
    132–134
  financial summary, sample form, 189
  goals and objectives, 26–33, 144–145
  in-house support, 51, 80, 132–133
  initiating, 25–53
  institutional support, 51–52, 133–134
  location, 13–14, 35–39
  management, 85–115
  organization, 17–18, 37–39
  outside support, 134
  procedure manual, 144–158
  procedures, 76–79, 103–105
  public relations, 80–83, 221
  quality of service, 103–112
  records, 79, 92–93
  sample budget, 49
  setting up, 27–28, 55–83
  staffing, 14, 39–40, 145–151
  statistics, sample form, 188
  vendor relations, 88–89
search strategy development, 199–200

searchers, 93–100, 195–216
  continuing education, 150–151,
    212–215
  division of requests, 95–98
  evaluation, 203–204
  expertise, 105–106, 313–314
  improving skills, 211–212
  procedure manual, 150–151
  qualifications, 201–202
  responsibilities, 75–76, 150, 197–201
  scheduling, 94–95
  selection of, 70–72, 93–94, 150,
    195–197
  software assistance, 257–260, 262–263
  training, 42, 72–75, 205–211, 269–270
  working with patrons, 202–203
searches
  distribution, 95–98
  scheduling, 98–100
searching
  delivery of results, 78
  preparation for, 77–78, 198–200
  quality, 79–80, 211–212
  scheduling, 76–77
security, 90–91, 159, 234
selective dissemination of information.
  See SDI
separate search service, 38–39
site selection, search service, 13–14,
  35–37
software for searching, 255–266
  aids for searchers, 257–259, 262–263
  downloading, 260
  for end-users, 258–259, 260–261
  for experienced searchers, 258, 260
  features, 256–257, 260–263
  level of assistance, 257–259
  postsearch processing, 257
  procedures for selection and use,
    268–269
  producers, 264–266
  reviews, 266, 325–326
  search accounting, 259
  selection, 261–263
  sources, 263–266
  technical specifications, 262
  training for use, 269–270
space requirements, 36–37
staffing, search service, 14, 39–40, 44

standardization of systems, 310
statistics, 156–157, 168–172
  sample forms, 188–191
  support materials. See search aids

technical services, impact on, 245–246
telephone connection, 13, 43, 69–70,
  250
terminals
  installation, 37
  search service, 11–13, 68–69
training end-users, 163, 291, 298–302
training searchers, 72–75, 205–211, 231
  advanced training, 74, 209–211
  in-house, 74–75, 207–209
  initial, 42
  library schools, 74, 207
  practicing, 209, 213, 224
  self-instruction, 208–209
  for using microcomputers, 269–270

undergraduate search request, sample
  form, 175–176
undergraduates, 9–11, 34–35, 240–242,
  278–279
user fees. See fees
user friendly systems. See end-user
  systems
user groups, 213–214, 320

variable costs, search service, 43–45,
  120–121
vendor charges, 61–63
  connect time, 43–44
  database, 44
vendor end-user systems, 281–282
vendor manuals, 14–15, 65
vendor software, 264
vendor systems, search language, 63–64
vendors, 8–9
  characteristics, 56–67
  contracts, 62, 88–89
  directories of, 317–320
  end-user systems, 281–282
  reliability, 65–66
  selection, 55–67, 151–152, 230
  services, 66
  training, 66–67, 74, 206

Janice Sieburth is head of the Pell Marine Science Library at the University of Rhode Island; she was previously head of reference and coordinator of online search services at the University of Rhode Island Library. Sieburth is the author of numerous journal articles on topics in online searching, reference services, biochemistry, and nutrition.